Black
Representation
and Urban
Policy

Albert K. Karnig
and Susan Welch

# Black
# Representation
# and Urban
# Policy

The University of Chicago Press
Chicago and London

The University of Chicago Press, Chicago 60637
The University of Chicago Press, Ltd., London

Library of Congress Cataloging in Publication Data

Karnig, Albert K
  Black representation and urban policy.

  Bibliography: p.
  Includes index.
    1. Municipal government—United States.  2. Afro-
American legislators.  3. Afro-American mayors.
I. Welch, Susan, joint author.  II. Title.
JS323.K35       352'.008'0973       80–16714
ISBN 0–226–42534–7

ALBERT K. KARNIG is director of the Center for
Public Affairs at Arizona State University.
SUSAN WELCH is chairman of the Department
of Political Science at the University of Nebraska,
Lincoln.

# Contents

# Preface

The age of demonstrations has passed, and the age of the ballot is upon the black man. [Stone 1970, p. 10]

The experience of blacks in the United States has been devastating. From the colonial period to the present, American history has been scarred by racial injustices too numerous to catalog: chattel slavery, lynching, Jim Crow segregation, and other horrors of post-Reconstruction years, as well as an extraordinary array of individual and institutional discriminatory practices, some of which persist. Nevertheless, blacks as a group not only have survived but have continued to improve their economic and political position in society, albeit by fits and starts. Gradually at first, then more rapidly, blacks have gained political and economic power.

This book addresses one aspect of black political power—the holding of public office. After the Civil War, Reconstruction brought a measure of political power to southern blacks. Some blacks were elected to Congress, and others held state and local office. For example, in 1873–74 seven blacks were members of congress, only three fewer than in 1968–69 (Walton 1972, p. 188). But by the end of the nineteenth century the short-lived flurry of officeholding was swiftly suppressed. Frequent intimidation and various laws and practices such as white primaries, poll taxes, and literacy tests stripped blacks of the franchise in the South. Between 1896 and 1901, twenty southern blacks served in the United States Congress; after 1901 no southern blacks were elected to that body for more than seventy years. Black elected officials in the South between 1900 and 1965 were largely officials of small all-black towns.

In the North, no blacks served in Congress until Oscar DePriest was elected from Chicago in 1928. Although at the time blacks made up only about 4 percent of Chicago's population (Patterson 1974, pp. 16–17), DePriest's district was well over 50 percent black. However, despite the growing number of these black majority districts in large northern cities, until the 1950s Chicago's William Dawson and New York's Adam Clayton Powell were the only black members of Congress.

At the state and local levels the situation was little better. Blacks in Chicago probably were more successful than those in other large cities in electing black representatives (Wilson 1960, p. 20). Still, these representatives were few. Records show a black elected to the Cook County Board

of Commissioners in 1871 (Patterson 1974, p. 19), the first black elected to
the city council in 1915, and another designated a ward committeeman five
years later. With its then larger black population, New York did not have
a black Tammany leader until 1935 (Wilson 1960, p. 26), and it was not
until 1944 that a black New Yorker was elected to Congress. In Detroit,
the first black city council member was elected only in 1957 (Wilson 1960,
p. 28). These were limited successes, and the election of blacks to state
and local offices was infrequent and only token.

Gradually the political system started to respond to blacks' demands.
First through court decisions that struck down "separate but equal" laws,
then through legislation giving statutory protection to blacks' rights to
public accommodations, equal employment, and the vote, their political
status began to improve. As more and more blacks were able to vote, the
number of blacks elected to public office increased dramatically.

In 1964, of the more than half-million elected officials in the United
States, 280 were black—6 members of Congress, 90 state legislators, and
184 other state and local officials (Fleming 1966). By 1975 the number of
elected blacks had increased more than tenfold to 3,503. And by 1978
there were 4,503 black elected officials in the United States (Joint Center
1978). This included 16 members of Congress and 4 state executives
below the gubernatorial level, 294 state legislators, 170 mayors, 1,618 city
council members, and 1,086 school board members (Joint Center 1978); the
rest were law enforcement officials, members of the judiciary and mis-
cellaneous local and state officials.[1] While the magnitude of the tenfold
increase must be viewed in light of the very small original base, it is no
longer surprising to hear that a black has been elected mayor of a large
community, to a congressional seat, or to a city council.[2] Indeed, though
black officials are a tiny fraction (less than 1 percent) of the more than
520,000 elected officials in the United States (Joint Center 1977), their
increase has been sudden and to some extent unexpected.[3]

The purpose of this book is to explore some of the conditions that affect
the number of black officials elected to urban offices. Focusing on black
mayors and council members, we will examine a number of propositions
about factors related to the election of blacks, then analyze the influence
of these officials on urban budgets.

Two possible methods of analysis immediately suggest themselves. The
first is to undertake a small-scale comparative investigation of several
cities having different levels of black representation. This type of study
would concentrate on from two to perhaps ten communities and seek to
determine how race relations, black-white coalitions, personal ambition,
and historical and current events affect the chances of blacks' gaining city
council and mayoral offices. To be sure, this mode of investigation can
prove highly valuable, because it can uncover rich detail and can allow
one to examine intensively the implications of social, political, economic,

organizational, personal, and historical developments in individual cities. The prototype of this type of research is the highly valuable study of Gary and Cleveland by Nelson and Meranto (1977). By employing the same concepts and modes of observation, limited comparative research ensures substantially better reliability than the pure case study.

A second method of studying black representation stresses large-scale aggregate data analyses of scores or even hundreds of cities. This approach does not deny the utility of studying in close detail the complex interactions of historical events, personalities, political compromises, and other conditions peculiar to individual municipalities. Indeed, any aggregate data study of several hundred cities must inevitably sacrifice insights that can be obtained only by rigorously observing one or a few communities over time.

However, large comparative studies have clear advantages of their own. Not only do they provide a higher degree of reliability, they allow greater generalization. Small comparative and case studies inevitably encounter problems of generalizability (or external validity). For example, if we conclude that particular political conditions such as a strong political party organization and district elections promote black city council representation in Chicago, can we generalize from that finding and infer that partisanship and district races tend to favor black representation in other cities? Obviously, conclusions drawn from one or a few communities must be tentative. Conversely, large comparative research on representative samples of cities—or, as in this instance, all cities of a particular size—permits one far greater confidence in generalizing about the influence of given conditions such as partisanship and district elections.

In addition, small comparative samples and case studies do not permit satisfactory controls, thus limiting our confidence in the findings. For example, let us say we are interested in determining how district elections and partisanship independently influence the percentage of council posts won by blacks. To test for the effect of one condition while controlling for the other, we would need at least four cities (see table 1). By focusing on numerous cases with dissimilar characteristics, we can begin to assess the effects of municipal conditions through comparisons. By introducing controls for various other factors that may be important, we improve our ability to generalize.

Table 1
Hypothetical Cities Matched on Election Type and Partisanship

| City | Election Type | Partisanship |
| --- | --- | --- |
| City A | District | Partisan |
| City B | At large | Nonpartisan |
| City C | District | Nonpartisan |
| City D | At large | Partisan |

If we examined only the first three cities in table 1, we would not know the role of partisanship independent of that of district elections. Furthermore, to discover the effects of another variable, such as percentage black in the city, we would need at least to double the number of cases to eight. Accordingly, we would have to find a set of communities (such as cities A to D) that had low proportions of blacks and a second set with higher percentages of blacks in the population. Indeed, for every additional variable considered we must again double the minimum number of cities under examination. Moreover, to analyze cities with intermediate percentages of blacks as well as those with high and low percentages, we would have to triple the number of cases.

Clearly, the more variables we examine, the more cases we require. Because we wished to include as many potentially relevant factors as possible, as a check against spurious findings, we opted for a large-scale comparative study. By doing so we have sacrificed the opportunity to gather some valuable in-depth information, but we will have gained greater confidence in the generalizability of our findings. Thus our basis for analysis is all United States cities over 25,000 in population that are at least 10 percent black.

The book is organized in the following way. In chapter 1 we review the large-scale societal changes that have contributed to an upsurge in the number of black elected officials in American cities. For the most part these changes will be taken as "givens" and will not be further explored. We also discuss how black officials compare with their white counterparts in background characteristics and in attitudes toward government. Finally, we present a brief preliminary discussion about the prospective influence of black elected officials.

In chapter 2 we will review some previous research on specific causes of black electional success in some types of cities and offer some propositions to be tested. This discussion will focus on four kinds of factors: demographic variables and white population characteristics, federal antipoverty efforts, municipal political and election rules, and black resources (including socioeconomic, organizational, population, and protest resources). Chapters 3 and 4 then will present the evidence on how these resources contribute to the election of black mayors and to the presence of mayoral candidates (chap. 3) and how they affect black candidacies for and election to city councils.

In these two chapters we ask the following kinds of questions: Do ward rather than at-large elections increase black representation? Does the presence in a community of a large number of black-owned businesses and media outlets help? Did the inflow of federal money in the 1960s aid in expanding the number of black elected officials? Are there any characteristics of the community at large that make it easier for blacks to be elected?

Chapters 5 and 6 consider the effects black officials have had on urban policy, specifically urban budgets: in chapter 5, we review previous findings on black influence, and in chapter 6 we present and review our own findings. Finally, in chapter 7 we summarize our findings and discuss some implications for black politics in urban settings.

# Acknowledgments

No study of this size could be completed without the assistance of many people. We are grateful to the Center for Metropolitan Studies of the National Institute of Mental Health for supporting the research with grant number 86-222-152-01. In particular, Mrs. Joan Schulman of that office was most helpful in expediting the project.

The efficient work of graduate assistants Ruth Grubel, Mark Williams, and Vernon Daniels of the University of Nebraska-Lincoln and Martha Rawls, Terry Kloris, and Arthur Maurice of Arizona State University lightened our load considerably. The speed and good cheer of our clerical staff—Velma Schroeder, Ramona Farmer, and Lori Davison of the University of Nebraska-Lincoln and Marion Buckley, Connie Comer, and Michelle Koch of Arizona State University—made the task of manuscript preparation nearly bearable.

We are also much indebted to colleagues who read part or all of the manuscript. Terry N. Clark, University of Chicago, Charles V. Hamilton, Columbia University, Susan M. Rigdon, University of Illinois, and Alan Booth, University of Nebraska, were especially helpful in improving the quality of the book.

Finally, we would like to thank our spouses, Marilyn Karnig and Alan Booth, who were always encouraging and almost always patient.

Of course it is traditional to absolve others of responsibility for errors remaining in the book, and we are happy to do so. After all, for overlooked shortcomings, we have one another to blame.

# 1 Black Electoral Success
## *The Setting*

American society is different today than it was in 1950 and is vastly different than in 1900. The nature of our laws has changed, individual attitudes have been transformed, we live in new places, and our general expectations about life, society, and government have undergone substantial revision. One of the aspects of American society that has seen the most change is race relations. In the first part of this chapter we will explore some of these broad societal changes over the past several decades that have resulted in dramatic alterations in black-white relations and have led to increased black electoral success. Though one might include numerous factors and events, at least four trends over the past two decades are specifically relevant: (1) demographic shifts of population, (2) legal protection for black voters, (3) changing black attitudes, and (4) reoriented white attitudes. To fully comprehend the expansion of black officeholding, familiarity with these developments is essential (also see Smith 1978).

Demographic Shifts

One certain reason for success in electing blacks to urban office is the rapid increase in the black proportion of central city populations (Patterson 1974; Cole 1976). A high percentage of black population is probably an important, though not sufficient, condition for black electoral victories in local, state, and national races as well. The movement of nonwhite minorities to the central cities has characterized demographic change in the United States since the 1930s, whereas until very recently the out-migration to the suburbs has been almost exclusively white (National Research Council 1975). Dramatic increases in the black proportion of central city populations are shown in table 2. Although the black proportion of the total United States population has remained relatively constant since 1900, this proportion has almost doubled in standard metropolitan statistical areas (SMSAs) and has more than tripled in the central cities. Overall, the black proportion in the central cities was almost 22 percent in 1970 and had probably reached 25 percent by the late 1970s. More than half the black population of the United States now lives in central cities (Caputo 1976, p. 82).

Table 2
Increase in Black Proportions of Urban Populations

| Year | Total United States | Total Central City | Total SMSA[a] |
|------|---------------------|--------------------|---------------|
| 1900 | 12.1% | 6.8% | 7.8% |
| 1910 | 11.1 | 6.9 | 7.3 |
| 1920 | 10.3 | 7.3 | 7.2 |
| 1930 | 10.2 | 9.0 | 8.1 |
| 1940 | 10.2 | 10.1 | 8.6 |
| 1950 | 10.7 | 13.1 | 10.1 |
| 1960 | 11.4 | 17.8 | 11.7 |
| 1970 | 12.3 | 21.9 | 13.7 |

*Source:* National Research Council (1975, p. 19).
[a]Standard metropolitan statistical areas.

Indicative of the migration pattern—that is, minorities streaming into the central cities and whites emigrating to the suburbs—is the fact that in the 1960s the black proportion of the central cities grew by more than 35 percent, while the white proportion decreased by 9 percent (National Research Council 1975, pp. 19–20; *U.S. News and World Report,* 1 March 1971, p. 24). Even though black movement to the suburbs now *proportionately* exceeds that of whites, this has had little effect on the accumulating numbers of black central city residents. During the 1960s, only three of the thirty largest cities failed to show an increase in the percentage of the population that was black (Cole 1976).

The black proportion in the central cities ranges widely from city to city and from region to region. It is highest in the Northeast, South, and industrial Midwest, considerably lower in the Plains and Far West. Table 3 displays the black populations of a number of representative large municipalities. By 1970 blacks were already a majority in three large United States cities (Washington, D.C.; Gary, Indiana; and Newark, New Jersey) and constituted more than 40 percent of the population of several more. During the 1970s, blacks were thought to have become majorities in New Orleans, Detroit, and other major cities. This growth in the black proportion of central cities is expected to continue. As long as whites flee the central cities and blacks continue to migrate there, an increasing black proportion is guaranteed.

The implications of such population shifts for black electoral power are obvious. As blacks become a larger part of a city population, they have a better chance of electing blacks to office. This is particularly true given the racially segregated housing patterns in most large cities (Taeuber and Taeuber 1965). Thus, if a municipality is 20 percent black, chances are very good that most of that 20 percent are clustered in one or two parts of the city. Whatever its deleterious consequences, this segregation provides a natural electoral base for black candidates. Given this housing pattern,

Table 3
Black Proportions of Some Urban Populations, 1970

| East | | South | | Midwest and Plains | | West and Southwest | |
|---|---|---|---|---|---|---|---|
| Washington, D.C. | 71% | Atlanta | 51% | Gary | 53% | Dallas | 25% |
| Newark | 54 | New Orleans | 45 | Detroit | 44 | Los Angeles | 18 |
| Baltimore | 46 | Richmond | 42 | Saint Louis | 41 | Denver | 9 |
| Cleveland | 38 | Jackson | 40 | Chicago | 33 | San Antonio | 8 |
| Philadelphia | 34 | Montgomery | 33 | Kansas City, Mo. | 22 | Seattle | 7 |
| New York | 21 | Charlotte | 30 | Indianapolis | 18 | Portland | 6 |
| Buffalo | 20 | Little Rock | 25 | Omaha | 10 | Tucson | 4 |
| Boston | 16 | Miami | 23 | Topeka | 8 | Albuquerque | 2 |
| Syracuse | 11 | | | Minneapolis | 4 | Honolulu | 1 |

*Source:* Caputo (1976, p. 82) and National Advisory Commission (1968, p. 216).

when the black population of an area reaches a large percentage, it is difficult to gerrymander district lines so as to exclude black majorities from every legislative or council district. Entrenched white leaders have of course attempted this by redrawing legislative district lines to split the black population, creating large districts, and supporting at-large election systems.[1] However, the larger the black population, the more difficult it becomes to deny blacks at least some representation.

Data from congressional districts illustrate nicely the relationship between electoral success and black proportion in the population. As of 1978, blacks held twelve of thirteen congressional seats in districts where blacks were a majority of the population;[2] two of the eleven seats where blacks were 40 to 49.9 percent of the population (Harold Ford of Tennessee and Mickey Leland of Texas, who has the seat formerly held by Barbara Jordan); but only one, that held by Ronald Dellums of California, of the 411 remaining seats where blacks were less than 40 percent of the population (Morris 1975, pp. 174–75; Joint Center 1973).[3] A substantial black percentage in an election district does, then, clearly promote the chances of gaining black representation.

Legal Protection for Black Voters

The legal changes that have most drastically affected the probabilities of black electoral success are the civil rights acts (particularly the Voting Rights Act of 1965). This series of laws, passed in 1957, 1960, 1964, 1965, and 1975, has been responsible for increases in black voter registration in the South. In recent years, the proportion of blacks registered in the heart of the South is only 11 percent less than the proportion of whites registered there (Congressional Quarterly Weekly Report [CQWR], 8 March 1975, p. 489). In six Deep South states, where black registration was only 29 percent in 1965, registration now stands more than 56 percent. Moreover, whereas in 1960 there were only a handful of black elected officials in these areas, as of 1977 more than 2,000 black officials held elective office in the South, including three members of Congress—Ford of Tennessee, Jordan of Texas, and Young of Georgia.

The tremendous growth in black voter registration is shown in table 4. Obviously, not all of this increase can be attributed to changes in federal laws. Other trends, such as urbanization, voter registration drives, and improved education of blacks have contributed substantially to black registration, at least in some parts of the South. Yet these federal civil rights laws have wrought tremendous changes in voter registration requirements and procedures (see Holloway 1969, p. 318).

The Fifteenth Amendment to the United States Constitution holds that neither a state nor the federal government may deprive a person of the vote because of race, color, or previous condition of servitude.

Table 4
Increases in Black Voter Registration in the Six Southern States
Covered by the 1965 Voting Rights Act

| State | 1952 | 1958 | 1962 | 1964 | 1968 |
|---|---|---|---|---|---|
| Alabama | 25,000 | 73,000 | 68,000 | 111,000 | 273,000 |
| Georgia | 144,000 | 161,000 | 175,500 | 270,000 | 344,000 |
| Louisiana | 120,000 | 132,000 | 152,000 | 165,000 | 305,000 |
| Mississippi | 21,000 | 22,000 | 24,000 | 28,500 | 251,000 |
| South Carolina | 80,000 | 58,000 | 91,000 | 144,000 | 189,000 |
| Virginia | 69,000 | 93,000 | 110,000 | 200,000 | 255,000 |

Sources: 1952 and 1958, Congressional Quarterly Almanac 16 (1960): 192; 1962 and 1964, Congressional Quarterly Almanac 21 (1965): 537; 1968, Congressional Quarterly Almanac 25 (1969):422.

Nevertheless, tactics for excluding blacks from the ballot box in the South were numerous and generally successful. By 1960, even though many of the more overtly unconstitutional tactics had been proscribed, remaining schemes ranged from legal conditions—such as requiring a prospective voter registrant to be vouched for by another registered voter or a well-known person in the community—to economic retribution for attempting to vote, to outright physical violence.[4] As a result, though black voter registration in the southern rim states and the more urban South had reached respectable levels by the late 1950s, registration of the huge black populations of the Deep South was pitifully small, as table 4 attests. Lest it be thought that the small registrations were due to apathy and poor education, the evidence of southern surveys (Matthews and Prothro 1966, chap. 3) shows that blacks' participation in political activities other than voting was reasonably similar to that of whites, and in some activities even higher. Black voting participation was substantially below white levels, and this trend was most marked in the most rural areas surveyed.

The 1957 Civil Rights Act was the first noteworthy national civil rights legislation. By empowering the attorney general to seek injunctions against deprivations of voting rights, it offered a remedy, though largely ineffective, for applicants denied the right to register to vote. The legislation also created a Civil Rights Commission with powers to investigate and report to the president and Congress about violations of voting rights (Congressional Quarterly Almanac [CQA] 1965, p. 536). The power of the attorney general was strengthened somewhat by the 1960 Civil Rights Act. Under this legislation, the attorney general could ask the court to find that a "pattern or practice" of depriving blacks of their rights existed. The court could then issue an order that some blacks were qualified to vote under state law and could appoint referees to help register them (CQA 1965, p. 537; Matthews and Prothro 1966). This procedure was cumbersome and depended upon several uncertain factors: local blacks willing to risk registering a complaint with the attorney general, a cooperative attorney general willing to actively prosecute such suits, and a sympathetic judge. Clearly, those blacks most intimidated would be the ones who would not use these procedures. Thus, despite this legislation, little success was forthcoming, as table 4 reveals. Relatively few blacks were registered between 1952 and 1962.

During this period many southern states had very restrictive legislation governing voter registration, leaving a good deal to the discretion of local registrars in deciding who could vote. This latitude made it easy for a registrar to find a black unqualified. For example, Alabama, Georgia, Mississippi, and Louisiana required that a candidate have good moral character, educational achievement, and the ability to read, write, and understand the Constitution or any other matter. South and North Carolina demanded an ability to read or write any section of the Constitution.[5] Tests of these abilities were often given orally, so that there was no written record of the applicant's abilities. Or the tests were given at the option of the registrar, so that a middle-class white might be asked only the simplest of questions, while a black was asked very detailed questions covering fine points of constitutional interpretation. Alabama and Louisiana also required that the applicant be vouched for by another registered voter.

The 1964 Civil Rights Act, best known for its provision on nondiscrimination in public accommodations, included a voting rights provision that considerably strengthened the 1957 and 1960 federal laws. The 1964 law made a presumption of literacy for anyone with a sixth-grade education.[6] It prohibited oral literacy tests for registration for federal elections. And, if fewer than 15 percent of blacks in an area were registered, the 1964 act permitted court-appointed referees to register blacks qualified under *state* law (with the above exceptions regarding literacy). The act also authorized a special three-judge court to handle voting-rights suits and established preferential treatment for the Justice Department to handle such suits (*CQA* 1965, p. 538).

Although by March 1965 the Justice Department had processed seventy voting-rights suits, so that thousands of blacks gained the right to vote, many argued that the judicial process was moving too slowly and was dealing with the problem only area-by-area. Furthermore, restrictive state laws were left untouched and, perhaps most important, the statute did nothing to protect the rights of blacks who were afraid to register complaints against discriminatory literacy tests and other unfair registration procedures.

The 1965 Voting Rights Act met these objections. The law had two key provisions. First, literacy tests were simply suspended. Second, the law authorized federal voting registrars to be sent to all counties where voter-qualification devices such as the literacy test had been used *and* where less than 50 percent of the voting-age population (of any race) was registered or had voted in the 1964 presidential election. These two conditions were automatic "triggering devices": no court order was needed to send the federal registrars into these affected areas (*CQA* 1965, p. 540). These areas also had to obtain Justice Department approval for any change in their voting laws. Affected were the six Deep South states shown in table 4, most counties in North Carolina, and a handful of counties in the North.[7] In the face of intense white hostility, and sometimes at great personal risk, the registrars went into these southern counties and registered thousands of voters.

The consequences of such actions also can be seen in table 4. In some cases the number of voters registered in the period from 1965 and 1968 more than doubled. In Mississippi the increase was ninefold. Overall, one report found that almost as many black voters registered in these six southern states in the four years after the act's passage as in the entire previous century (*CQA* 1970 [vol. 26], p. 198). Before the act, 5,900,000 whites and 920,000 blacks were registered in these six states; by 1968 an additional 900,000 blacks and 1,000,000 whites were registered (*CQA* 1970, p. 198); and by 1970 it was estimated that a million new black voters had registered since 1965 (*CQA* 1972 [vol. 28], p. 258). In 1969, nonwhite registration in the six states ranged from a low of 51 percent in South Carolina to a high of 59 percent in Mississippi.

The original law had a five-year life. It was extended for another five years in 1970, and in 1975 it was extended for seven years, so that the act would not expire in the midst of the expected redistricting controversies of 1980–81. The 1975 act made permanent the bar on literacy tests and extended the protection of the law to other minorities such as Spanish-speaking Americans, native Americans, Asian Americans, and Alaskan natives.

All in all, these civil rights acts, especially that of 1965, must be seen as important catalysts helping to precipitate the increase in black elected officials. Although their direct effect was confined to the South, it is in that region that a substantial part of the nation's black population still lives. This enlarged black voter strength has had influence other than electing blacks to office. Most recently, the ability of Jimmy Carter to carry the southern states in 1976 and hence win the election was attributed to his strong support among black southern voters.

## Black Attitudes

The increase in the numbers of black elected officials has been made possible in part by certain attitude changes on the part of both blacks and whites. Among these new attitudes held by blacks is an intensified political consciousness. Although various elements seem to make up this black consciousness, we will focus on three: increased distrust and hostility toward whites; increased positive reactions toward blacks; and belief in some variety of what might be called black power as a way of gaining an equal share in society (Aberbach and Walker 1973, pp. 109, 165 ff).

Some general themes can be found among the myriad recent studies on black attitudes. Blacks are increasingly distrustful of white people (Aberbach and Walker 1973) and exhibit a lack of trust in governments run by whites, especially at the local level (Aberbach and Walker 1973). At the national level, black trust in government has plummeted in the past ten years (Miller 1974). Campbell and Hatchett (1974, p. 117) concluded from a longitudinal study of blacks in Detroit that between 1968 and 1971 black attitudes become more militant, with more blacks seeing whites as hostile and oppressive. More blacks were willing to consider extreme measures to redress their grievances. Despite this increasing alienation, however, only 11 percent in the Campbell study believed violence was the optimal way for blacks to try to gain their rights, with about 40 percent reasoning that laws and persuasion were best and nearly 50 percent mentioning nonviolent protest (1974, p. 8). Still, many studies showed widespread black sympathy toward the rioters of the 1960s (Campbell and Schuman 1968; Aberbach and Walker 1973), and most blacks believed the riots were the result of legitimate grievances rather than constituting criminal behavior (Sears and McConahay 1973). Many preferred to call the incidents "rebellions" or "insurrections," terms obviously indicating extreme alienation from government. Related to this alienation was the belief of the vast majority of blacks that whites consider blacks inferior, that they give blacks a break only when forced to, and that whites really are sorry that slavery was abolished (Harris 1973, p. 233).

Perhaps more important than antiwhite feelings is the development of racial pride that has recently been articulated by blacks. The thesis of "black power" enunciated by Carmichael and Hamilton in 1966 evoked a response from many blacks. Although initially dismaying to some black leaders (see Barker and McCorry 1976), the term black power began to have positive connotations to the black masses. Aberbach and Walker (1973) found that blacks interpret black power to mean getting a fair share of what society has to offer, rather than to mean using violence and causing insurrection. A number of examples illustrate various aspects of this racial pride. Sears (1969) discovered that blacks believed that black elected officials could be trusted more than white elected officials. In a response to the question, Who really represents the Negro? 58 percent of the Los Angeles blacks in Sears's sample named some black group or individual, while only 9 percent named a white group or individual. Respondents had very positive attitudes toward both protest and assimilationist groups. Campbell and Hatchett (1974) found that about 40 percent of their Detroit sample believed that black teachers take more interest in black children than white teachers do, and an equal percentage believed there should be black principals in schools with black children.

However, this black pride does not extend to separatism. Only about one-fifth of a 1969 black sample responded positively to the notion of a separate black nation. Black leaders, too, enunciated the black power theme in terms of black pride and tried to channel these attitudes toward effective political work. Kenneth Clark, for example, argues that "The most important unintended benefit of the black power movement was that it became a most effective smoke screen behind which the hard, thorough job of planning, seeking and obtaining genuine direct political power for blacks could proceed with a minimum of interference" (Clark in Dymally 1971, foreward [n.p.]. Leaders as diverse as Shirley Chisholm, Adam Clayton Powell, and Julian Bond all stressed obtaining black power through organizational activity (see various articles in Dymally 1971).

The confluence of these various attitudes points toward an increase in black elected officials. Blacks are alienated from government, which they correctly see as white dominated. They are becoming increasingly militant, but most spurn violence and hope for change through legislation. Black leaders also stress these themes. Therefore, organizing to elect members of the black race to public office, so as to change the laws by exercising control over parts of the government structure, seems a logical and reasonable extension of these beliefs. As Bayard Rustin (1965) urged, the era of protest had to give way to efforts to exercise political power.

## White Attitudes

A fourth factor contributing to an increase in black officials is change in white attitudes. To say that white attitudes toward blacks have become more positive is not to say that reservoirs of distrust and even hatred do not exist among the white population. But the attitude changes among whites in the past thirty years have been striking.

Probably the best documentation of white attitude change toward blacks is contained in a series of studies done by the National Opinion Research Center from 1942 to 1970 (see Hyman and Sheatsley 1956, 1964; Greeley and Sheatsley 1971). In these reports, remarkable shifts in white attitudes were found. Some previously quite controversial issues—for example, segregation in public transportation—are now not even salient. Even on issues that are still controversial, such as school and residential integration, the increase in pro-integrationist responses by whites has been steady. And most people no longer oppose, for example, the principle of school integration—they have shifted their objections to the ways it is implemented. While all major segments of the white population have intensified their pro-integration stance, the change has been most noticeable among groups formerly the most hostile: those who are rural, poorly educated, unskilled, and southern. Differences in attitudes between different groups in society have decreased.

Harris (1973, pp. 230–37) has uncovered additional attitude changes among whites. In the past ten years the number of whites who admit that they believe traditional negative stereotypes about blacks has decreased, though a sizable minority holds steadfastly to each of the stereotypes. Less than 50 percent now believe that blacks have lower moral standards than whites, though a bare majority (52 percent) still believes that blacks are less ambitious (down, however, from 66 percent in 1963). Twenty-two percent say they believe blacks are inferior to whites, about a quarter think blacks care less for their families and breed crime, and about one-third believe that blacks have less native intelligence. The proportion of whites holding each of these beliefs has decreased since 1963. Harris also points to a hopeful trend when he shows that whites under thirty are more likely to believe that blacks are discriminated against than are whites over fifty (1973, p. 214).

The increased acceptance of blacks in various social settings is also evident. In one sample of white opinion, more than 80 percent said they would not mind having a black supervisor (Campbell and Schuman 1968), and more than half said they would not mind having a black family live next door (Campbell and Schuman 1968). Most pertinent to the topic at hand, well over 60 percent said they would vote for a qualified black candidate for mayor. In an overall evaluation of current white attitudes toward blacks, Campbell (1971) found that whites vary greatly in their attitudes, but that one-fifth to one-third can be called generally positive and supportive while an equal number are negative or hostile, with the remainder possessing very ambivalent and changing feelings.

In sum, these altered white attitudes are important to potential black candidates. Only in a few instances can a black candidate completely diregard white voters. In all statewide races, in most congressional and mayoral races, and in many elections in smaller districts, the black candidate must attract some white voters, if only a minority. That there are a substantial number of whites who seem ready to support black candidates is another reason for increased black electoral success. The victories of a number of black candidates such as Carl Stokes, Barbara Jordan, Tom Bradley, Ronald Dellums, and others who were elected from white majority districts is evidence that many whites will support black candidates.[8] Murray and Vedlitz (1978), after examining 109 elections in five southern cities, conclude that white support for black candidates varies according to a number of factors, including the social class of the voter, the context of the election, and the office for which the black is campaigning. Generally, however, middle- and upper-class whites are more likely to support black candidates than are lower-class whites.

We have discussed four major factors that appear to have been important conditions for the surge in black electoral success. Without demographic shifts it would be more difficult for blacks to be elected in large central cities; without the Voting Rights Act, black aspirants in the Deep South would be unable to count on much black electoral support; without mass racial pride, enough to overcome alienation from government in general, few black candidates and organizations would be able to rally enough enthusiastic black supporters; finally, without nationwide shifts in white feelings about blacks, few black candidates would be able to win that margin of white votes necessary in many elections.

These factors provide an essential background to any understanding of why blacks are now being elected to office in far greater numbers than previously. Other contributing factors include the increase in black educational levels that has provided a larger pool of candidates and the tremendous organizational efforts of the black community in the 1950s and 1960s to protest the evils of segregation and discrimination. These factors and others will be examined in succeeding chapters as we try to identify the conditions that characterize cities successful in electing blacks to office.

## Some Characteristics of Black Officials

Are black elected officeholders different in any important senses from their white colleagues? Our information on this is drawn largely from two recent books focusing on the background and attitudes of black elected officials (Cole 1976; Conyers and Wallace 1976). Cole compares black mayors and council members with their white counterparts in New Jersey, and Conyers and Wallace report the results from a nationwide sample of black and white elected officials. This latter sample includes legislators and other state officeholders as well as local officials.

What kinds of differences can be found between black and white officials? Public officials in general are better educated than the general public, and black officials appear to be even better educated than white officials. For example, Conyers and Wallace found that 41 percent of the black officials had two degrees, compared with only 34 percent of white officials. Less than a quarter of the blacks and 26 percent of the whites had no college degrees. Similarly, Cole found that only 10 percent of his black New Jersey sample, but 29 percent of the white sample, had only a high-school education or less, while 41 percent of the whites and 52 percent of the blacks had some postgraduate studies or a postgraduate degree.

Interestingly, Cole determined that black local officials are much less likely than whites to be lawyers (3 percent compared with 20 percent) but are more likely to be other professionals such as teachers, engineers, and accountants. Blacks were not, however, more prone to be laborers or members of other non-middle-class occupations. Browning et al. 1971*a*, p. 15) also found that a disproportionate number of minority officials came from "relatively prestigious occupations." The Cole and the Conyers and Wallace studies found that fewer than 10 percent of all black officials in their samples were women. Paulsen (1979) also found that almost all black mayors in his nationwide sample were men (see also Karnig and Welch 1979).

The views of the typical black official appear to be a mix of social liberalism and racial moderation. For example, the black official is much less conservative that the white official in matters of social policy and ideology. In the Cole study (1976, p. 94), 16 percent of the blacks saw themselves as radical and 52 percent as liberal, with 26 percent responding "other" or "none." Of the white officials, however, none saw themselves as radical, 34 percent were liberal, 42 percent were middle of the road, 14 percent were conservative, and only 10 percent responded "other" or "none." In the Conyers and Wallace (1976, p. 31) study, blacks were much more likely than whites to favor social programs such as housing and were less likely to agree that the United States is moving toward socialism.

Nonetheless, black officials appear moderate on the continuum of black strategies for racial justice. In assessing which strategies black officials thought important to black progress, 86 percent said increasing black-owned businesses; 71 percent, black involvement in white businesses; 70 percent, racial integration in schools and universities; and 59 percent, working through party structures (Conyers and Wallace 1976, p. 28). Only a quarter responded that more black-controlled schools and universities were needed, and only 9 percent said a black political party would be an important strategy. Indeed, Paulson (1979) found that 93 percent of black mayors favored integration. Further, while 89 percent of the Conyers and Wallace (1976, p. 20) sample believed court actions and legislation were very important in achieving real progress and 65 percent thought petitions or delegations were very important, only 16 percent believed that mass demonstrations, sit-ins, and marches were similarly important, and just 9 percent ranked violence as important.[9]

Pronounced differences of perspective were found among public officials with respect to the "black power" theme. Of those expressing unqualified opinions, a majority of whites (53 percent) but only 7 percent of blacks evaluated the phrase in an unfavorable manner. On the other hand, 61 percent of the black officials and only 24 percent of the white officials in Cole's sample had a favorable impression of the term "black power," but the dominant interpretation by the blacks was that it meant getting one's "fair share": "It means that black people would like to have slice of the political and economic pie of the country. It doesn't mean overthrow or riots or things of that nature. Black power means that black people would like to have a share of jobs, opportunities, decent housing, religious institutions, playgrounds, all kinds of recreational facilities, senior citizens housing. We would like not to be denied anything" (Cole 1976, pp. 101–2). Seventy-seven percent of the black officials strongly agree that it is important to the community that blacks hold elective office; curiously, only 13 percent of the black public "strongly" agree, though an additional 69 percent agree (1976, p. 111)

Finally, in assessing the sources of their electoral support (Conyers and Wallace 1976, p. 106), black officials overwhelmingly credited black organizations and leaders as well as the rank-and file black community. A substantial majority also gave credit to party leaders and workers of both races. Interestingly, only a bare majority credited white organization, and just 43 percent mentioned white government leaders. Black officials felt that they obtained more white help in the North but more solid black support in South (1976, p. 132).

In general, then, black officials tend to be liberal or occasionally "radical" with respect to social welfare policy, but basically moderate on strategies to achieve racial justice. And they attribute their electoral victories in large measure to the activity of fellow blacks. Given their overall concern with problems experienced by lower-class blacks and their inclination to advocate social welfare policies, what are the likely effects of electing black officials at the municipal level? In the next section, we briefly address this question, and in chapter 6 we attempt to measure one type of possible policy change—that related to municipal expenditures.

## Prospective Effect of Black Elected Officials

The final topic to be considered here is the effect these newly elected black officials are expected to have on the city or area they represent and on the larger society. The policy influence of black elected officials as a group has not been systematically analyzed, though there do exist case studies and comments on individual black officials in a few selected communities (Nelson 1972; Nelson and Meranto 1977; Cole 1976). The influence of these men and women might be usefully analyzed both for policy achievements and for their importance as symbols to the black community.

In terms of material benefits, it is clear that some people have clung to unrealistic hopes about the effects these black elected officials might have. Some believed that they would be "supermen and superwomen" who could cure the ills of three centuries overnight. Blacks, especially those elected to mayoral positions, were somehow expected to have the answers to problems of housing, unemployment, and education that have been festering for decades.

The black elected official, in any circumstances, must be, as Lamb puts it, "an uncommon man" (Lamb, in Dymally 1971, p. 36). While faced with overwhelming problems, the black official is also perched "on a tightrope" (Lee in Dymally 1971, p. 83). The official must move fast enough so that blacks do not believe they have been "sold out," yet there are countervailing pressures from the white community to move cautiously. These whites must be heard, because most often they control the financial institutions, media, and other resources that the black official depends on in any proposed policy change. Trying to balance these pressures can cause loss of confidence by the black community, the white community, or both.[10]

Even if he has the political support to move ahead with actions to benefit the black community, the black official may not be able to do so. A mayor is apt to be faced with either a very small rural community with few resources or a large municipality blighted by urban decay. In either case, the problems of the community usually cannot be solved by local government alone but require extensive state or national assistance (see Walton 1972, chap. 11). If the black official holds state or national office, it is usually as a legislator or a minor executive official, one of a small minority unable to take decisive action—certainly not unilateral action. Stone (1970), for instance, has shown that in 1970 the percentage of blacks in state legislatures ranged from zero to a high of 8 percent in the Michigan lower house. Although these numbers have grown since 1970, they still are not nearly representative of the black percentages in many states. In any case, if blacks were represented in true proportion, black officials would still constitute scarcely more than 10 percent of elected decision-makers in the nation.

Despite these special dilemmas and limitations of black elected officials, they have had influence in many ways. Keech (1968) found that black votes can bring about some policy changes in southern communities; the potential effect of actually electing black officials is even greater. Cole has already documented black success in having at least some policy preferences adopted by city councils in New Jersey. Further, Mack Jones (1971) and Campbell and Feagin (1975) indicate that the ascendance of blacks to political power in smaller southern towns has resulted in policies beneficial to black citizens. And the election of blacks to Congress has moderated the southern Democratic delegation.

Perhaps one of the most important effects of black elected officials is their symbolic effect on both blacks and whites. This is eloquently stated by Howard Lee, mayor of Chapel Hill, North Carolina (Dymally 1971, pp. 85–86), when he describes his success in winning some degree of rapport with young blacks. After telling how he joined a group of young blacks in a protest march and later sat down to talk with them about their problems, he says: "It is this kind of activity that I think makes the black elected official very effective. It makes him effective because he can identify with the frustrations of the blacks, both young and old, who can know what it feels like to want someone in government who can be trusted." Some empirical evidence of the importance to the black community of a black elected official is found in Cole's New Jersey study. In cities with black mayors, 87 percent of the black community could identify their mayor, compared with 72 percent in cities with white mayors (1976, p. 109). And only 19 percent of the black community sampled disagreed with, or had no opinion about, the statement "It is important to the city that blacks hold elective office" (Cole 1976, p. 111).

Election of black officials may also be important to whites. Cole reported that nearly two-thirds of the whites interviewed also agreed that it is important for blacks to be elected to public office (Cole 1976, p. 111). Some of these responses doubtless grow out of genuine concern for representative government or for blacks as a group. Others are rooted in self-interest, perhaps based on the belief that, until blacks are given a fair share of political power in this country, the danger of widespread violence will continue. As Chuck Stone, a former aide to Congressman Adam Clayton Powell, has suggested: "[As long as] the white community continues to reject black candidates for public office ... the comparative moderation of the political process will be increasingly disowned by young blacks as a meaningless exercise in the quest for power" (Stone 1970, p. 228). In perhaps a bit of hyperbole, Gerald Lamb, former state treasurer of Connecticut, called black officials "the last great white hope for peace in this land." To the extent that people believe that political tranquillity and order are in the common interest, then electing representative numbers of blacks to public positions serves the aims of blacks and whites alike.

## Summary

In this chapter we have discussed four key historical developments: shifts of black and white population, legal protection for the black electorate, modified black attitudes, and more progressive white attitudes toward blacks. Collectively and individually, these phenomena helped to produce a watershed break with the past, easing the entry of blacks into elective office. We have also drawn a profile of the educational and social background and the political viewpoints of black officials. Finally, we have highlighted some potential benefits of electing blacks as well as some of the obstacles that must be hurdled if black officeholders are to be truly effective.

These factors are important to an understanding of the recent great increase in black elected officials and the likelihood of their producing significant social changes. But they do not explain why certain communities provide reasonably proportional representation for blacks whereas others persist in underrepresentation or even nonrepresentation of the black population. Numerous explanations have been advanced to account for different rates of black representation, and in the next chapter we will review literature dealing with these often competing views.

# 2 Election of Blacks to Office
*A Review*

The sweeping demographic, attitudinal, and legislative trends sketched in chapter 1 have helped foster formidable growth in black respresentation during the past decade. There are now many more black elected officials than ever before in American history. Nevertheless, even a cursory observation indicates that the general improvement has not resulted in equal levels of black representation in all cities. For example, Atlanta, Gary, Los Angeles, Newark, and New Orleans have black mayors, whereas Miami, Indianapolis, San Francisco, New York, and Dallas have never had one. Similary, black council representation ranges from very low in Mobile, Alabama, to substantial in Atlanta and Richmond. Obviously, not all cities provide the same level of black representation. What might account for these differences? The following pages will discuss previous findings, offer some hypotheses, and describe our research procedures.

## Review of the Literature

Past research on urban politics and black studies points to numerous city characteristics that may affect black representation in municipal offices. One group of characteristics pertains to the white population profile (such as income of whites) and to the overall demography of the community (such as city size). A second set of factors deals with the influence of federal antipoverty efforts, such as presence of a Community Action program. A third group of characteristics relates to formal political and election rules adopted by the city, such as partisanship and term of office. And, finally, there are characteristics of the black community that may influence black representation, such as black income levels and population size. Our discussion will be organized around these different types of factors that may affect black candidacy for, and election to, mayoral seats and city council posts.

### White Population and Demographic Factors

Previous studies, some dealing explicitly with the election of blacks and others focusing on past or present race relations, suggest a number of general white population and demographic factors that may influence the chance of blacks' winning elections to municipal offices. In general, where we find groups most opposed to blacks or in competition with them, we expect fewer black mayors and city council members. Conversely, in cities containing groups more sympathetic to black interests, we anticipate a higher degree of black municipal representation.

One of the demographic factors that has received considerable attention is region. In particular, most past research has confirmed that racial inequities are most acute in the South. To be sure, no region in the nation has been spared the legacy of racism. But the overt and extreme forms of racial discrimination—lynching, acts of general violence, Jim Crow legislation, and rigid stratification—have been practiced with greater frequency in the South (Lewinson 1932; Key 1949). There is related evidence of a stubborn southern white resistence to the creation and maintenance of black political organization. Opposition tactics have ranged from subtle economic pressures to blatant physical intimidation (Matthews and Prothro 1966).

There has, however, been a marked reduction of regionalism in recent years, as the South has grown more similar to the other regions (McKinney and Bourque 1971; Niemi 1975). And there has been much current discussion about the "New South." Indeed, blacks recently have won important electoral victories at all levels of southern government (Bond 1969). Many blacks have been returning to the South, reversing the early flow of black migration to the North. Perhaps these changes augur well for southern blacks. Yet, the findings of attitude research still indicate that southern whites tend to express attitudes that are more racist than those of their northern counterparts (Glenn and Simmons 1967; Kelley 1974, pp. 29, 36; Greeley and Sheatsley 1971). These findings suggest that southern whites may continue to be more reluctant than whites elsewhere to support blacks seeking elective office. With evidence of this type in mind, Jones (1971, pp. 50–51) has concluded: "The essential desideratum of white southerners is white supremacy, and southern politics still revolves around it."

Even if the attitudes of northern and southern whites were similar, blacks in the South might still be less represented than northern blacks. Past discrimination, having retarded southern black organizational and economic development, may result in lower black municipal representation. Numerous studies have documented the dramatic inequality between the races in the South, especially with respect to income (e.g., Dye 1969b; Weingarden 1972). And a very recent examination demonstrates that not only is black income lower in the South, so is black education. In addition, this study shows that overall levels of black poverty and black unemployment are greatest in the South (Karnig 1979b). Black representation on councils (Jones 1976; Karnig 1976) and in the mayor's office (Marshall and Meyer 1975) has also been found to be less in southern cities. Another study discovered that the lower southern representation of blacks on councils was due primarily to the greater gap in socioeconomic resources between the races (Karnig 1979a), and this finding is congruent with Marshall and Meyer's (1975) conclusion with respect to black victories in mayoral races.

Overall, then, these studies indicate that black representation in mayoral and council positions should be lowest in the South. However, a recent examination by Robinson and Dye (1978) found that, once other factors such as socioeconomic inequalities are held constant, a northeastern location had the most negative influence on black council representation. This study does not explain why northeastern cities should have lower black representation scores, but we will comment on possible reasons for this in later chapters.

City size is a second demographic characteristic that may affect black chances of election. Blacks apparently perceive large cities as affording good opportunities. For instance, the editors of Ebony (1974, p. 300) have written that "Instead of wanting to abandon big cities, increasing numbers of blacks see them as suitable arenas for their economic, political, and cultural development." This view is supported by Karnig's (1979b) findings that in larger cities black income and educational levels are higher; black financial institutions, civil rights groups, and black media exist in greater numbers; and blacks are more likely to be elected to city councils.

Such findings are consistent with a good deal of literature on urban politics and sociology that concludes that groups tend to be better organized in big cities (Hawkins 1971; Turk 1970), especially groups that are numerical minorities (Fischer 1976). Further, big cities tend to provide a more open and pluralistic local political arena (Clark 1968a; Gilbert 1968). Also, big cities are thought to provide political institutions that are responsive to the interests of the less affluent as well as ethnic and minority groups (Lineberry and Fowler 1967; Karnig 1975; Lyons 1978). Thus we hypothesized that greater city size is favorably related to the election of blacks to municipal office.

Although there have been no systematic efforts to discern whether the proportion of workers employed in education would be positively associated with the selection of blacks as mayors and council members, we expected to find such a relationship. There is a widespread belief that educators are more liberal than others on racial matters, and there is at least case-study information suggesting that educators and blacks sometimes form supportive coalitions (Keech 1968). Some further impressionistic evidence supports this; sites of large universities, such as Chapel Hill, North Carolina, and Berkeley, California, were among the first predominantly white cities to elect black mayors.

We also expected the presence of a large middle class to be positively associated with black representation. Over the past few decades there have been an impressive number of social science surveys inquiring into the racial attitudes of white Americans of different social classes. In the past, at least, these studies ordinarily found that middle-class whites—of higher income and education—tended to be less prejudiced toward blacks (e.g., Lipset 1960; Key 1964; but see also Jackman 1978). A reason for their less racist attitudes is that middle-class whites tend to be better educated and thus to have been exposed to the limitations of racial stereotypes. Also, middle-income whites are more secure in their financial and social positions and may be less threatened by improved conditions for blacks. In contrast, working-class whites may react unfavorably to black progress because such improvement triggers status insecurity and fears of economic threat among the less affluent whites.

Leonard Cole's (1976) examination of council members and mayors in New Jersey cities did find that black representation varied directly with the median income of the community, and he interpreted the findings to indicate that blacks gained better representation in these cities because middle-class whites are less antagonistic to black success. Cole used 1972 information in his study. Karnig (1976) replicated part of the Cole research and also employed 1972 information in his analysis of a national sample of 139 cities. Instead of using median community income, he utilized black income and white income as separate measures. The findings led him to conclude that white income levels have *no* significant effect on black representation, and that the significant link is between black income and black representation. The view that white social class has little bearing on black representation is also supported by recent survey research that indicates that "racial attitudes are so similar among people of high, medium and low income that knowing family income helps us very little in explaining differences in racial orientation" (Campbell 1971, p. 53). Karnig's research dealt with a larger set of cities and actually tested the relative effects of black and white income. However, Cole's conclusion that the white middle class is more sympathetic to black representation is intuitively appealing. Further, Murray and Vedlitz (1978) did find that white voting for black candidates was at least in part a function of the voter's social class, regardless of the partisan or nonpartisan nature of the election. Moreover, both Karnig and Cole used 1972 data. Therefore, it will interesting to determine whether white social class composition has any effect on black mayoral chances at a later time—in our 1978 information on black representation.

The final white population characteristic we will examine in the percentage of the population that is foreign-born. This category is composed largely of those whites that have been referred to as "white ethnics." There is substantial documentation from case studies (Nelson 1972; Nelson and Meranto 1977) that white ethnics frequently fail to support black candidates. Further, an earlier comparative test of the effect of white ethnicity on black representation found that, when other factors are held constant, the larger the percentage of white ethnics in the city the less the chances of blacks' gaining office (Karnig 1979a).

Why might foreign stock influence black representation? White ethnics tend to be more affluent than other whites (Greeley 1976); hence any depressing effect on black representation is not due to white ethnics' being of lower social class. Neither can it be shown that white ethnics are more hostile to blacks than are other white groups (though Slavs may be an exception—see Greeley and Sheatsley 1971). Instead, the rationale for the proposition is the dominant position that those of foreign stock have had in the politics of many cities. Black efforts to achieve greater representation clash directly with the historical emphasis white ethnics have placed on gaining local elective offices. Indeed, as Lane (1959) has suggested, city politics has traditionally been the "seat of ethnic politics."

At the highly visible mayoral level, the competition between blacks and white ethnics is apparent. When blacks win big-city mayoral races, they frequently must defeat the Perks, Adonezios, and Massels. Voting for fellow ethnics may be founded upon the same justification as blacks voting for fellow blacks—a positive statement of the need for group representation and the capacity of group numbers to manage municipal affairs effectively. At this time the Voinoviches and Rizzos still dot the urban landscape, and, given the past propensity of white ethnics to support their own candidates (Pomper 1966; Gordon 1964; Parenti 1967; Gordon 1970), the opportunities for black electoral success may be weakened in cities containing large concentrations of white ethnics within the overall white population.

In sum, we will test five hypotheses concerning the effect of white population and demographic factors on the municipal representation of blacks:

$H_1$ Cities in the South or the Northeast tend to have lower rates of black representation.

$H_2$ Larger cities tend to have greater black representation.

$H_3$ Cities with higher proportions of workers employed in education tend to have greater black representation.

$H_4$ Cities with higher white median incomes tend to have greater black representation.

$H_5$ Cities with higher proportions of white ethnics tend to have lower rates of black representation.

*Federal Antipoverty Efforts*

The second set of potentially important factors explaining black representation pertains to federal antipoverty programs. A number of scholars have commented on the effect that federal antipoverty efforts of the 1960s have had in stimulating black leadership. These programs, especially the Community Action program (CAP) of the Office of Economic Opportunity (OEO) and the Model Cities program, called for community and neighborhood participation by the poor in making decisions about how federal money was to be spent. Some observers believe that developing leadership of the poor was one of the main goals of CAP agencies (Clark and Hopkins 1969); others suggest that it was simply an important, though perhaps unintended, result.

Daniel Patrick Moynihan (1969), one of the most influential critics of the overall antipoverty program, has argued that possibly "the most important long-run impact of the Community Action Program of the 1960s will prove to have been the formation of an urban Negro leadership echelon at just the time when the Negro masses were verging toward extensive commitments to urban politics." Moynihan commented that New York City's old Tammany machine itself would have been jealous of the political apprenticeship positions provided by the antipoverty program. Other commentators have also remarked on the leadership training function proved by OEO projects. Piven and Cloward (1971, pp. 275–76) argue that the programs helped integrate blacks into the political system. They point to several black leaders of poverty organizations who later sought elective office, such as Kenneth Gibson, mayor of Newark, who began his political career as vice-president of the local Community Action program. Thus, Piven and Cloward believe the programs were an effective source of political patronage and leadership training for blacks and other non-white minorities, just as municipal departments once served for the Irish, Italians, and Jews.

The effect of the CAP and Model Cities agencies in stimulating black political leadership and organization has also been discussed by other scholars (e.g., Bachrach and Baratz 1970; Kramer 1969; Perrotta, 1977; Pressman 1975; Greenstone and Peterson 1973). In general, these works indicate that, despite formidable obstacles, opposition by entrenched authorities, and internal divisions among the poor, antipoverty programs gave previously powerless groups—notably blacks—the opportunity to generate some organization and thus stimulated the development of political leadership within black communities.

In contrast, there is a popularly held view that OEO and Model Cities programs were mismanaged and of little use. Moynihan's criticisms are relevant here. This view is not confined to whites: James Hicks, a black writer, suggested that "the greatest rip-off that has occurred in this country in the last ten years has been not a rip-off of whites against blacks but a rip-off of poor blacks by upper middle class blacks" (Hamilton 1976). According to Hicks, OEO and Model Cities served to line the pockets of a favored few and had little effect on the development of black leadership or greater equality.

Hamilton (1979) argues that in New York there is little evidence that the federal antipoverty funds stimulated much effort by blacks to elect black officials. In fact, he shows that participation in electoral politics has actually *decreased* since the activation of the federal programs and that black candidates have done poorly even in black-dominated districts. He argues that federal antipoverty money has simply generated an intracommunity struggle over these funds and channeled attention away from the more important battle to gain public office toward an effort to win control of the "hard" dollars allocated by the city itself.

In recent years there have been two general tests of the role of antipoverty programs in fostering greater black municipal representation. Browning and Marshall (1976) found that San Francisco Bay Area communities with Model Cities programs had a more rapid increase in black representation on city councils than did Bay Area municipalities without such programs. And Eisinger (1978), in his survey of more than two hundred black elected officials in the United States, discovered that about one-third of them had been involved in some capacity with Community Action programs. Both these studies, then, suggest that federal antipoverty funds (both Model Cities and CAP) aided the election of blacks to municipal office, probably because they afforded blacks experience in political bargaining and negotiation and allowed them opportunities to build support and make useful political contacts in several segments of the community.

These two studies were capably done and are of substantial interest. However, Browning and Marshall focused on only ten San Francisco Bay Area cities, and we cannot confidently generalize from this one circumscribed area of the nation. The Eisinger study, though provocative, does not examine whether other socializing agencies exist in cities without Community Action programs or whether the number of officials with experience in a CAP agency represents a small or a large fraction of all those involved in CAPs. It is possible that, in the absence of CAPs, other channels exist to introduce blacks to political activities. It is also possible that those already interested in political leadership gravitated to the CAPs.

Although the debate is still open, the balance of evidence indicates that OEO and Model Cities programs do promote black political activity and leadership—and hence greater representation in elective office. Both the existence of antipoverty agencies and the infusion of larger amounts of federal funding probably allow more opportunity for the development of leadership experience for blacks. Further, a well-financed antipoverty agency probably has leverage in city politics, thus permitting actual experience in negotiating on some issues. Specifically, we will test the following propositions:

H6 Cities with OEO programs (Community Action and Neighborhood

Youth Corps) and Models Cities programs tend to have greater black representation than cities without these antipoverty programs.

H7 Cities spending more federal antipoverty funds, both per capita and in absolute amount, tend to have greater black representation than cities spending less.

### Electoral and Political Conditions

Electoral and political conditions are the third cluster of potentially influential variables. Several rules are worthy of scrutiny. In our examination of the probability that blacks will be elected to the mayoralty or the city council, we will look at five political variables: term of office, salary level, independence of local elections from state and national voting, form of government, and partisanship. When we focus on city councils, we will also consider the role of at-large versus district elections and of council size.

Longer terms of office and higher salary may result in *lower* black representation. When an office is made more attractive, it is likely that more candidates of both races will seek the position. Longer terms and improved salary levels may trigger enhanced activity in the black community, thus resulting in more black candidacies. But, when the seats are more desirable, not only may more whites enter the contests, they may be willing to commit greater resources to their attempts to win office.

If one scans the general structure of American government, it soon becomes clear that blacks have the least representation in the most desirable and prestigious posts. In legislative bodies, blacks win a larger share of city council positions than of state legislative seats, and a larger share of state legislative posts than of congressional posts. Similarly, blacks do better in lower houses than in upper houses of state legislatures and Congress. In the executive branch, blacks have won an increasing share of mayoral races and minor state offices, but of course no black has ever been elected to the governor's office or to the presidency.

Long terms of office and higher salary presumably make an elected office more attractive. With longer terms, officials have a better opportunity to achieve their policy and other objectives. They are less frequently involved in fund-raising and reelection campaigns. The reasons for the greater attractiveness of positions providing higher salaries is obvious. Given that blacks are less frequently elected as the desirability and status of a position rise, we would expect that blacks will receive less representation on city councils and in mayoral posts when salary is high and term of office is long.

Non-simultaneous local and national elections may have a similar unfavorable influence on black representation. Several studies have contended that a chief explanation for the typically dismal voter turnout in city elections is the separation of many municipal races from contests at the state and national level. Apparently, cities holding elections along with contests for higher office usually have considerably higher voter turnout (Alford and Lee 1968; Karnig and Walter 1974, 1977). We would guess that lower turnout probably means a greater reduction in the black vote than in the white vote. When state and particularly national elections are held, there is usually greater interest in the campaign and the issues than in purely local elections. Morever, political party identification spurs more participation, notably among the lower- and working-class groups to which a disproportionate number of blacks belong. Furthermore, Hansen (1975) has found that cities with higher turnout tend to have municipal officials whose political preferences are more in line with the policy predilections of the city's lower and working classes. It may be that one reason for the greater congruence between officials and citizens in high-turnout cities is that high-turnout communities elect a more representative cross-section of citizens. This outcome could include the more frequent election of blacks, especially to the city council.

Higher voter turnout may, then, favorably affect black representation both by signaling the fuller participation of blacks and perhaps by resulting in a more representative set of city officials. On the other hand, Pettigrew (1976) found that in Cleveland, Gary, Los Angeles, and Newark, when blacks ran for mayor the first time, turnout was very high but the outcome was not always favorable to the black candidate. A black candidate stimulated antiblack white voters as well as enthusiastic black supporters. On the other hand, the second time a black candidate ran, turnout declined, especially among whites, and black success was more frequent.

Regrettably, we had no information on actual voter turnout for the years in which we measured black representation. Since holding elections simultaneously with state or national races is evidently the single most important local election rule in patterning turnout rates, we employed the distinction between independent and simultaneous elections as a rough proxy for turnout. We would expect cities with simultaneous races to provide somewhat greater black representation than cities with purely independent elections.

Partisanship and government form are two more political conditions that pertain to both mayors and council members. Both of these characteristics of cities have been much studied in general, and a limited number of examinations have attempted to assess their specific effect on black representation. Let us discuss them in turn.

There are two general interpretations of the influence partisanship may have on minority representation. On one side, reformers have long argued that political parties tend to exclude newcomers and to give unjustified influence to groups that have traditionally supported the party. Evidence of this can be found, for example, in the continuing overrepresentation of certain ethnic groups, especially the Irish in Chicago, and the relative underrepresentation of blacks. According to this view, parties are an aspect of the established interests that must be overcome by outgroups such as blacks. Indeed, various case studies do show how political parties may act to thwart black candidacies (e.g., Nelson and Mertanto 1977).

The other view of partisanship is expressed by a number of political and social scientists who see partisanship as a useful vehicle for minority representation. Banfield and Wilson's (1963, p. 158) classic account, for instance, suggests that "in a partisan system, being a member of a minority group may be a positive advantage. The party runs a 'ticket' or 'slate' which it 'balances' with candidates who represent the elements within the party in due proportion to their voting strength." In its extreme form, Banfield and Wilson's assertion is probably an exaggeration. Local parties, at least, rarely have the capacity to "slate," and normally they have not been inclined to foster perfect balance. Yet even some semblance of concern for representing diverse elements of the party may enhance black representation. Hawley (1973) goes so far as to suggest that the adoption of partisanship may be a key feature in the development of fair representation for minorities. Several studies (Pomper 1966; Gordon 1970) have also discovered that there is less ethnic voting in partisan than in nonpartisan races, because in partisan elections the party acts as a bridge between different ethnic groups. And the Pettigrew (1976) study cited above found that partisan elections tempered white racial attitudes in the voting for a black mayoral candidate. Thus, in cities with partisan elections, there is probably more white voting for blacks and black voting for whites. Because blacks, as a minority, need white support to win more often that white candidates need the votes of blacks, nonpartisanship may impede black representation.

A number of investigations have examined the effects of partisan-nonpartisan election rules on black representation. The findings are somewhat mixed. Kramer (1971) and Campbell and Feagin (1975) suggest some positive influence of partisanship in a small set of large cities and in the South. Similarly, Robinson and Dye (1978) uncovered a mild but favorable link between partisanship and black council representation in 105 cities of more than 50,000 population that were at least 15 percent black. Conversely, Cole (1974) found no connection between partisanship and either black mayoral or council representation in 16 New Jersey cities.

The evidence appears to indicate a positive but not very strong relationship between partisanship and the election of black candidates. Parties may play a favorable but limited role in fostering black representation. The trend among American cities, however, has been toward nonpartisanship. There have been allegations that partisan systems are more corrupt and suffer the unnecessary intrusion of national parties and "irrelevant political issues" that interfere with the supposedly businesslike operation of local government. This trend may have the effect—intended or not—of depressing blacks' chances of winning election to municipal office.

The effect of form of government on black representation is unclear. Some research has concluded that both partisanship and mayor-council government are generally more responsive to working and lower classes (e.g., Lineberry and Fowler 1967; Karnig 1975), yet no studies have, to our knowledge, linked partisanship or form of government to both the selection of black candidates and the unfolding of programs favored by blacks. The mayor-council form of government or, as some refer to it, the "unreformed system," calls for the mayor to play a visible leadership role in local government. However, there are numerous permutations of this model, ranging from very strong to very weak mayoral control. Cole (1974) found no relationship between form of government and black victory in council or mayor contests, but Robinson and Dye (1978) offer data suggesting that mayor-council government tends to favor the electoral success of blacks. This finding is left unexplained: presumably, the greater politicization of mayor-council cities leads to greater participation and perhaps the kinds of racial compromises that improve blacks' chances of gaining municipal office.

Robinson and Dye mention "manager government" as a factor that was found to "contribute to a decline in black representation." Again, there was no discussion of the reasons underlying the relationship. We may speculate that the presence of a city manager may depoliticize local government, thereby lowering voter turnout (Karnig and Walter 1974), as well as perhaps creating a system that stresses a middle-class reform style in which black candidates often do not fit well.

A third form of municipal government, which has fallen into disfavor of late, is the commission form. In mayor-council and manager-council cities, the city council constitutes the legislature. In commission cities, each of the elected commissioners sits as a legislator as well as being the head of an executive branch department. Each commissioner, then, takes responsibility for a major local government department (e.g., police, fire, and public works). Robinson and Dye (1978) do not mention commission government, but there is cause to believe commission institutions may be the least representative of blacks. Commission cities are most frequently found in the South, the area we expect will have the lowest rates of black electoral success. Further, commissioners are paid more, and commission seats are therefore highly desirable. To anticipate our discussion of council size, commission cities elect few commissioners. The mayor is generally selected by the commission (from among the commissioners) or is the commissioner with the most votes. Since we expected black representation to be lowest in the South, in contests for desirable seats, and where only a small number of council members are elected, we hypothesized that commission cities would be the most unrepresentative of blacks. The extent to which the commission form contributes to underrepresentation of blacks even after taking these other factors into account will be discussed in chapters 3 and 4.

A variable of interest in explaining black mayoral presence is the mode of election of the mayor. Most cities (217) elect the mayor separately. In some, however, the mayor is chosen by the council, or the council member with the most votes in the election becomes the mayor. In both cases, the public does not directly choose one person to be mayor. There has been no prior research examining the effect of these structural arrangements on minority representation; we might speculate, however, that taking selection out of the hands of the public might promote black representation.

Council size and district elections complete our inventory of the political and electoral conditions presumed relevant to black representation. We expected both of these characteristics to have positive independent effects on the selection of blacks of the city council. These topics, especially the question of district versus at-large elections, have drawn wide attention from social scientists and from the courts as well.

Jones's (1976) comparative study of cities that were at least 5 percent black showed that, in 1972, municipalities with larger councils tended to have greater black representation. It may be that the greater the number of council seats available, the more prone whites are to cast votes for black candidates. If the council is small, say fewer than five seats, the election of a single black will give blacks a substantial share of decision-making authority. With larger councils, say with ten or twelve members, the election of one black will not necessarily give blacks any goodly amount of power; hence, whites may be more willing to support a black candidate. Moreover, posts on smaller councils are generally more attractive, since a council member shares authority with fewer colleagues. Consequently, more whites may seek the office. Finally, council size may be especially critical in district cities. The larger the council, the smaller the districts from which council members are drawn. Given the prevalence of racial segregation in American cities, larger councils—those with smaller districts—are more apt to provide districts that contain black majorities. Since there is much racial voting in the United States, with blacks and whites casting ballots overwhelmingly for candidates of their own races (Hahn, Klingman, and Pachon 1976; Halley, Acock, and Greene 1976; Walton 1976), black majority districts may be a key step in the development of black representation.

There has been much controversy on whether at-large elections affect black representation. A majority of the nation's cities use an at-large election of one kind or another—usually a "pure" at-large system, in which candidates can live in any area of the city and are elected by the citywide citizenry, or a modified at-large election, in which candidates must live in specified districts of the municipality but are nevertheless voted upon by citizens in all parts of the community. In a district city, candidates must reside in the districts they wish to represent, and they are chosen exclusively by residents of those districts. At-large contests are an aspect of "reform" government. It has been argued that at-large elections tend to ensure council members with citywide interests rather than parochial concerns, and that at-large elections also make it possible for the "best people" to be selected regardless of where they live.

Most research has revealed a significant but not always powerful link between district elections and greater black electoral success (Campbell and Feagin 1975; Gelb 1970; Jones 1976; Karnig 1976, 1979b; Karnig and Welch 1978; Kramer 1971; Robinson and Dye 1978; Taebel 1978; Sloan 1969). In fact, if there is one question to which scholars interested in black representation have repeatedly returned, it is surely whether district elections promote—and whether at-large elections impede—blacks' chances of winning council seats.

Why would district elections favor black victories? Ostensibly, it is because black candidates seeking district seats can steer clear of direct competition with white candidates. Owing to racial segregation, black candidates running in districts often face electorates that are primarily black; on the other hand, given the minority status of blacks in most United States cities, black aspirants in at-large contests must almost always contend with white majorities. Just as black voters are much more likely to cast ballots for black candidates, the white electorate is prone to support white candidates. At-large elections are also said to increase campaign costs, to more often require endorsements by civic associations, newspapers, and the media, and to stress widespread name recognition. All these elements may be expected to diminish the chances of black success in city council elections. In fact, case studies of the effect of switching from at-large to district elections usually do show an increase in black candidates and council members (Mundt 1979; Heilig 1978; Cottrell and Fleischmann 1979).

Despite these findings and interpretations, there is reason to be cautious about the influence of district elections in promoting the election of blacks. For instance, Cole (1974) has shown that black representation in New Jersey cities is not deleteriously affected by at-large elections. Moreover, MacManus (1978) has argued that once controls are introduced for socioeconomic and other factors, the effect of district elections on black city council representation vanishes. In addition, Welch and Karnig (1978) have provided evidence that large school districts with at-large contests actually have greater black representation on school boards than do communities with mixed or pure district school elections, though their sharply limited sample of district cities make confident generalization impossible.

The issue of at-large or district city elections is no longer confined to the pages of academic journals or "good government" literature. Cities such as San Antonio and Fort Worth, Texas; Charlotte and Raleigh, North Carolina; and Mobile, Alabama, have recently changed their election systems from at-large to district-based. In San Antonio, pursuant to the 1975 Voting Rights Act, pressure apparently was exerted on San Antonio by federal authorities before the shift to district elections. Arguments challenging at-large elections as discriminatory to blacks and other minorities have also reached the courts. Many have decided that at-large systems have been used to discriminate against blacks and Hispanics. For example, in *Paige* v. *Gray* (1971), *Beer* v. *United States* (1974), *Blacks United for Lasting Friendship, Inc.* v. *The City of Shreveport, Louisiana* (1976), and *Bolden* v. *City of Mobile, Alabama* (1976), federal district and appellate courts have ruled that at-large voting systems are unfair to blacks in Albany, Georgia; New Orleans; Shreveport; and Mobile.[1] Similar findings have been issued for county offices of various sorts.[2] Although in each of these cases the courts have decided in favor of single-member districts, they have not asserted the general unconstitutionality of at-large elections. Instead, the judges look for a pattern of discrimination behind the election system. For example, in several cases not only has the court determined that no blacks had ever been elected to the council or commission, it also searched to see if there was a pattern of discrimination in the kind of services the city accorded black neighborhoods and in the city's employment record for blacks, and it looked for other indications that the city in fact intended to or did discriminate against blacks or other minorities. When a pattern of discrimination or intended discrimination could *not* be shown, the courts have upheld the constitutionality of the at-large systems.[3] All the cases where the at-large systems have been struck down are from the South. None of these decisions has as yet been tested in the Supreme Court.[4]

In sum, we have isolated seven political and election rules that may influence black representation in city offices. The first five pertain to both mayoral seats and council posts. The last two focus exclusively on city councils. They give rise to the following hypotheses:

$H_8$ Cities offering higher salaries to municipal officials will tend to have lower rates of black representation.

$H_9$ Cities with longer terms of offices will tend to have lower rates of black representation.

$H_{10}$ Cities holding municipal elections simultaneously with state or national contests will tend to have greater black representation.

$H_{11}$ Cities with the mayor-council form of government will tend to have the greatest black representation, and commission cities will tend to have the lowest rates.

$H_{12}$ Cities with partisan elections will tend to have greater black representation.

$H_{13}$ Cities with larger councils will tend to have greater black representation.

$H_{14}$ District cities will tend to have greater black representation.

*Black Resources*

Distinct from the clusters of variables that concern city conditions external to the black community, this group of characteristics, which we call "black resources," deals with potentially important dimensions of the black population itself. James Coleman (1971) has outlined in detail the different ways particular educational, economic, population, civil rights, media, and protest resources of the black community may be employed to improve the lives of blacks. We hypothesized that black success in winning mayoral and council seats would be higher in municipalities with better-educated and more affluent blacks, where black constituted the majority of the population, where civil rights group, black-owned banks, savings and loan associations, and media are present, and where blacks have previously engaged in civil disturbances (riots).

Black economic and educational resources are potentially the most important of all. Both Wolfinger (1965) and Altshuler (1970) suggest that the electoral participation and success of an ethnic group grows in accordance with the size of the ethnic middle class. Greater affluence and attainment in education probably signal an increase in the number of blacks with the money, time, political talent, interests, and role status requisite for effective political activism. Further, where blacks have greater education and income, they are likely to register, vote, and participate more cohesively than in less affluent and less educated black communities. Indeed, there is abundant evidence that social class characteristics are strongly related to electoral participation (Milbrath 1965; Matthews and Prothro 1966; Verba and Nie 1972).

As Wilson (1966) concluded in an often-cited study, even if racial prejudice were to come to an abrupt halt and a color-blind society were created, blacks would probably continue to suffer low political participation because of their very poor socioeconomic positions.[5] Orum (1966), Danigelis (1978), Olson (1970), and Verba and Nie (1972) provide evidence that, when controls are introduced for socioeconomic measures, recent black political participation is equal to or higher than that of whites. Social class characteristics of the black community may, then, be instrumental in assuring greater representation. Hence we hypothesize that, in cities where blacks are better educated and have higher incomes, blacks receive greater representation.

A few previous studies have supported this proposition, although their findings are somewhat inconsistent on whether black education or black income is the more critical socioeconomic dimension. For example, Karnig (1976, 1979*b*) emphasized the influence on council representation of economic development among blacks, and Marshall and Meyer (1975) discovered that black income factors were more important than black education in predicting the location of black mayors. But Robinson and Dye (1978) found that black education was a more powerful determinant of black council representation than was black income. Despite the present lack of consensus on the specific effects of social class, there is consistency in the general findings that the higher black social class, the greater the chance of blacks' gaining fuller representation.

Black population size may also affect black success in winning municipal office. We had two different kinds of expectations concerning the role of black population size. The first dealt with blacks' chances in winning mayoral races or a larger share of council seats. We anticipated that cities with higher percentages of blacks would more often have black mayors and black council members. Our reasoning needs little elaboration; there is ample documentation that, when possible, both blacks and whites overwhelmingly vote for candidates of their own races. Thus, the higher the black portion of the population, the greater are blacks' chances of winning. Marshall and Meyer (1975) show that the percentage of the population that is black is related to the chances of black mayoral success, and Browning, Marshall and Tabb (1979b) find that the absolute size of the black population is related to ability to mobilize, which in turn leads to increased representation.

However, as we will explain below, it is necessary to examine not only absolute representation of blacks, but also "proportional representation." Especially with reference to city council elections, it is useful to determine the conditions under which blacks gain representation at or above their share of the population. There is reason to suspect that proportional black representation may be affected by the black percentage in the city population. Literature examining this question has reported no relationship between percentage black and city council representation (e.g. Karnig 1976; Robinson and Dye 1978). However, neither of these examinations presented evidence on black representation levels in cities of different black population sizes. There may be a curvilinear relationship in which there is a negative association between percentage black and proportional council representation when blacks are minorities and a positive association after blacks become majorities. A linear test of the proposition will show no association at all. Therefore finer inspection of the pattern is called for, especially since there is other evidence (Key 1949; Schoenberger and Segal 1971; Wright 1977; Blalock 1967) indicating that whites tend to be more threatened by and opposed to blacks as the concentration of blacks in the population increases. Giles (1977), however, argues that this effect is found only in the South. We will, then, test the influence of percentage black on the proportionality of council representation, and we will look especially for any curvilinear patterns.

Black civil rights groups, financial institutions, and media form another group of potentially important black resources. Various studies have suggested that the mobilization of civil rights organizations is related to public policies of benefit to the black community (Morlock 1973; Dunlop 1973; Karnig 1975). Of course, case studies of black campaigns provide evidence of useful electoral activities undertaken by civil rights organizations, not the least of which are voter registration drives. Black candidates are themselves frequently drawn from the ranks of civil rights groups in the community (Salamon 1973). Also, civil rights organizations can provide their members with highly valuable organizational experience—the kind of experience that is exceedingly useful in promoting effective campaigns for office. In communities with well-organized civil rights groups, there are already established channels of communication that simplify the task of the campaign workers in getting the black electorate to the polls. We would guess that, where civil rights organization is weak, campaign efforts will also be weak. By and large, as Crain (1968, pp. 352, 353, 369) has suggested, "more complex...leadership structure" in civil rights groups in a community results in "greater levels of action." With numerous civil rights groups organized in the black community, we would expect more successful black electoral campaigns (Browning, Marshall, and Tabb 1979*b*).

The presence of black banks and savings and loan associations in a city may also have a favorable influence on black electoral success. Blackwell (1975, p. 171) has written that black financial institutions can be significant because of "their present services as well as their potential in the rehabilitation of the black community." Blackwell is doubtless correct about the long-range importance of such enterprises. More immediately, black financial institutions can also be instrumental in aiding black candidates for office. The existence of black financial institutions may indicate more readily available funding sources for black candidates, including campaign contributions and perhaps relatively unsecured loans that allow candidates to wage electoral campaigns. With black financial institutions organized in the city, blacks may be able to reduce their dependence on monetary support from outside the black community. We will test these speculations in chapters 3 and 4.

The presence of black media outlets, too, has implications for black electoral success. The value of black-owned media has been underscored by discussions of the subject (Garret 1970; Blackwell 1975). And black leaders, understanding the potentially profound influence of the media, have challenged the ownership of unresponsive media franchises operated by whites (Congressional Caucus 1973). Black-owned or black-operated newspapers and radio are likely to provide more black political news and information. Newspapers and radio programming directed at the black community enhance black candidates' opportunities to bring their viewpoints directly to that public that is most disposed to vote for blacks. Moreover, the black media can be of use not merely in organizing the vote for a given candidate but also in promoting voter registration drives and raising the probability that blacks will participate in the election.

Although the incidence and severity of racial disorders of the 1960s have been extensively studied (Caplan and Paige 1968; Downes 1970; Morgan and Clark 1978; Sears and McConahay 1973; Spilerman 1970, 1971; Feagin and Hahn 1973), their effect has barely been analyzed (for exceptions, see Hahn 1976; Button 1978; Welch 1975). We do not know whether a link exists between the disorders and black electoral outcomes. Still, there is reason to believe that racial disturbances may be positively associated with the election of blacks to mayoral seats and city councils. Two complementary reasons led us to expect that cities that had experienced civil disturbances would tend to have greater black representation. First, it seems intuitively plausible that the anger that led to a civil disturbance and the political interest that results in enhanced black representation may stem from a common political consciousness. It is clear that the riots were to some degree political acts, directed in part against societal conditions believed to be oppressing to blacks (see Feagin and Hahn 1973). Blacks in cities that experienced disorder, then, are possibly more politicized. Second, after the riots, whites may have better understood the starkness of conditions in the ghetto. The greater understanding and perhaps a disposition to "keep a lid" on the situation could result in more whites' voting for at least some black candidates. Even if the rationale was the provision of token black officials whose election would decrease the chances of further violence, the result would be greater black representation in cities that had riots during the 1960s.

To summarize our propositions concerning the implications of black resources for the election of blacks to mayoral posts and council positions:

$H_{15}$ Cities in which blacks have higher income will tend to have greater black representation.

$H_{16}$ Cities in which blacks have attained higher educational levels will tend to have greater black representation.

$H_{17}$ Cities with black population majorities will tend to have greater black representation.

$H_{18}$ Cities with a greater number of civil rights groups will tend to have greater black representation.

$H_{19}$ Cities containing black financial institutions will tend to have greater black representation.

$H_{20}$ Cities with black-owned or black-operated media will tend to have greater black representation.

$H_{21}$ Cities that experienced civil disturbances during the 1960s will tend to have greater black representation.

## Data and Methods

The focus of our study is the 264 American cities over 25,000 in population (as of the 1970 census) that are at least 10 percent black. This group of municipalities is substantial enough to allow rigorous empirical testing, and the threshold of 10 percent black permits us to concentrate on those communities that have a solid likelihood of blacks' winning election, especially to city council posts.

The information on black representation comes from multiple sources. Different measures will be further discussed in the chapters that concentrate on particular aspects of black representation. Chapter 3 examines black candidacy and success in winning mayoral races; chapter 4 examines black candidacy for council positions, the proportionality of black council representation, and the total share of council seats won by blacks. The data, then, are of two general kinds. One set deals with black candidacy for the mayoralty and council offices; the second set concerns the actual representation of blacks.

Candidacy data were taken from a 1975 mail survey of city clerks, conducted by Albert Karnig and Oliver Walter (1977) in cooperation with the International City Managers' Association, which compiled candidacy information on cities over 25,000 in population. This questionnaire inquired into the number of black and other minority candidates in the last municipal election.

Indicators of black representation in city offices were collected for several points in time. The *National Roster of Black Elected Officials* (1970, 1972, 1975) was used to determine black electoral success during the early and mid-1970s. Since the *National Roster* listing is incomplete (MacManus 1978; Robinson and Dye 1978; Taebel 1978), we undertook a mail survey of city clerks to gather the requisite data for 1978. Information on black mayors and black council members was collected for all 264 cities. When responses to the questionnaire were ambiguous, or if no response was forthcoming after two mailings, the information was gathered by telephone interviews.

Turning to the independent variables, our literature review indicated that a considerable number of indicators had been employed in testing hypotheses about the effects of demographic, antipoverty, political, and black resources on black candidacy and election. Essentially the same set will be used in chapters 3 and 4. The following is a brief description of the measures used in testing these hypotheses.

### White Population and Demographic Factors

Out of the myriad city and black population characteristics, the following were chosen as most relevant to a study of black representation. Except for the region variable, all data on these characteristics were taken from the 1970 census. First we determined in which of the United States regions each city was situated. We began with a fourfold regional categorization: South, including the deep and peripheral South; Northeast, Midwest; and West. The latter two regions were combined in the multivariate analysis because of the small number of western cities. Our analysis demonstrated that the West and the Midwest were very similar in their relationship to the variables under consideration. In our classification, southern states are Alabama, Arkansas, Florida, Georgia, Louisiana, Mississippi, North Carolina, Oklahoma, South Carolina, Tennessee, Texas, and Virginia. The Northeast includes Connecticut, Delaware, Maryland, Massachusetts, New Jersey, New York, and Pennsylvania. Midwestern states were Illinois, Indiana, Kansas, Kentucky, Michigan, Missouri, Ohio, West Virginia, and Wisconsin. Western states included California and Nevada. States not mentioned here had no cities that fit our criteria of 25,000 population including at least 10 percent black.

Second, we utilized city population size, drawn from 1970 United States census. For initial display, we grouped the cities into five population categories: 25,000 through 49,999; 50,000 through 99,999; 100,000 through 249,999; 250,000 through 499,999; and 500,000 and over. In our regressions, these and the following variables are used in their uncategorized, raw form.

Third, the median income of whites was used as an indicator of the social class characteristics of the white population in each city. Subcategories used in the presentation include cities where white income was less than $8,000, $8,000 through $9,999, $10,000 through $12,499, and $12,500 and over.

Our fourth indicator of white population and city demographic characteristics was the proportion of the *non*black community that was foreign-born. The cut-offs for our categories were: less than 10 percent foreign-born, 10 percent to 29.9 percent, and 30 percent and over. This measure includes those whites who have been labeled "white ethnics": the Irish and those of Southern and Eastern European descent, largely Roman Catholic. However, the proportion foreign-born is only a crude measure because many of those we would term "white ethnics" are not foreign-born, but rather are two, three, and four generations removed from immigration, and some foreign-born are not those commonly referred to as "white ethnics." Small fractions of the foreign-born would be Protestants of British and Canadian descent, for example. Still others would be Asians or Hispanics. Even though Hispanics may behave in a somewhat different way politically from people of Eastern and Southern European heritage,[6] we do not believe that the presence of Hispanics in our measure of the percentage foreign-born seriously distorts our analysis. First, the overwhelming majority of Hispanics are not among the foreign-born. Puerto Rican immigrants, for example, are not "foreign-born." Other Hispanics have been in the United States for two or three generations, or in some cases much longer. Second, most of the cities in our universe have very small proportions of Hispanics. More than 100 cities have less than 1 percent, and 214 have 5 percent or less. Only in 20 cities is there more than 10 percent Hispanic population. In those 20 cities, a great (but unknown) proportion of Hispanics would not be counted among the foreign-born. Thus, only in a very few cities would the presence of Hispanics pose a threat to the validity of our foreign-stock measure. Thus we conclude that, though "foreign-born" is far from a perfect measure of the concept "white ethnicity," its limitations are not so serious as to prevent its use.

Finally, we examined the proportion of the population employed by educational institutions. Thus, "college towns" had higher scores on this variable than either towns without colleges or bigger cities with modest-sized colleges or universities. The coding for this variable in the bivariate tables was: less than 7 percent, 7 to 9.9 percent, and 10 percent and over.

## Federal Antipoverty Programs and Funding

Five indicators were used to assess the amount of federal antipoverty activity in each community. First we determined whether each city had participated in the Community Action program, the Neighborhood Youth Corps program, and the Model Cities program. A city was coded 1 if it had participated and 0 if it had not. Information for the first two variables was drawn from the University of Wisconsin's government units analysis data set. The data were originally collected by Robert Alford and Michael Aiken of the University of Wisconsin. The Model Cities participation measure was coded from information contained in George J. Washnis's (1974) work on Model Cities. Our last two variables are a measure of the total antipoverty funds that went into the city at the high point of the antipoverty program (1966), and the amount of money per capita spent in that same year.

These five variables captured different aspects of municipal benefits from the War on Poverty and later Model Cities programs. The presence of a Community Action program indicates that the city was involved in one of the keystone efforts of the War on Poverty. CAPs were also the programs that tried most clearly to stimulate participation by poor communities. Therefore CAPs possibly had the greatest effect on later black leadership mobilization. The presence of Neighborhood Youth Corps programs was a further measure of community acceptance of the antipoverty efforts; fewer cities in our sample were involved in this program (102) than in the CAPs (133). While the Model Cities program was not limited to as few municipalities as its early proponents advocated, those communities selected for Model Cities were relatively few. Being chosen for the program meant the infusion of additional money and the further development of organization for the city's antipoverty effort. Finally, the two indicators of the amount of federal dollars flowing into the community measured the magnitude of federal aid rather than just its presence.

## Political and Election Rules

Accurately determining the political characteristics of various cities is a difficult process. Although the *Municipal Yearbook* has published information on several political and electoral characteristics of municipalities, this information is often incomplete, omits many cases, and is occasionally inaccurate. Consequently, from surveys completed in 1975 and 1978, we have compiled data on city political and election characteristics. The 1975 survey, conducted by Karnig and Walter, asked a series of questions concerning each city's "last" local election and the city's political structure. The sample included 257 out of the possible 264 municipalities over 25,000 in population that are at least 10 percent black. The 1978 survey, sent to the city clerks of the communities, was undertaken by the present authors and was successful in obtaining information on each of the 264 cities under examination here.

Seven political variables were used in the study. Unless noted, these were drawn from the 1978 survey. First, we examined the form of government in each city. The forms include the standard triad of commission, mayor-council, and manager-council government. Second, we coded whether the city was formally partisan or nonpartisan. Although we realized that in some cities formal nonpartisanship masks heavy partisan activity and that in others nominal partisanship conceals moribund local parties, we believed this variable is worth exploring because of the importance attributed to it in prior works on city politics and public policy.

Third, from the 1975 survey we assessed whether local elections are held simultaneously with races for state or national office. This measure was used essentially as a proxy for voter turnout. Next we focused on two characteristics of the council and mayoral offices. From the 1975 survey, we determined the terms of office. We recoded these so that the alternatives were two years or less in office and more than two years. The great majority of all terms of office were, in fact, either two or four years. Fifth, the salaries of the mayor and council members were coded. For tabular displays, council salaries were placed into four categories: less than $1,000, $1,000 to $4,999, $5,000 to $9,999, and $10,000 and over. Mayoral categories reflect the generally higher pay for mayors than for city council members: less than $7,000, $7,000 to $15,999, $16,000 to $25,999, and $26,000 and over.

The type of election was dichotomized into district and at-large systems. Races in which a candidate must live in a district of the city but is elected at large were classified as at-large elections. Similarly, cities with

mixed systems with some seats elected at large and others by district were
also classified as at-large cities. Our rationale for these decisions is based
on a prior analysis of the data (Karnig and Welch 1978) that showed that
pure district cities were significantly different from the other types, hence
constituting a separate category. On the other hand, even with multiple
controls established, there were no significant differences between pure at
large, at large with district requirements, and mixed cities. Therefore we
collapsed these three types into one at-large category.

The seventh political and election characteristic we examined was
council size. After determining the number of council seats, we
categorized council size as less than five members, five or six members,
seven to nine members, and ten or more members.

*Black Resources*

Several measures of black resources were drawn from the 1970 census.
These include the proportion of the city population that is black, the
ratio of median black income to that of whites, and the median education
of blacks in the community. For purposes of the bivariate analysis, the
categories for display for the first variable were coded as less than 20
percent black, 20 to 34.9 percent black, 35 to 49.9 percent black, and 50
percent black and over. The income ratio measure was divided into
categories where black income was less than 60 percent that of whites, 60
to 79.9 percent of white income, and 80 or over. Median education was
trichotomized into fewer than 9 years, 9 to 10.9 years, and 11 years and over.

Data on black civil rights groups, financial institutions, and media were
collected for other projects (cf. Karnig 1979a,b). The variables are somewhat crude, and in some instances the data are older than we would have
preferred. However, in the absence of better indicators, our measures at
least give us some insights into the potentially supportive role of black
organizational, financial, and media resources in promoting black representation. Information on the locations of black civil rights organizations
was gathered in 1971 from correspondence with the national headquarters
of the NAACP, Southern Christian Leadership Conference, and National
Urban League, while the CORE (Congress on Racial Equality) locations
were taken from a 1966 roster of CORE affiliates. We coded cities into
categories with 0, 1, and 2 or more civil rights organizations. Next we
ascertained which communities had black financial institutions—that is,
black-owned banks or savings and loan associations. We coded a city 0 if
it had no such enterprise and 1 if it possessed either a bank or a savings
and loan association. The financial institution data were drawn from Ploski and Kaiser, eds., *The Negro Almanac* (1971, p. 927), and *The Ebony
Handbook* (1974, pp. 246–47). To assess the presence of black media
outlets, we obtained information on which cities were served by black

newspapers and black radio programming (Ploski and Kaiser 1971, pp. 845–53, 859–62). The cities were then coded into those that had 0 black media, 1 black medium, or 2 or more types of black media.

Last, to measure protest resources, we counted the number of racial disorders in the community during 1961 and 1968. These data, utilized by Welch (1975) in a previous project, were collected from the *Congressional Quarterly* (1967, pp. 3–6); the National Advisory Commission (1968, pp. 158–67, 481–631); the Lemberg Center for the Study of Violence (1968); and the *New York Times*. Incidents were included if they had more than thirty participants.

These, then, are the independent variables we will employ in the following two chapters. We have tried to compromise between being so comprehensive that we exhaust the reader with dozens of conceivably relevant variables and being so parsimonious that we omit some important predictors of black electoral activity and success. Therefore we have used multiple indicators of each of our concepts but have tried to eliminate from this report redundant analyses of those indicators.[7]

*Methods*

We employ similar methods in each of the next two chapters. First we present simple tabular displays showing bivariate relationships between the various dependent and independent variables. For example, we present tables displaying the proportion of partisan and nonpartisan cities that have black candidates for the council; the proportion of southern, midwestern, and northeastern cities with black mayors; and so forth. This form of presentation provides valuable descriptive insights into the kinds of cities that have black candidates and officeholders. Yet the more sophisticated reader will immediately recognize, for example, the possibility that, though cities containing black financial institutions have a higher proportion of black council members than do cities without such enterprises, the differences may have nothing directly to do with these financial institutions. Rather, cities with a large black population can be expected to have both black-owned financial institutions and more black officeholders; it may be the size of the black community rather than the financial enterprises that promotes black electoral success. Hence black financial institutions may be only spuriously related to black representation.

It is necessary to determine the relative influence of each indicator upon the black representation variable. We accomplish this by multiple regression, a statistical technique that enables us to sort out the effects of each of our factors while simultaneously controlling for each of the other factors. By using a process—described in the next chapter—that eliminates independent variables with no significant effect on black representation, we arrive at final estimates of the relative influence of those factors that are significantly linked to black representation. Our intention is to present a multivariate analysis simple enough so that most readers can grasp the results and implications, yet sophisticated enough so that we can have confidence in the accuracy of our findings.

# 3 Black Mayors

## Introduction

The central figure in urban politics is the mayor. In most cities, the mayor plays a major role in setting the tone of politics. Indeed, even when the formal powers of the office are circumscribed, the mayor usually has a prominent role in establishing policy priorities, in budgeting, and in appointing individuals to city offices and commissions. Thus the mayor can make at least a moderate amount of difference in the city's political environment and the types of policies adopted.

For the past several decades, racial conflict has been one of the most pressing problems of American cities. City mayors have often played important parts in cooling or aggravating racial tensions. Mayors have taken a variety of stances, from advocating hold-the-line segregationist policies at one extreme to encouraging racial harmony and equality at the other. In recent years, of course, few mayors anywhere have overtly endorsed segregation. Virtually all municipal officials now at least verbalize agreement with the goal of improving conditions for blacks. Of course, there is a profound difference between endorsing black progress and actually working to develop favorable policies, and gross variations still exist in the commitment of mayors to racial equality.

Until the late 1960s, the mayoral contest in most American communities was among whites—candidates were differentiated by their policy stands, but rarely by their skin color. In 1967, however, Richard Hatcher of Gary, Indiana, and Carl Stokes of Cleveland, both black men, were elected to mayoral seats. Blacks in these and other municipalities came to believe that they could move toward resolving pressing urban issues by electing someone of their own race. The success of black mayors in dealing with such issues will be addressed later in the book, but, however well or poorly they fared in altering public policy, the symbolic importance of black mayors cannot be denied. Indeed, this symbolic value may have increased as black mayors have been elected with reasonable frequency during the past ten years.

Growth in the number of black mayors has been slow but significant. By 1978, nearly 10 percent of our 264 cities had black mayors, a figure essentially unchanged from 1975, but one that represents a significant increase from 1972 (7 percent) and 1970 (4 percent). Overall, nearly 16 percent of these cities had a black mayor at some time between 1970 and 1978. Since the black population in these cities was about 25 percent, in 1978 blacks held mayoral posts at about 40 percent of the rate one might expect by chance alone (i.e, 10 percent black mayors/25 percent black population=40 percent). While far from directly proportional, this does represent a dramatic increase over the 16 percent proportionality rate of 1970. The absence of change in the rate of blacks winning mayoral elections between 1975 and 1978 may indicate that the period of rapid growth among black mayors has ended. It is too early to draw firm conclusions, and only time will allow us to determine whether 1975–78 reflected a temporary pause or a halt in the increase of black mayors. It is of some interest to note that all black mayors in these cities in 1978 were male; black females were conspicuously absent (Karnig and Welch 1979).

Unlike the systematic research on which urban settings are most conducive to the election of black city council members, little work has been done in connection with black mayors. The one example of large-scale comparative research on black mayors (Marshall and Meyer, 1975) was able to explain only about 10 percent of the variation in the presence of black mayors during 1960–71. The researchers' conclusions are limited by the use of a long time frame (the types of cities electing black mayors probably changed radically during that twelve-year period), by the inclusion of vice-mayors with mayors, and by the use of only socioeconomic and demographic predictor variables. They did find, however, that the existence of black mayors is affected by such factors as black income, education, and occupational status relative to whites; region; and proportion of blacks in city population. Theirs was an important first step, but a full analysis would include other factors.

Among these factors are our four categories of potentially significant variables: white population and demographic factors; educational, organizational, income, size, communication, and protest resources of the black population; political and election characteristics of the city; and federal antipoverty funds injected into the community in the late 1960s through the War on Poverty and Model Cities programs. Using these same factors, we will analyze the presence and success of black mayoral candidates. Examining black candidates, which has not so far been done, seems essential in understanding black officeholding. The obvious prerequisite for electing a black mayor is a black candidate. If blacks are not elected mayor, it could be because blacks are simply not recruited (or self-recruited) to become candidates or because black candidates are not elected by the citywide constituency.

Of the cities for which we have data, only 27 percent had black candidates in their last mayoral election before 1975, and only 7 percent (13 cities) had more than one black candidate. Overall, blacks averaged 9.4 percent of all the candidates running for mayor. This percentage, then, indicates that the representation ratio for blacks as candidates was only 0.40, almost identical to the representation ratio for blacks as mayors. Thus, blacks are represented equally as candidates and as mayors. This may suggest that blacks have about the same chance of election as whites once they become candidates for office.

The evidence thus seems to indicate that the chief obstacle to the election of black mayors is encountered before formal candidacy. Our data do not allow us to judge whether no qualified blacks are interested in the post, whether interested blacks simply anticipate defeat and therefore do not seek the office, whether they do not possess satisfactory resources to vie with whites in gaining candidacy, or whether racist practices by political parties or by the electorate in primaries operate to exclude black candidates. It is possible that all these processes work to limit black candidates. But once blacks become mayoral candidates, their opportunities for victory are roughly equivalent to those of whites who have become formal candidates.

Only a minority of cities have had black mayoral candidates, let alone black mayors. Are black candidates and mayors likely to come from cities of a particular demographic category, region, political structure, or type of black community? Or are they more or less randomly distributed among cities with at least a modest share of blacks? In answering these questions, we can help to predict the kinds of communities likely to continue electing black mayors.

## Data and Procedures

The independent variables were described in chapter 2. The dependent variables are several. First, we have data on the number and location of black mayors holding office in 1970, 1972, 1975, and 1978—a rather comprehensive account of black mayoral presence in United States cities in recent years. We examined each year separately, then aggregated the years so that a city had a score of 1 if it had a black mayor during any of the years under analysis, 0 if it did not. By examining each year separately, then all years together, we can see whether aggregating black mayoral presence over a longer time span adds to our knowledge of what city characteristics promote the election of black mayors.

The data on blacks as candidates pertain to 1974–75 elections. In all, 184 of the 264 cities over 25,000 that were at least 10 percent black had a mayoral contest in those elections. We examined two indicators of black candidacy. First, we created a dichotomous variable to indicate the presence of any black candidate. Then, for cities with black candidates (N=54), we analyzed the differences between those communities where blacks won the mayoralty and those where they were unsuccessful.

These indexes are imperfect, because they do not tell us whether blacks were "serious" candidates—that is, whether they mounted a "real" campaign and received a substantial number of votes. Especially where we have many black candidates (or many total candidates of both races, for that matter), we can assume that not all of them were serious contenders. Yet our measures do tell us something useful about the willingness and ability of blacks in various cities to enter citywide political contests. As we shall see later, there are in fact some key differences between cities on this important variable.

Our presentation is divided into two parts. First, we display simple frequencies to pinpoint the kinds of cities that black mayors and black candidates come from. We will compare our black mayoral and candidate variables on each of the independent variables, organizing our discussion around the four categories of variables discussed earlier and describing the incidence of black mayors and candidates in the various types of cities. This mode of analysis is especially helpful in answering the question, What kinds of cities nominate and elect black mayors? These tabular displays will also provide preliminary indications of what factors may significantly influence black mayoral candidacy and success. In the second part of our presentation we try to reach some conclusions about which relationships are spurious and which are not. Although it is impossible to completely determine causal patterns, we will use multiple regression to sort out variables whose influence seems to be strong even when other factors are held constant.

## Black Candidates and Mayors: A Descriptive Analysis

Becoming a candidate is the first formal step in the process of being elected to office. Among most American cities, there are three common methods of candidate nomination, determined by city statutes or state laws. One can file for the race as an individual, be nominated by a political party, or collect enough signatures on a nominating petition. In only a handful of cities is the process accomplished in some other fashion. Individual filing is the most common path in these 264 cities.

Even where the candidate needs no formal group endorsement, becoming a candidate usually involves being asked to run or at least obtaining pledges of support from friends, associates, and perhaps others (Seligman et al. 1974). The decision to seek elective office is almost always made in a social context: it is rare for a candidate to run in isolation from any organized or ad hoc grouping. Therefore it is important to examine black candidacies in terms of potential environmental resources. A reasonable person knows that an election campaign takes time and money; before spending that time and money, he or she must believe there is some possibility of election. So it is important for the candidate, as well as the researcher, to survey the community resources and conditions that might influence his chances of success.

The factors actually promoting the success of a black candidate may in some cases, but not all, mirror those encouraging the candidacy itself. To win a citywide race, a black candidate usually must have resources that reach beyond the black community. If a city is dominated by whites, numerically or otherwise, then at least some support must come from the white community, ordinarily from its more "liberal" elements. We would therefore expect to find slightly different correlates of black success than of black candidacies. Further, the election of a black mayor can be thought of as the joint product of the conditions that cause blacks to be nominated (or to choose to run) and those that affect their chance of election once they are candidates.

*White Population Demographic Factors*

We will first examine the association between black candidacy and general demographic and white population factors. Table 5 indicates that few of these factors are related to the incidence of black candidacy. One exception is the regional location of the city. As predicted, black candidates are less frequent in the South (24 percent of all southern cities) than in the Midwest and especially the West.

The Northeast also has a relatively small number of black candidates compared with other regions outside the South. This low number of northeastern candidacies (23 percent of northeastern cities) is consistent with Robinson and Dye's (1978) study of black council members. The low candidacy score has developed even though blacks in the Northeast have the resources that would enable them to participate more effectively in electoral politics: large black communities with relatively high socioeconomic resources. We will explore this puzzle in more detail in the multivariate analysis.

Moreover, black candidates tend to be generally more successful in the West and Midwest, winning 58 percent and 33 percent respectively of the races in which blacks are candidates. In the South and Northeast, black candidate success rates are only 17 percent and 25 percent. Since regional location is strongly related to the presence of black candidates and modestly related to their success, it follows that the presence of black mayors is also associated with region. In fact, the effect is similar, with the Northeast occupying roughly the same position as the South, while the Midwest and West tend to elect more black mayors (table 6). Only 10 percent of the southern and northeastern cities had a black mayor at any time during the 1970s. Yet, in the Midwest and West, approximately

Table 5
Black Mayoral Candidacy and White Population and Demographic Factors

| White Population and Demographic Factors | Proportion of Cities Having a Black Candidate | Black Candidate Success[a] |
|---|---|---|
| Region | | |
| South (95)[b] | .24 | .17 |
| Northeast (35) | .23 | .25 |
| Midwest (43) | .28 | .58 |
| West (8) | .75* | .33 |
| Population size | | |
| 25,000–49,999 (73) | .23 | .24 |
| 50,000–99,999 (41) | .22 | .33 |
| 100,000–499,999 (52) | .31 | .44 |
| 500,000 and over (18) | .39 | .14 |
| Median white income | | |
| Less than $8,000 (12) | .25 | .33 |
| $8,000–$9,999 (95) | .27 | .15 |
| $10,000–$12,499 (70) | .29 | .50* |
| 12,500 and over (7) | .00 | — |
| Percentage foreign-born | | |
| 0–9 (90) | .20 | .22 |
| 10–29.9 (60) | .33 | .31 |
| 30 and over (33) | .33 | .40 |
| Percentage in educational services | | |
| 0–6.9 (61) | .31 | .21 |
| 7–9.9 (64) | .30 | .37 |
| 10 and over (59) | .19 | .36 |
| Overall mean | .27 | .31 |

[a]Based only on cities with black candidates (N=54).
[b]( )=N for each category.
*The relationship between black candidacies and the demographic factor could be considered statistically significant at the .05 level. Since we do not have what is, strictly speaking, a sample (in most cases it is a universe of a defined set of cities at one point in time), two interpretations of this level of significance may be considered. First, one might want to view those relationships that are starred as simply strong relationships by some defined criterion. Others might choose to view our universe of cities as a sample of cities across time and therefore interpret a relationship that is significant at .05 more traditionally—that the sample will reflect true relationships in the population from which it was drawn 95 out of 100 times.

one-third of the municipalities had chosen a black to be mayor at least once in the decade.

No consistent relationships with black candidacies appear among the other white population and demographic indicators. City size shows no clear pattern. Surprisingly, the income level of whites also appears to have no effect. The richest communities do show fewer black candidates

Table 6
Presence of Black Mayors and White Population and Demographic Factors

| White Population and Demographic Factors | 1970 | 1972 | 1975 | 1978 | Ever Had, 1970–78 |
|---|---|---|---|---|---|
| Region | | | | | |
| South[a] (128) | .00[b] | .02 | .04 | .06 | .10 |
| Northeast (50) | .04 | .04 | .08 | .04 | .10 |
| Midwest (163) | .08 | .19 | .18 | .16 | .31 |
| West (19) | .11 | .11* | .21* | .26* | .37* |
| Population size | | | | | |
| 25,000–50,000 (108) | .05 | .07 | .08 | .07 | .17 |
| 50,000–99,999 (61) | .05 | .08 | .12 | .11 | .19 |
| 100,000–499,999 (73) | .01 | .08 | .11 | .10 | .14 |
| 500,000 and over (20) | .05 | .00 | .10 | .15 | .20 |
| Median white income | | | | | |
| Less than $8,000 (13) | .00 | .08 | .08 | .15 | .15 |
| $8,000–$9,999 (135) | .02 | .06 | .07 | .07 | .13 |
| $10,000–$12,499 (107) | .06 | .09 | .15 | .12 | .22 |
| $12,500 and over (9) | .11 | .00 | .00* | .00 | .11 |
| Percentage foreign-born | | | | | |
| 0–9.9 (121) | .00 | .03 | .04 | .05 | .09 |
| 10–29.9 (79) | .05 | .13 | .13 | .11 | .24 |
| 30 and over (63) | .10* | .10* | .18* | .16 | .22* |
| Percentage in educational services | | | | | |
| 0–6.9 (84) | .03 | .06 | .10 | .11 | .17 |
| 7–9.9 (118) | .05 | .08 | .10 | .11 | .16 |
| 10 and over (57) | .03 | .07 | .10 | .06 | .17 |
| Overall mean | .04 | .07 | .10 | .10 | .17 |

[a]( )=N for each category.
[b]The figures are the proportion of cities in each category that have had black mayors.
*$p \leq .05$. See table 5.

than the other cities, but the number of cities with affluent whites is very small, and, in any case, there are apt to be few blacks in wealthy white cities. Contrary to our expectation, municipalities with the lowest percentage of foreign-born residents have fewer black candidates than other cities, though there is no difference between communities with moderate and high percentages of foreign-born residents. One explanation for this is that the cities with fewer foreign-born residents are more likely to be southern cities—those treating blacks least well. Finally, cities with large educational establishments seem to have fewer black candidates, contrary to our hypothesis. It may be that this too reflects the relatively small percentage of blacks in these cities.

The relationships are only slightly different for the presence of black mayors. The association between black mayors and percentage foreign-born is the reverse of what we expected: the *more* foreign-born in the city, the more likely the city is to have a black mayor. There are several reasonable explanations for this finding. First, it may be that recent immigrants are not more antiblack than are others. Percentage foreign-born is an imperfect measure of ethnic competition. Ethnic identification persists beyond the first generation, and the political strength of an ethnic population may increase as its proportion of first-generation ethnics decreases, because the ethnic group becomes acculturated to American politics. Third, the percentage foreign-born includes a small number of Spanish-speaking immigrants from Mexico and Cuba. Although this population is not necessarily supportive of black candidates (see Hahn Klingman, and Pachon 1976), its position as a minority is quite unlike that of Eastern and Southern European ethnics. Spanish-speaking immigrants do not have the political muscle that Eastern European ethnics possess in many cities and therefore probably do not provide the political competition to blacks that the other groups do. Finally, cities with large ethnic populations are generally not southern, and thus these ethnics may be more supportive of black election than are whites in southern cities.

As with black candidacies, the percentage employed in education, city size, and white income appear unrelated to the presence of black mayors. Since these and other variables are associated with the percentage black in a city, we will withhold generalizations until the multivariate analysis.

## Federal Antipoverty Efforts

We hypothesized that cities that had substantial federal antipoverty programs in the 1960s would be the most likely to have black candidates and mayors. There is some evidence that these antipoverty efforts stimulated the development of a black leadership cadre that later could be turned toward electoral politics (Eisinger 1978; Moynihan 1969). To look for this effect, we recorded whether the city participated in the Community Action program (CAP), the Neighborhood Youth Corps program, and the Model Cities program. We also assessed the amount of federal poverty aid going into the city in one of the early, more prosperous years of the programs (1966). The factor we thought would have the most influence in stimulating black leadership formation was the presence of CAP agencies. However, when we examine table 7, we find that Model Cities and Neighborhood Youth Corps programs are most strongly related to the presence and success of black candidates. For example, roughly twice as many communities with Model Cities programs had a black candidate (39 to 21 percent); black candidates in these cities won at a robust rate of 46 percent, whereas black mayoral candidates in municipalities with no Model Cities experience won at only 18 percent. Neither candidate presence nor success is apparently linked to participation in CAPs. These patterns are also reflected in our data on black mayors. The incidence of black mayors is strongly tied to Model Cities participation, very weakly related to Neighborhood Youth Corps participation, and not related at all to the presence of CAP agencies.

Table 7
Black Mayoral Candidacy and Federal Antipoverty Efforts

| Federal Antipoverty Programs and Funds | Proportion of Cities Having a Black Candidate | Black Candidate Success[a] |
|---|---|---|
| Community Action program | | |
| Present (104) | .27 | .29 |
| Absent (80) | .26 | .32 |
| Neighborhood Youth Corps | | |
| Present (78) | .35 | .37 |
| Absent (106) | .21* | .22 |
| Model Cities | | |
| Present (56) | .39* | .46* |
| Absent (128) | .21 | .18 |
| Total antipoverty funds, 1966 | | |
| 0 (68) | .40 | .13 |
| $1–20,000 (33) | .24 | .30 |
| $20,001–70,000 (30) | .19 | .43 |
| $70,001 and over (52) | .23 | .33 |
| Per capita antipoverty funds, 1966 | | |
| 0 (24) | .12 | .17 |
| $1–$149 (32) | .29 | .29 |
| $150–$649 (62) | .26 | .31 |
| $650 and over (48) | .31 | .40 |

[a]Based only on cities with black candidates (N=54).
$p \leqslant .05$. For explanation see note to table 5.

As table 8 shows, black mayors are as apt to be found in cities with or without CAPs and Neighborhood Youth Corps programs. About 16 to 18 percent of cities of either kind have had a black mayor. In contrast roughly twice as many Model Cities communities (27 percent) have elected black mayors as municipalities without this program (13 percent). Whether this relationship is real or is spuriously produced because cities chosen for Model Cities programs have large black populations will be explored in the multivariate analysis.

The presence and the success of black candidates are also associated with the amount of per capita poverty money spent in the city. Although these relationships are not statistically significant, they are in the predicted direction. However, the antipoverty measures have only negligible effect on the presence of black mayors.

We can conclude, then, that cities that had more antipoverty resources in the 1960s, particularly Model Cities and Neighborhood Youth Corps pro-

Table 8
Presence of Black Mayors and Federal Antipoverty Efforts

| Federal Antipoverty Programs and Funds | 1970 | 1972 | 1975 | 1978 | Ever Had, 1970–78 |
|---|---|---|---|---|---|
| Community Action program | | | | | |
| Present (139) | .04[a] | .07 | .10 | .09 | .16 |
| Absent (125) | .04 | .07 | .10 | .10 | .18 |
| Neighborhood Youth Corps | | | | | |
| Present (107) | .05 | .08 | .12 | .11 | .18 |
| Absent (157) | .03 | .07 | .08 | .08 | .16 |
| Model Cities | | | | | |
| Present (75) | .07* | .12* | .19* | .19* | .27* |
| Absent (187) | .03 | .05 | .06 | .06 | .13 |
| Total antipoverty funds, 1966 | | | | | |
| 0 (33) | .03 | .09 | .09 | .06 | .12 |
| $1–$100,000 (96) | .04 | .09 | .04 | .09 | .15 |
| $200,001–$700,000 (46) | .04 | .04 | .07 | .02 | .15 |
| $700,001 and over (63) | .03 | .14 | .10 | .17* | .21 |
| Per capita antipoverty funds, 1966 | | | | | |
| $0 (33) | .03 | .09 | .09 | .06 | .12 |
| $0–$149 (47) | .06 | .06 | .09 | .11 | .17 |
| $150–$649 (91) | .03 | .05 | .08 | .06 | .14 |
| $650 and over (61) | .03 | .08 | .13 | .16 | .20 |

[b]The figures are the proportion of cities in each category that have had black mayors.
*$p \leq .05$. For explanation, see note to table 5.

grams, subsequently have had more black candidates as well as more successful black candidates, and hence a higher probability of having a black mayor. Apparently this positive effect has persisted beyond the immediate infusion of funds. Whether the antipoverty money caused the proliferation of black candidates and their success is a question we will turn to in the multivariate analysis later in the chapter.

*Political and Election Rules*

If we shift our attention from federal antipoverty efforts to the political characteristics of cities, we find the relationships with black electoral activity much less strong. For example, neither mayor-council nor city-manager communities are significantly more likely to have black candidates. Black candidates do seem to be somewhat more successful in council-manager systems (table 9), though this pattern is not reflected in black mayoral presence (table 10). Despite the findings that mayor-council cities produce policies more in accord with minority needs (e.g., Lineberry and Fowler 1967), mayor-council systems do not appear to increase the election of black mayors. Indeed, during 1970–78, only 13 percent of such communities had a black mayor, whereas 18 percent of the commission cities and 20 percent of those with manager systems have had a black mayor during the 1970s.

Table 9
Black Mayoral Candidacy and Political and Election Rules

| Political and Election Rules | Proportion of Cities Having a Black Candidate | Black Candidate Success[a] |
|---|---|---|
| Partisanship | | |
| Partisan (75) | .21 | .25 |
| Nonpartisan (100) | .33* | .33 |
| Form of government | | |
| Commission (15) | .30 | .14 |
| Manager-council (75) | .25 | .37 |
| Mayor-council (86) | .27 | .30 |
| Mayor's term of office | | |
| Less than four years (66) | .20 | .23 |
| Four years (118) | .31* | .33 |
| Mayor's salary | | |
| $0–$6,999 (64) | .25 | .38 |
| $7,000–$15,999 (26) | .19 | .20 |
| $16,000–$25,999 (50) | .24 | .08 |
| $26,000 and over (41) | .37 | .47 |
| Independence of elections | | |
| Simultaneous (77) | .29 | .30 |
| Independent (99) | .27 | .32 |

[a]Based only on cities with black candidates (N=54).
* $p \leq .05$. For explanation, see note to table 5.

Black candidates emerge more often in nonpartisan systems, though the reason for this is unclear. Certainly, in some cities where political parties are powerful, the party leadership may try to keep blacks from running for this most important citywide office and may slate them for minor offices instead. However, many partisan systems operate without strong parties capable of slating candidates. Rather, candidates are chosen in primaries without much party organization directed at "turning out the loyalists." Likewise, many presumably nonpartisan systems behave in some respects like party systems, with candidates sponsored and supported by political parties even though no party name is on the ballot. Black candidates are more successful in nonpartisan systems, and this is reflected in the presence of black mayors. In the 1970s a mere 8 percent of partisan cities had a black mayor, while 21 percent of nonpartisan communities had elected a black mayor. In light of arguments favoring partisanship—since it putatively promotes black representation—these findings are provocative. At the mayoral level, at least, it is possible that party elections actually reduce blacks' chances of gaining the mayoralty.

Whether local elections are held simultaneously with national or other elections seems to make no difference in either the presence of black candidates, their success, or the consequent incidence of black mayors. We hypothesized that simultaneous races would foster more black mayors, because simultaneous elections encourage turnout, which in turn might stimulate black voting. However, it appears that the timing of these elections is irrelevant to black activity or success.

Table 9 indicates that there are more black candidates when the mayor's term of office is four years than when the term is shorter. Given the relatively low economic status of blacks, it may be that potential black candidates would not want to sacrifice economic security for the possibility of only a two-year term. Further, as noted above, longer terms of office are more attractive for several reasons. In general, there should be more candidates of both races when the mayor's office is more desirable. This reasoning is further supported by the lack of a relationship between term of office and either success for black candidates or the presence of black mayors. We would not expect term of office to enter into voter calculations, at least not in ways favoring black candidates. In fact, it appears that voters are somewhat more likely to favor blacks when the term is two years instead of four, suggesting that they are more willing to "take a chance" on a black mayor if the term if brief.

We developed a similar hypothesis concerning mayoral salary. We

Table 10
Presence of Black Mayors and Political and Election Rules

| Political and Election Rules | 1970 | 1972 | 1975 | 1978 | Ever Had, 1970–78 |
|---|---|---|---|---|---|
| Partisanship | | | | | |
| Partisan (88) | .02[a] | .03 | .07 | .06 | .08* |
| Nonpartisan (174) | .04 | .09 | .12 | .12 | .21 |
| Form of government | | | | | |
| Commission (28) | .07 | .07 | .07 | .04 | .18 |
| Manager-council (118) | .03 | .08 | .11 | .12 | .20 |
| Mayor-council (118) | .03 | .07 | .09 | .09 | .13 |
| Mayor's term of office | | | | | |
| Less than four years (109) | .04 | .06 | .09 | .08 | .21 |
| Four years (150) | .04 | .08 | .11 | .11 | .14* |
| Mayor's salary | | | | | |
| $0–$6,999 (107) | .06 | .10 | .12 | .09 | .23 |
| $7,000–$15,999 (43) | .00 | .05 | .09 | .09 | .14 |
| $16,000–$25,999 (56) | .00 | .02 | .02 | .00 | .02 |
| $26,000 and over (49) | .08 | .10 | .16* | .18* | .20* |
| Independence of elections | | | | | |
| Simultaneous (106) | .02 | .09 | .10 | .09 | .17 |
| Independent (144) | .05 | .07 | .10 | .10 | .17 |
| Mode of election | | | | | |
| By people directly (217) | .04 | .06 | .09 | .09 | .13 |
| Other ways (47) | .04 | .11 | .15 | .13 | .34* |

[a]The figures are the proportion of cities in each category that have had black mayors.
*$p \leqslant .05$. For explanation, see note to table 5.

expected that a higher salary would attract blacks to run for office. The professions of many white officeholders—lawyer, insurance agent, realtor, and so forth—are not as prevalent among blacks. These occupations allow one to withdraw for a time without suffering financial ruin or loss of job. In fact, members of these occupations may benefit from contacts and information gained while holding office. The black middle class, however, is primarily salaried, and members can less easily take time off to run for and hold office. Therefore the salary of the office by itself would have to be sufficient.

The evidence indicates that a high salary is mildly related to the presence of black candidates, with 37 percent of the high-salary cities having black candidates but only 25 percent or less of those offering lower salaries. However, there is an interesting curvilinear relationship between black success and mayoral salary. It may be that, when the salary is low, the competition for office is also relatively low; hence blacks have a greater chance of winning (see an analogous argument made for women in Diamond 1977). This curvilinear relationship also is reflected in the presence of black mayors, since 20 percent or more of the low- and high-salary communities have had black mayors in the 1970s compared with only 14 percent or less of those offering intermediate salaries (table 10). Finally, we see that when mayors are not chosen directly by the people, blacks have a slightly better chance of being selected. This is especially true in looking at the aggregate statistics for 1970–78. The other methods include selection of the council member with the most votes or selection by the council itself. It appears that blacks will have a better chance of winning the mayoralty when the decision is not made directly by the electorate.

## Black Resources

Our final group of explanatory variables refer to characteristics of the black population— the organizational, financial, and other resources possessed by members of the black community. The group of black resources measured here appears to have an impressive influence on black political life. All seven black resource indicators are significantly related to the incidence of black mayoral candidates; three are significantly linked to candidate success; and six demonstrate a significant association with the presence of black mayors in 1978 or during 1970–78. These patterns strongly suggest that black socioeconomic and other resources have greater effect on number of black candidates and electoral success than any other set of factors we have considered.

Not surprisingly, one of the most important black resources is the percentage of blacks in the community. Clearly, black population size can act as a key resource in improving black candidacy and election rates. When we examine the presence of black candidates, however, the relationship is not a linear one. Cities that are 10 to 20 percent black are as likely to have black candidates as are cities that are nearly 50 percent black (table 11), providing some support for our expectations about a curvilinear pattern. Blacks are progressively more underrepresented as candidates as their population increases, until they become a population majority.

Table 11
Black Mayoral Candidacy and Black Resources

| Black Resources | Proportion of Cities Having a Black Candidate | Black Candidate Success[a] |
|---|---|---|
| *Socioeconomic resources* | | |
| Black/White income ratio | | |
| Less than .60 (89) | .23 | .15 |
| .60–.799 (81) | .27 | .46 |
| .80 and over (14) | .50* | .29* |
| Median black education | | |
| Less than 9 years (49) | .20 | .10 |
| 9–10.9 years (109) | .23 | .39 |
| 11 years and over (26) | .50* | .31 |
| *Population resources* | | |
| Percentage black in city | | |
| 10–19.9 (80) | .20 | .19 |
| 20–34.9 (63) | .29 | .17 |
| 35–49.9 (31) | .23 | .27 |
| 50 and over (10) | .80* | .88* |
| *Organizational resources* | | |
| Black banks or savings and loans | | |
| Present (44) | .38* | .31 |
| Absent (220) | .24 | .31 |
| Black media outlets | | |
| 0 (99) | .21 | .29 |
| Radio *or* newspaper (38) | .29 | .36 |
| Radio *and* newspaper (25) | .36* | .29 |
| Number of civil rights groups | | |
| 0 (43) | .12 | .20 |
| 1 (48) | .25 | .33 |
| 2–4 (74) | .35* | .35 |
| *Protest resources* | | |
| Number of racial disturbances, 1961–68 | | |
| 0 (127) | .24 | .19 |
| 1 (36) | .22 | .50 |
| 2 or more (19) | .53* | .50* |

[a]Based only on cities with black candidates (N=54).
*$p \leq .05$. For explanation, see note to table 5.

The profound effect of black population size is obvious in tables 11 and 12. For instance, though there were black candidates in fewer than 30 percent of cities in which blacks were population minorities, there was at least one black candidate in a full 80 percent of communities with black majorities. Black candidates won in fewer than 30 percent of the cities with lower black population levels, but in 88 percent of the cases with black majorities in the electorate. Parallel evidence is found in the data on black mayors in the 1970s. Once again, black majority cities have an extraordinarily high rate of black mayors—more than 80 percent had a black mayor during the time period. But no more than 17 percent of the cities with black minorities had a black mayor during the decade. Black population size, then, has a profound effect, but only after the 50 percent mark is reached. A closer inspection reveals that the proportion of black mayors does increase slightly (though not proportionately) as black population increases in the North, but it has no such effect in the South until blacks become a majority.

Other black resources also seem to be instrumental in promoting black candidacies and representation. In particular, black income and education have a notable effect. As the ratio of black to white incomes increases, so too does the number of black candidacies as well as their rate of success. In cities where the black income gap is less than $3,000, the presence of black candidates and the probability of their election is more than double that in cities where the gap is more than $5,000. Black candidacy is also strikingly more likely where black educational attainments are higher and is markedly more frequent where blacks have a median educational level of at least eleven years. Black success in winning elections, however, is not so strongly affected by black community education levels, though there appears to be a difference between those with less than nine years' education and all other communities. Blacks are ten times more likely to be elected mayor in cities where blacks have a high median education than where median education is less than nine years, and the differences between cities with high and low black income resources are also clear. These data show beyond question that blacks tend to profit politically in environments where they are relatively properous and have gained more education. Of course, these findings are not startling. Social science research has uncovered a consistent positive linkage between political activity and individual social class characteristics, though Alford and Lee (1968) found the opposite relationship between class and activity in examining city-level data with controls for political factors. Our findings, however, provide preliminary support for our original proposition that black socioeconomic characteristics strongly affect black representation.

The incidence of black candidates, their success, and the consequent presence of black mayors are associated with black organizational and protest resources as well as with simple demographics. Though the relationships are not perfect, all three of the organizational resources— black civil rights groups, financial institutions, and media outlets—are significantly linked to the presence of black mayoral candidates. Although none of these resource indicators are significantly associated with candidate success scores, the cities with more civil rights groups and black financial institutions do tend to have black mayors more often. However, since these organizational measures are also related to black population size and other aspects of the black community, we must await the multivariate analysis before we develop a final assessment of their effect on black representation.

Table 12
Presence of Black Mayors and Black Resources

| Black Resources | 1970 | 1972 | 1975 | 1978 | Ever Had, 1970–78 |
|---|---|---|---|---|---|
| *Socioeconomic resources* | | | | | |
| Black/white income ratio | | | | | |
| Less than .60 (126) | .02[a] | .03 | .05 | .04 | .10 |
| .60–.799 (114) | .05 | .09 | .11 | .12 | .19 |
| .80 and over (24) | .08 | .21* | .29* | .25* | .42* |
| Median black education | | | | | |
| Less than 9 years (62) | .00 | .02 | .02 | .03 | .03 |
| 9–10.9 years (158) | .03 | .08 | .10 | .10 | .17 |
| 11 years and over (44) | .11* | .14* | .21* | .18* | .34* |
| *Population resources* | | | | | |
| Percentage black in city | | | | | |
| 10–19.9 (119) | .01 | .05 | .08 | .04 | .13 |
| 20–34.9 (90) | .02 | .06 | .06 | .07 | .13 |
| 35–49.9 (41) | .07 | .02 | .07 | .10 | .17 |
| 50 and over (12) | .33* | 58* | .75* | .83* | .83* |
| *Organizational resources* | | | | | |
| Black banks and savings and loans | | | | | |
| Present (44) | .05 | .07 | .14 | .20* | .25* |
| Absent (220) | .04 | .07 | .09 | .07 | .15 |
| Black media outlets | | | | | |
| 0 (152) | .05 | .08 | .08 | .08 | .16 |
| Radio *or* newspaper (54) | .04 | .09 | .15 | .11 | .19 |
| Radio *and* newspaper (58) | .02 | .03 | .10 | .12 | .17 |
| Number of civil rights groups | | | | | |
| 0 (61) | .00 | .02 | .05 | .02 | .05 |
| 1 (77) | .05 | .08 | .09 | .09 | .18 |
| 2–4 (152) | .05 | .09 | .12 | .14* | .20* |
| *Protest resources* | | | | | |
| Number of racial disturbances, 1961–68 | | | | | |
| 0 (180) | .04 | .06 | .07 | .08 | .13 |
| 1 (57) | .02 | .09 | .11 | .07 | .29 |
| 2 or more (25) | .08 | .16* | .28* | .28* | .36* |

[a]The figures are the proportion of cities in each category that have had black mayors.
*$p \leq .05$. For explanation, see note to table 5.

Finally, as we expected, black candidacy, black candidate success, and the presence of black mayors are more likely in cities that experienced racial disturbances in the 1960s. The pattern is particularly evident in table 12. In 28 percent of the cities having had two or more riots there was a black mayor in 1978, yet only 7 to 8 percent of the communities with fewer than two riots had a black mayor. And over 1970–78, cities with two or more riots had about twice as great a likelihood of having a black mayor as those with one disturbance or none. The multivariate analysis to follow will tell us whether this relationship is spurious.

In sum, all the black resources we examined are related to the presence of black candidates. The link to candidate success was weaker, though black income, population, and protest resources were related. Except in the small number of cities where blacks are a majority, black resources may not be the compelling factor in a citywide victory; a successful candidate needs to attract white organization and financial resources as well. This is somewhat substantiated by the distribution of black mayors. Black population size, black income and educational resources, and black protest are still important in predicting which cities will have black mayors, but black organizational, financial, and media resources evidently recede in influence.

## Conclusions: Where Black Mayors Are Found

Of our four types of factors, black resources and the inflow of federal poverty money appear to be most closely related to the presence and success of black candidacies and to the overall incidence of black mayors. If we were to extrapolate into the future, the black resource findings in particular would augur well for possible improvement in the level of black mayoral representation. For example, black educational attainment is rising appreciably; and, though the relative incomes of blacks and whites have remained fairly stable, the absolute income of blacks has grown. One might venture to predict that, as a result of rising black social class characteristics, black victories in mayoral elections will become more frequent. Even more important, perhaps, blacks continue to increase their proportion in many city populations, a factor that becomes a key determinant of black success once blacks achieve majority status. Despite these changes, however, there has been *no* increase in the incidence of black mayors between 1975 and 1978. Any speculation about "trends" in these findings therefore remains hazardous.

We have sought to determine the types of cities where black candidates and mayors are most often found. But various characteristics of cities are very much interrelated. Cities with large black populations, for example, are more likely to have had both federal poverty programs and more riots. It is necessary to untangle the relative effects of these diverse characteristics before we can ascertain with confidence the factors that promote black electoral success at the citywide level. Therefore we move on to a multivariate presentation, where we attempt to uncover the comparative importance of our variables in promoting black candidacy and electing blacks to office. We will use mutiple regression. This technique allows us to eliminate factors whose relationship with the mayoral variables is spurious and to evaluate the comparative effect of the remaining variables in explaining the black mayoral outcomes.[1]

## Black Candidates and Mayors: A Multiple Regression Analysis

We begin our multivariate analysis by examining the combined effect of each cluster of variables on our dependent measures. Table 13 presents the results of this analysis. There are too few cases to assess accurately the effects of independent variables on candidate success. Therefore, we focused exclusively on three measures of black mayoral politics: (1) the presence of a black candidate in 1974–75 elections; (2) the election of a black mayor during 1970–78; (3) the presence of a black mayor in 1978. The results from the 1978 data give us a very up-to-date picture, and the 1970–78 composite variable provides a check against 1978 being an atypical year.

Table 13
Variation in Black Mayoral Candidacy and Mayoral Presence Explained by Variable Clusters

| Variable Clusters | Black Candidacy | Black Mayor, 1978 | Black Mayors, 1970–78 |
|---|---|---|---|
| Black resources | 15.8% | 20.3% | 24.5% |
| White population and demographic factors | 8.6 | 11.4 | 7.3 |
| Federal antipoverty efforts | 7.1 | 5.8 | 6.5 |
| Political and election rules | 3.7 | 5.8 | 5.5 |

We see that, for all three dependent variables, the black resources cluster accounts for the most variance, ranging from slightly less than 16 percent for the candidacy variable to almost 25 percent for the 1978 mayoral indicator. White population and demographic factors are the next most potent set of characteristics, though their contribution to explained variance in the dependent variables amounts to only 7.3 to 11.4 percent. Federal antipoverty efforts and municipal election and political rules make even smaller contributions, running from 5.8 to 7.1 percent for the antipoverty indicators and from 3.7 to 5.8 percent for the political measures. This analysis indicates, then, that the black resource cluster is by far the best single predictor of black mayoral candidacy and election.

However, this form of analysis does not inform us which of the independent variables, taken together, are the most powerful. It may be, for example, that many of the black resource variables appear important in explaining black success in mayoral elections only because of their relation to other variables, notably black population size. It may be that federal antipoverty efforts or city political characteristics have *no* effect once black resources are controlled. Ideally, we would like to know the relative influence of each of our twenty-three variables in explaining the occurrence of black candidates and black mayors. As a practical matter, however, that is impossible because of the strong interrelationships among the variables. The presence of very powerful interrelationships (i.e., multicollinearity) does not permit us to undertake an analysis utilizing all twenty-three variables. In a multiple regression equation, if two variables are related at a substantial level—for example, at $r=.70$—then one of the measures may show a strong positive relationship to the dependent variable and the other a very small association or even a large negative one. This happens because the first factor has captured all the joint variation that is shared with the dependent and the second independent variable, leaving the second independent variable with little residual variation to explain.

To minimize the problem but still portray as accurate a picture as possible of the relative effect of each of these variables, we used a several-stage process to winnow the number of independent variables. We decided to enter into a regression equation any measure that had been significantly related to the dependent variable in either bivariate relationship; a multiple regression that included all variables in its category (e.g., all black resource variables); or a multiple regression where the dependent variable was regressed on all twenty-three variables. An indicator that was significantly associated with the black representation rates in any of these three analyses would then be considered for the final multiple regression.

Our second step was to enter the variables that remained after this weeding-out into a second regression procedure. At this stage, seventeen variables remained in the two black mayoral regressions, nine in the candidacy analyses. An inspection of the regression output revealed further problems of multicollinearity that the first step had not solved. For example, community size was strongly related to a number of other characteristics, such as black financial and media resources, some of the political variables, and so forth. A further pruning was therefore needed. At this step we eliminated all variables that had an $F$ ratio of less than .50. The procedure allowed us a way to obtain a multivariate result free of large errors owing to multicollinearity without mistakenly omitting from the anlaysis some independent variable that might have a substantial effect on the dependent variable. We were left with thirteen variables in the black mayoral regressions and seven variables in the black candidacy regression.

Our regression of black candidacy on the independent variables reveals that very few factors have a significant effect on the presence of black candidates (table 14). As one might expect, the proportion black in the community has the largest effect ($\beta = .36$). The median education of the black population makes a strong contribution to explaining black candidacy as well ($\beta = .30$). Contributions of the other variables are less strong, though cities that participated in the Model Cities program are more likely to have black candidates than those that did not. Of the political characteristics, only nonpartisanship has a statistically significant relationship with black candidacy. Cities with nonpartisan systems are slightly more likely to have black mayoral candidates than cities with partisan systems. This might be due to the greater ease of being nominated in some nonpartisan systems. None of the city demographic characteristics have any bearing at all on black candidacy. The only variable that remained until the final regression model was northeastern region, and its regression coefficient was negligible.

Table 14
Significant Variables in Final Black Mayoral and Candidacy Multiple Regressions

| Variable | Black Candidacy | Black Mayor, 1970–78 | Black Mayors 1978 |
|---|---|---|---|
| Percentage black | .36 | .38 | .46 |
| Black/white income ratio | — | .24 | .19 |
| Percentage in educational services | — | .24 | .16 |
| Median black education | .30 | .20 | .21 |
| Number of racial disorders | — | .13 | — |
| Mayor's salary | — | — | — |
| Midwestern locale | — | .13 | — |
| Northeastern locale | — | −.10 | −.17 |
| Partisanship | −.11 | −.11 | — |
| Mayor's term of office | — | — | — |
| Model Cities participation | .22 | — | — |
| Mode of election | — | −.12 | — |
| Total R² | .23[a] | .37[c] | .32[b] |

[a]The Northeast region, the mayoral term of office, and the per capita poverty funds received had insignificant relationships with the black candidacy variable in this final regression.
[b]Midwest locale, median white income, racial disorders, mayoral salary and term of office, partisanship, and Model Cities participation were not significantly related to the mayoral variable.
[c]Median white income, commission form of government, mayoral salary and term of office, and participation in Model Cities were not significantly related to the mayoral variable in this equation.
*All variables significant at .05. For explanation, see note to table 5.

In sum, it appears that the presence of black mayoral candidates is most strongly related to black resources, especially the proportion and the educational level of the black population. Partisanship had a very modest effect on this candidacy variable. And participation in the Model Cities program has the expected positive effect on the presence of black candidates, even with other factors controlled. Table 15 summarizes these findings. It is clear that black resources are by far the most powerful predictors of black candidacy, contributing uniquely 13 percent of explained variance. The political variables explain only 2 percent uniquely and 4 percent in combination with the others, and the final two clusters explain even less. In fact, city population characteristics explain no variation whatever.

Table 15
Unique and Shared Contributions to $R^2$ in Black Candidacies by Variable Clusters

| Variable Clusters | Unique | Shared | Total |
|---|---|---|---|
| Black resources | .13 | .04 | .17 |
| Political and election rules | .02 | .04 | .06 |
| Federal antipoverty effort | .03 | .02 | .05 |
| White population and demographic factors | .00 | .00 | .00 |

An analysis of the black mayoral measures yields somewhat different findings (table 14). Again, however, the greatest predictor of black mayoral presence is the proportion of blacks in the city. The beta weights of .46 in 1978 and .38 in 1970–78 are by far the strongest of any of our independent variables. In 1978 the next strongest predictor of the presence of black mayors is median black education, with a beta of .21, whereas in 1970–78 the black/white income ratio is even more strongly related with a beta of .24. In all, four of the nine significant variables in the 1970–78 equation and three of the five in the 1978 equation are black resource variables.

The contributions made by white population and demographic characteristics are substantially smaller. In both regressions, the percentage in educational services is related in a moderately positive way, and the northeastern locale of the city is related in a modestly negative way. Although the former relationship was predicted, the latter was not. Thus the location of a city in the Northeast was a stronger negative predictor of its having a black mayor than was location in the Deep South. In referring to the bivariate findings along with the multivariate ones, it is not difficult to see why, in a statiscal sense, this is so. Cities in the Northeast had approximately the same percentage of black mayors as did those in the Deep South (in fact slightly fewer in 1978). At the same time, however, in contrast to the South, the northeastern cities have black populations with greater resources—particularly education and income, but also protest resources—and that would lead one to predict higher rates of black mayoral leadership in the Northeast. Thus there is reason to expect the Northeast to have more black mayors than the South because of its wealthier and better-educated black populations. In an important sense, the absence of black resources in the South accounts for the low rate of black mayors there, but the small number of black mayors in the Northeast is largely unaccounted for by other factors in the regression. Hence, northeastern location is negatively related to the dependent variable. This explanation does not give us substantive answers to why cities in the Northeast should have fewer black mayors than those in other nonsouthern regions. One reason may be that blacks are a larger minority in northeastern cities than they are in either the West or the Midwest. And the environment of which they are a part is undergoing greater decline than are cities in either of the other two nonsouthern regions—or in the South, for that matter. Consequently, many whites in the Northeast may feel especially threatened, politically as well as economically, by these two factors in conjunction. In none of the other regions that we examined are both these factors present; in the West and Midwest the black urban populations are not as large as they are in the Northeast, and in the urban South, though the black populations are at least as large, the cities are growing and expanding economically, rather than shrinking and losing economic resources.

Further, a number of large northeastern cities continue to be machine-dominated; where the machine prevails, it may be unlikely that a black would be encouraged to run for mayor. Black mayoral success is often achieved by casting aside the machine-sponsored candidate (as happened with Hatcher in Gary). If the machine thrives, black chances are diminished, because the machines traditionally have been controlled by white ethnic groups not predisposed to allow others to gain political power. However, machine behavior cannot be considered the sole cause of the relationship. We have thirty-five northeastern cities in our sample, and only a small fraction could be said to experience any kind of machine control.

Political characteristics make a slight but significant contribution to explaining the presence of black mayors. Nonpartisanship seems to have a small positive effect on black election in 1970–78, as it did with black candidacy. This effect is smaller than any we have discussed but is still statistically significant. Further, if we look at the nine-year time span, we see that the mode of mayoral election is also slightly and negatively related to the presence of black mayors. Black mayors are less often found in cities where the mayors are elected directly by the public. None of the other political variables are significantly related to the presence of black mayors.

Finally, with all the controls introduced, the participation of a city in the Model Cities program or other federal antipoverty programs does *not* have a significant effect. Apparently, its bivariate relationship with the presence of black mayors was due to its intercorrelation with black population and other black resources. Even though the Model Cities experience appears to have stimulated black candidacy, this does not carry over to black electoral success. Presumably, whatever boost the program gave black interest and skill in politics, it did not give the impetus necessary to ensure victory with a predominantly white electorate.

Table 16 summarizes the relationships of the independent variable clusters to black mayoral presence. The unique variance explained by each cluster, along with the variance it explains in common with the other variables and its consequent total variance, are outlined in that table. The findings there reaffirm the previous discussion. The lion's share of the variance explained is accounted for by the unique contribution of black resources. It alone explains 22 percent of the 31 percent explained variance in 1978, and 21 percent of the 34 percent in 1970–78. Its shared variance is negative, indicating a suppressor effect on the part of the other variables.[2]

As we noted earlier, the key black resources are population size and socioeconomic development. When blacks constitute a majority of the population, they tend to elect a black mayor. In fact, when black population size exceeds 50 percent, blacks obtain a disproportionately large number of mayoralties. For example, blacks won more than 80 percent of the mayoral posts in these cities, though they constituted, on the average, less than 60 percent of the total population. There is, then, as expected, a high degree of racially determined voting in mayoral elections. Where blacks constitute a majority, there is actually underrepresentation of whites in the mayoralty—and, where whites are in the majority, there is underrepresentation of blacks.

Our evidence also indicates the powerful role of socioeconomic resources—that is, black education and income. Where the black population is better developed socioeconomically, it is more capable of vying with whites for elective office. It is likely that better-educated and more affluent black communities have a greater number of "qualified" aspirants for office, higher rates of electoral participation, and enhanced financial capacity to elect black officials. Even with multiple controls established, therefore, as the black middle class grows in size, so do the chances of electing a black mayor.

In 1978 white population and demographic characteristics make the only other important unique contribution to predicting black mayoral presence, though political characteristics do contribute some shared variance. In 1970–78 the unique variance contributed by white population and demographic factors and by political and election rules increased somewhat over the 1978 findings. Still, in this latter regression, black resources claim by far the largest share of the explained variation.

## Conclusions

Some explanation may be offered for the slightly different findings for the one-point-in-time data (1978) and the longitudinal data (1970–78). In both cases, black resources are clearly the most important predictor of success

Table 16
Unique and Shared Contributions to $R^2$ in Black Mayoral Variables by Variable Clusters

| Variable Clusters | 1978 | | | 1970–78 | | |
|---|---|---|---|---|---|---|
| | Unique | Shared | Total | Unique | Shared | Total |
| Black resources | .22 | .02 | .24 | .21 | −.02 | .19 |
| City and white population factors | .04 | −.02 | .02 | .08 | −.01 | .07 |
| Political and election rules | .01 | .04 | .05 | .04 | .00 | .04 |
| Federal antipoverty efforts | .00 | .03 | .03 | .00 | .02 | .02 |

in electing a black mayor. In the longitudinal analysis, however, other factors seem to be more important than they are for 1978 alone. One logical explanation for this is that, at any given point in time, the relatively small number of mayors holding office in these cities leads to measurement error in estimating the effects of city characteristics on electoral success; that is, there are so few black mayors that the effects of various characteristics are likely to be overestimated or underestimated slightly at that point. The defeat of a black, or the election of a black mayor by one or two other cities, may cause a considerable shift in the size of the estimators. However, when we examine a nine-year period, the number of black mayors is considerably larger, and the correlates of the presence of those mayors is more stable. As we mentioned earlier, if the period covered is so long that there are important shifts in the kinds of cities that elected black mayors, one's conclusions could be questionable. However, referring back to the bivariate relationships displayed earlier in the chapter, we can see that the relationships between presence of a black mayor and the whole array of city characteristics stayed fairly constant. The same kinds of cities that elected blacks in 1970 were likely to do so in 1978, though the relationships often grew somewhat stronger. Given the vagaries of these kinds of data, however, we believe that the findings across the four data points are remarkably consistent.

If we turn from measurement problems to the substance of our findings, what do we have? Our major finding, it seems, is obvious, yet very important. That is, blacks are increasingly able to convert population and socioeconomic resources into representation in municipal office. As black populations grow larger, better-educated, and less poor, the chances of having a black mayor improve. Since, in fact, black urban populations are growing proportionally larger and are raising their educational and income standing, it is reasonable to expect that more and more cities will have black mayors. In examining the phenomenon of black mayors, then, researchers should not focus on political and general demographic factors to the exclusion of resources within the black community itself.

Generally speaking, demographic shifts in the black population are not trends over which we have much control; many would like to see the income and educational status of the black population improve, not necessarily so blacks could win political office, but to make their everyday lives easier. Winning political office, for most, would be a goal very secondary to improving employment, housing, and other conditions of life.

Do our findings yield any policy recommendations? Are there other factors, under the control of policymakers, that might be changed to promote the election of black mayors? At this point the answer seems to be a qualified no. We would not want to decrease mayors' salaries to attract more black candidates; improving the income of blacks would certainly be a more desirable goal. The effect of partisanship on black officeholding is so minimal that it would be difficult to generate enthusiasm for promoting nonpartisanship. And the relationships between black mayors and each of the other political and poverty inflow characteristics are so low that we are not even sure that nonspurious relationships exist, let alone that we should begin changing institutions to promote the election of blacks.

However, the mayoralty is probably the most difficult urban office to win in terms of the financial resources and name recognition necessary. It is certainly possible that political and other characteristics outside the black population itself are relatively random with respect to the election of a black mayor but that, if we look at other urban offices, more systematic findings will emerge. With this in mind, we turn to a consideration of black candidacy and election to the legislative branch of urban government—the city council.

# 4 Black City Council Candidacies and Representation

## Introduction

Members of the city council ordinarily are not as visible or as powerful as mayors. Though not quite household words, Maynard Jackson, Kenneth Gibson, Tom Bradley, and Richard Hatcher are at least easily recognized inside and frequently outside their cities. On the other hand, few people outside their own communities have heard of black—or, for that matter, white—council members. Indeed, they are often not even well recognized in their home communities.

Nevertheless, council members individually and collectively possess a good deal of political authority. There are, of course, great variations from city to city. In some a city manager recommends an initial budget and hires and fires personnel. In other communities that have a strong-mayor form of government, the mayor submits the budget, hires and dismisses department heads, and exercises veto power over legislation. In still other municipalities, the council alone is responsible for the budget, personnel practices, and so forth. Regardless of these differing institutional arrangements, however, the council has ultimate authority over most municipal policies. Spending, taxing, and lawmaking responsibilities give the council, at the minimum, a great measure of potential power over local policy.

Because only one mayor serves at a time, the chances that a city's mayor will be black are slim indeed, as we have found. But the probability of blacks' winning election to the council is considerably higher, since a greater number of council members serve at any one time. In fact, roughly 85 percent of our cities have five or more council members, making it far more likely that blacks will be able to achieve at least some council representation. The all-or-none situation that marks the mayoral race, in which blacks either win it all or lose it all, does not augur well for the electoral chances of blacks. The win some, lose some situation of city councils, in which blacks can be defeated for certain council seats yet win other seats, provides a more favorable opportunity for blacks to gain representation.

As we suggested in chapter 2, the issue of black council representation is many faceted. Any comprehensive analysis must focus on conditions related to blacks' becoming candidates for city council posts; blacks' obtaining council seats in proportion to their numbers in the city population; and the absolute percentage of the council composed of blacks, irrespective of their numbers in the city population.

This chapter will deal with these aspects of black representation. As in the previous chapter, we will first present simple frequencies to display the effects of demographic and white population factors, municipal, political, and election characteristics, federal antipoverty funding, and black resources on black council representation and candidacy levels. Subsequently, we will use mutiple regression to assess the relative influence of particular conditions on black candidacy, equitable representation, and absolute voting power on city councils.

## Data and Measures

Our data on black candidacy are taken from the 1975 Karnig and Walter survey of cities described in chapter 2. Unfortunately, because the candidacy information was gathered as part of a larger examination undertaken for other purposes, there are limitations in our ability to treat the data. In analyzing council candidacy, three special problems exist. First, though we know the number of council members elected and the number of black candidates, we have no way of ascertaining the number of black candidates for any specific council seat. For example, in a given municipal election there may have been five council positions contested and two black candidates. The survey information specified neither the number of white candidates nor whether the two blacks were candidates for the same seat or were running for different council positions. Second, the data are less than ideal because in some cities candidates run for specified positions. That is, in district elections the candidates always run for particular seats; in some at-large races candidates also run for place one, place two, and so forth. Other cities, however, have at-large elections with the highest vote-getters capturing the available council positions. The third problem is that some cities have runoff elections with only the top finishers in the primary designated as candidates, whereas other communities have no provisions for a runoff if one candidate obtains a majority of the vote during the first balloting.

The three limitations noted above somewhat restrict our ability to generalize confidently about how various factors affect black candidacy. However, we are aware of *no* previous comparative examinations of rates of black candidacy in city council elections. Thus even an examination of less than perfect information can prove highly valuable.

Given the demonstrated underrepresentation of blacks in local government, we will assume that a larger number of black candidates per council seat is a favorable outcome for blacks. Undoubtedly there are occasions when too many black candidates seek a given office and thereby split the votes that would otherwise go to a single black aspirant. Yet, on balance, the presence of too many black candidates is the exception rather than the rule. Many cities had no black city council candidates whatever. Our underlying assumption that having more black council candidates favors black council representation is supported by the fact that black candidacy is strongly and significantly related to overall black council representation ($r = .48$; $p \leq .001$). In sum, despite its shortcomings, our information will permit at least some preliminary judgments about the probable effects of a number of city characteristics on black candidacy.

We use two measures of black council candidacy. The first, the ratio of the number of black candidates to the available council seats (the candidate representation rate), takes the following form:

$$\text{Candidate representation rate} = \frac{\text{Number of black candidates}}{\text{Number of council seats voted on}} .$$

This formula takes into account that the number of black candidates is largely a function of the number of council positions available by dividing the number of black candidates by the number of council seats available for election. Although there are exceptions, we will presume that, where there are more black candidates per seat, blacks are candidates for a greater share of council posts. The candidate representation scores, then, will serve as crude indicators of the number of council seats for which blacks are candidates.

We would expect, our course, that the larger the black population the greater the black candidacy rate. Consequently we developed a second important statistic, the candidate equitability score. It is the black candidate representation rate divided by the size of the black population.

$$\text{Candidate equitability score} = \frac{\text{Black candidate representation rate}}{\text{Percentage of blacks in city population}} .$$

The candidate equitability score takes into account the proportion black in the city population and therefore better measures the "fairness" of the number of black candidates for the city council.

We have also created two measures of council representational equity. One, which we shall call the black council equity ratio, takes the following form:

$$\text{Black council equity ratio} = \frac{\text{Percentage of seats held by blacks}}{\text{Percentage of blacks in the city population}} .$$

The black council equity ratio, then, indicates how closely the percentage of council posts won by blacks reflects the black proportion in the city population. Table 17 illustrates four possible black council equity patterns in cities that are 20 percent black.

City A has no black representative, and therefore black council equity

Table 17
Possible Patterns of Black City Council Representation

| City | Blacks on City Council | Blacks in City Population | Black Council Equity Ratio |
|------|------------------------|---------------------------|----------------------------|
| City A | 0.0% | 20% | 0.00 |
| City B | 10 | 20 | 0.50 |
| City C | 20 | 20 | 1.00 |
| City D | 40 | 20 | 2.00 |

equals zero. City B, which possesses only half as much black representation as the black population warrants by sheer numbers (10 percent of the council is black, but blacks constitute 20 percent of the city population), accordingly is assigned a council equity score of .50. In city C blacks have precisely the same share of the council as their percentage of the population; hence the council equity rate is 1.00. Finally, city D's equity value is 2.00, indicating that blacks are actually overrepresented on the council because they have twice as many council posts as their percentage of the population would justify. In sum, black council equity has the attractive quality of being set at zero when there is no black representation, as in city A; greater than zero but less than 1.0 when black representation is present but not proportional, as in city B; 1.0 when the black percentage of the council is exactly the same as the black percentage of the municipal population, as in city C; and over 1.0 when the level of black representation exceeds the proportional representation rate, as in city D.

The ratio indicator of black council equity is intuitively easy to understand, but it has two primary limitations. First, a number of cities have no black representation; the presence of many zeros creates some mild difficulties in undertaking statistical analyses such as correlation and regression. Second, there is a conceptual problem. Consider two cities, one with 10 percent of its population black and the other with a black proportion of 20 percent. Assume that neither city has a black city council member. Both municipalities are assigned a 0 equity ratio, though we should expect more representation in the community that is 20 percent black. The equity ratio simply does not capture the difference between these cities. Consequently, Taebel (1978) and MacManus (1978) have suggested another measurement approach: Black council equity equals black percentage of city council minus black percentage in city population.

For this subtractive technique, a negative value indicates underrepresentation of blacks (the black population is proportionately larger than the black share of the council); a zero shows fair representation (the black share of the council and the black share of the population are precisely the same); and a positive sum suggests overrepresentation of blacks (the black council share is proportionately larger than the black population).

However, the subtractive measure also has shortcomings. Compared with cities that have large black populations, cities with small black populations have a much narrower range of possible negative values and a greater possible range of positive values. Consider three examples: City 1 has a 10 percent black population; it can have a minimum score of $-10$ percent $(0-10=-10)$ if the city has no black representative and a maximum score of 90 $(100-10=90)$ if all council members are black. City 2, with 50 percent of the population black, has a possible minimum of $-50$ and a maximum of 50. City 3, with a population 90 percent black, has a potential minimum of $-90$ and a maximum of 10. Thus it is evident that the possible scores are inversely related to the percentage of the population that is black. As a result, in our group of cities, though the percentage of blacks is unrelated to the ratio measure, there is a significant negative relationship between the subtractive score and the percentage of the population that is black $(r= -.18; p \leqslant .01)$. Furthermore, it is often difficult to interpret the subtractive measure. For instance, while the ratio measure permits an interpretation that blacks are twice as fairly represented in cities where the ratio is .5 rather than .25, subtractive scores do not permit a parallel interpretation. Therefore, given the strengths and weaknesses of both the ratio and the subtractive approaches, we will present the results of analyses using both.

The data on black council representation come from our 1978 mail survey of the 264 American cities over 25,000 in population and at least 10 percent black. In addition, the data drawn from the *Roster of Black Elected Officials* in 1970, 1972, and 1975 provide benchmarks against which to judge any possible changes in the level of black representation on city councils.

After we compare the rates of council equity for different time periods in the 1970s, we will concentrate on the 1978 levels of black representation—that is, the absolute rate of black council representation regardless of the percentage of blacks in the city population.

A Descriptive Analysis

Of the cities in our sample, 73 percent had at least one black candidate in their city council elections. This is a highly encouraging statistic. With blacks constituting only 10 percent of the population in many of these cities, this is a considerable proportion. However, we must bear in mind that sixty-eight cities (27 percent of the sample) had no black candidate and therefore could elect no black council members. It should be noted, too, that all of these cities had appreciable black proportions in their populations, often more than the minimal 10 percent.

On the average, there were 4.07 black candidates for every 10 council positions being voted upon. When standardized for black population, the candidate equitability score suggests there was a mean of 1.62 black candidates for each seat that we would expect blacks to win based on their share of the population. That is, for an election for 10 council posts in a city with a population 20 percent black, there would be about 3 black candidates. If the black population were 30 percent, there would be about 5 black candidates for the 10 council seats, and so forth.

How successful are black candidates in getting elected to office? In our 264 cities, blacks constituted 17.3 percent of the elected council members in 1978—twice the rate of mayorships they acquired. Given that blacks average 24.7 percent of the population in these cities and occupy 17.3 percent of the council seats, they have about 71 percent of the representation that their share of the population would justify. The black council equity ratio, then, is .71, and the equity score reflects black underrepresentation of −7.36 percent. Clearly, though not suprisingly, blacks are underrepresented on city councils. Additional evidence of this underrepresentation is evident when one notes that seventy-five cities (more than 28 percent of the sample) have no black representatives, about the same proportion that have no black candidates. Moreover, we find that 70.5 percent of these cities have an equity ratio below 1.0 and thus underrepresent blacks on city councils, while only 29.5 percent have an equity ratio of at least 1.0. Thus, although it is obvious that by the late 1970s blacks continued to be underrepresented on city councils, they were not universally underrepresented, since almost 30 percent of the cities did provide equitable, or more than equitable, representation.

Further, there has been substantial progress in securing more equitable levels of black representation during the 1970s. Improvement in the rate of black council equity has been dramatic. In 1970, 61 percent of the cities had no black council member, and blacks obtained only 27 percent of the expected representation. By 1975 the proportion of cities with no black representation had dipped to 46 percent, and blacks obtained about 50 percent of the council seats their numbers warranted. By 1978 the proportion of cities without black representation had dwindled to 28.4 percent, and blacks gained representation at 71 percent of the expected level.

Viewed somewhat differently, in 1970 blacks had at least some representation in 31 percent of the municipalities; in 1975 they had representation in 54 percent. And in 1978 they captured at least some representation in roughly 72 percent of the sample communities. By any measure, then, black representation has become far more equitable over the 1970s. The equity rate is still low, and many cities still lack black candidates as well as black representatives, but equity is now far higher than the alarmingly unrepresentative rates of the early 1970s and before. The evidence presented to this point suggests both substantial progress by blacks in obtaining more proportional representation on city councils and appreciable disparities in the equitability of black representation in different cities as well as in candidacy rates. In the rest of this chapter we will seek to ascertain what municipal characteristics affect the equity of black representation and the incidence of black candidacy on these United States city councils.

## White Population and Demographic Factors

We first sought to determine whether black council equity varied in cities marked by different white population and demographic factors. We expected that several of these characteristics would influence the strength of black council representation and candidacy.

Previous research suggested that black representation would be higher in larger cities, because larger cities would have better organized black populations and because whites would be a bit more liberal in their acceptance of black representation. But, as tables 18 and 19 show, there is no clear pattern of variation among cities of different sizes. The relationships are mixed. City size, then, is unrelated to any of our measures of black council equity or candidate representation.

Previous examinations have reached different conclusions on whether black representation tends to be more proportional in cities with higher socioeconomic status (Cole 1976; Karnig 1976). Our analysis shows that, though the patterns are not strong, black candidacy rates tend to be somewhat higher in cities where whites are the *least* affluent and where a *smaller* percentage of the work force is employed in education. Common wisdom would have us believe that middle-class whites are more sympathetic to black interests and that persons involved in education are more liberal. These findings should at least make us pause before drawing such conclusions. At best, white socioeconomic status is unrelated to black candidacy, and black candidates may actually do less well in communities of prosperous whites. Moreover, in cities where whites are the least affluent and where there are fewest educational workers, black equity is the greatest (.85 of the expected rate and only 2.4 percent underrepresentation). But this lowest category of white income, less than $8,000 annually, includes only 13 cities. If we divide the sample of cities into two categories, below and above $10,000 income, there do appear to be generally higher equity levels in communities with more prosperous whites. In cities where white income averages under $10,000 a year, the equity rate is considerably lower (.66) and the underrepresentation amounts to $-9.2$ percent. White income may thus have some mild beneficial effect on the fairness of black representation, even though its effect on candidacy is the opposite. This suggests that, when black candidates actually appear. they are somewhat more likely to be elected in upper-income areas.

The percentage foreign-born in the city is unrelated to black candidacy and positively related to council equity. Since first- and second-generation immigrants have emphasized local public sector representation in the past, we felt their traditions could clash with the aspirations of blacks for greater council representation. The actual equity figures are most favorable in communities with more than 10 percent foreign-born, with blacks gaining .79 of the fair rate. Levels are lowest in cities with less than 10 percent foreign-born, where the equity rate is .61 and underrepresentation is −.10.7.

Perhaps we should not be surprised at these findings. They conform to our bivariate findings concerning mayors. Andrew Greeley (1976) has argued that there is no public-opinion evidence to suggest that those of foreign parentage harbor any more racial prejudice than other groups. On the other hand, since the foreign-born are concentrated in the North and in areas with greater black resources, we must withhold firm conclusions until later in this chapter.

The final demographic characteristic is region. As table 18 indicates, black candidacy varies considerably by region. As one might expect, the rate is lowest in the South, the region suffering the most severe legacy of racial bigotry and inequality. However, the candidacy levels are barely higher in the Northeast. In the Midwest and especially the West, with

Table 18
Black Council Candidacy and White Population and Demographic Factors

| White Population and Demographic Factors | Black Candidate Representation | Black Candidate Equity |
|---|---|---|
| Region | | |
| South (128) | .36 | 1.33 |
| Northeast (48) | .42 | 1.46 |
| Midwest (62) | .41 | 1.97 |
| West (15) | .83* | 3.21* |
| Population size | | |
| 25,000–49,999 (109) | .41 | 1.78 |
| 50,000–99,999 (59) | .36 | 1.24 |
| 100,000–249,999 (50) | .38 | 1.60 |
| 250,000–499,999 (20) | .58 | 1.98 |
| 500,000 and over (19) | .40 | 1.57 |
| Median white income | | |
| Less than $8,000 (13) | 64 | 2.39 |
| $8,000–$9,999 (134) | .42 | 1.52 |
| $10,000–$12,499 (102) | .38 | 1.67 |
| $12,500 and over (8) | .25 | 1.45 |
| Percentage foreign-born | | |
| 0–6.9 (121) | .44 | 1.87 |
| 10–29.9 (76) | .44 | 1.58 |
| 30 and over (59) | .29 | 1.39 |
| Percentage in educational services | | |
| 0–6.9 (81) | .34 | 1.32 |
| 7–9.9 (116) | .45 | 2.13 |
| 10 and over (57) | .48 | 1.56* |

*$p \leqslant .05$. For explanation, see note to table 5.

traditions of greater egalitarianism and more limited histories of racial antagonism, the levels are the highest. There are also robust differences in the rates of black council equity in the various regions. And, as with candidacy levels, the poorest council equity is obtained by blacks in the South. Indeed, the .54 southern equity ratio is a scant one-half of the expected level, resulting in a prominent degree of underrepresentation (−12.4 percent). In the northeastern cities, council equity levels are somewhat greater, with blacks gaining roughly .73 of their warranted share.

Table 19
Black Council Equity and White Population and Demographic Factors

| White Population and Demographic Factors | Council Equity Ratio | Council Equity Score |
|---|---|---|
| Region | | |
| South (128) | .54* | −12.4%* |
| Northeast (50) | .73 | −6.1 |
| Midwest (63) | .93* | − 0.6* |
| West (19) | 1.05* | − 0.2* |
| Population size | | |
| 25,000–49,999 (109) | .67 | −8.7 |
| 50,000–99,999 (62) | .84 | −4.9 |
| 100,000–249,999 (53) | .59 | −8.7 |
| 250,000–499,999 (20) | .74 | −5.5 |
| 500,000 and over (20) | .80 | −5.8 |
| Median white income | | |
| Less than $8,000 (13) | .85 | −2.4 |
| $8,000–$9,999 (135) | .64 | −9.9 |
| $10,000–$12,499 (107) | .78 | −5.0 |
| $12,500 and over (9) | .71 | −5.2 |
| Percentage foreign-born | | |
| 0–6.9 (121) | .61 | −10.7 |
| 10–29.9 (79) | .79 | −5.0 |
| 30 and over (63) | .79* | −4.0* |
| Percentage in educational services | | |
| 0–6.9 (84) | .87 | −3.5 |
| 7–9.9 (118) | .65 | −8.5 |
| 10 and over (57) | .59* | −10.8* |

*$p \le .05$. For explanation, see note to table 5.

In contrast to the Northeast and in stark contrast to the South, midwestern communities provide almost perfect numerical representation for blacks (.93) and barely underrepresent them, at less than 1 percent (−0.6 percent). This high degree of proportional representation is itself exceeded by the substantial council equity afforded in the 19 western cities. In fact, as measured by the ratio approach, blacks are slightly overrepresented in the West (equity=1.05); as gauged by the subtractive score, blacks are represented at nearly precise equitability (underrepresentation= −0.2 percent). In the Midwest and West, then, the black community overall has won essentially the level of numerical representation that the size of the black population justifies.

Regional differences in black representation may depend upon the attitudes of white voters in the various areas of the country. There is some evidence that southern whites actually are more racially prejudiced than whites elsewhere. However, southern cities are also marked by less black resource development, fewer antipoverty programs, and allegedly unfavorable election rules such as at-large elections. In the multivariate research reported later in this chapter, we will be better prepared to judge whether southern location directly impedes the fairness of black representation—through, say, less favorable white voters—or whether it simply reflects the fact that southern blacks have fewer resources.

## Federal Antipoverty Funds

One of the primary goals of the Office of Economic Opportunity's War on Poverty policies, especially the Community Action program, was to develop enhanced political power on the part of the poor, particularly blacks. Of course, antipoverty funding was also aimed at reducing social dependence, decreasing unemployment, and fostering social equality. Regardless of the motivation, and there is an abundant literature suggesting that the motives were mixed, we would expect that heightened politicization, diminished social dependence, greater employment, and more social equity should be linked favorably with blacks' ability to nominate and elect candidates in city council elections.

The candidacy data, however, with one exception, are generally unsupportive of such expectations. In table 20, for example, cities with the highest and lowest levels of overall antipoverty funding had somewhat more black candidates, and cities with intermediate funding had the least. Only meager differences existed based on per capita funding as well. Totally unrelated to black candidacy was the presence of Community Action programs, the policy innovation that we were most interested in, and Neighborhood Youth Corps programs. Office of Economic Opportunity (OEO) programs may have had socially equalizing and politicizing effects on blacks and on the poor generally, but they had no measurable effect on the rates of black candidacy.

The presence of Model Cities programs in a city was the one federal antipoverty program that was significantly connected to the number of black candidates per council seat. Interestingly, Model Cities was not an OEO program, and it was intended to be less "political" than its OEO predecessors. However, that Model Cities is not significantly associated with black candidate equity leads us to believe that the relationship with candidate representation is probably spurious. That is, there are more blacks in cities with higher black candidate representation scores, and

Model Cities programs are related to percentage black in the population. Model Cities were in part responses to black poverty; and cities with larger black populations are apt to have a larger number of black candidates. The multivariate analysis at the end of the chapter will allow us to see if Model Cities influences black candidacy or if it is spuriously related.

Table 20
Black Council Candidacy and Federal Antipoverty Efforts

| Federal Antipoverty Programs and Funds | Black Candidate Representation | Black Candidate Equity |
|---|---|---|
| Community Action program | | |
| Present (133) | .41 | 1.57 |
| Absent (122) | .40 | 1.68 |
| Neighborhood Youth Corps program | | |
| Present (102) | .42 | 1.58 |
| Absent (153) | .40 | 1.65 |
| Model Cities program | | |
| Present (72) | .55 | 1.76 |
| Absent (185) | .35* | 1.57 |
| Total antipoverty funds | | |
| $0 (44) | .51 | 1.86 |
| $1–$200,000 (104) | .32 | 1.48 |
| $200,001 and over (112) | .45 | 1.66 |
| Per capita antipoverty funds (1966) | | |
| $0 (52) | .46 | 1.42 |
| $1–$149 (46) | .32 | 1.45 |
| $150–649 (95) | .34 | 1.55 |
| $650 and over (59) | .54 | 1.69 |

$*p \leqslant .05$. For explanation, see note to table 5.

Though poverty programs and funds may not strongly affect candidacy rates, it is nonetheless possible that such funding and programs may result in a higher election rate—and thus more equitable representation. In fact, the statistics presented in table 21 show a weak but consistent tendency for higher council equity to be found in communities that had antipoverty programs and greater funding. Again, we must emphasize that the relationships are weak and in no case quite statistically significant. However, almost without exception, the patterns reveal that council equity is a bit higher where federal antipoverty resources were introduced into the community. For example, the rates are lower in cities without Community Action programs, without Model Cities programs, and without Neighborhood Youth Corps programs. Moreover, cities with some antipoverty funding and those with the greatest per capita share tend to represent blacks in closer line with their proportion of the overall city population.

Of course, even if the patterns were statistically significant, we could not say categorically that federal funds have worked to create viable black political organizations that propel blacks into council office. It is possible, too, that cities that took part in these programs may have already been more sensitive to the needs of the black population. The information displayed here does suggest, however, that communities with antipoverty program experience may perform a little better in providing proportional black representation. And, if this is true in the multivariate analysis, one likely explanation is that federal funds were instrumental, despite some abuses, in helping to organize black communities.

Table 21
Black Council Equity and Federal Antipoverty Efforts

| Federal Antipoverty Programs and Funds | Council Equity Ratio | Council Equity Score |
|---|---|---|
| Community Action program | | |
| Present (137) | .74 | −6.2% |
| Absent (125) | .67 | −8.7 |
| Neighborhood Youth Corps program | | |
| Present (105) | .72 | −5.9 |
| Absent (157) | .69 | −8.4 |
| Model Cities program | | |
| Present (75) | .71 | −6.5 |
| Absent (189) | .71 | −7.7 |
| Total antipoverty funds | | |
| $0 (46) | .64 | −10.4 |
| $1–$200,000 (104) | .73 | −7.1 |
| $200,001 and over (112) | .71 | −6.4 |
| Per capita antipoverty funds (1966) | | |
| $0 (33) | .61 | −10.7 |
| $1–$149 (47) | .69 | −7.6 |
| $150–$649 (97) | .67 | −8.3 |
| $650 and over (61) | .72 | −5.2 |

## Political and Election Rules

We expected that black candidacy rates would be higher where the council office was more prestigious or attractive. For instance, council positions would be more desirable when few council seats were available, thus increasing the importance of any given seat; when the term of office was long; and when the salary was greater. We also anticipated that black candidacy would profit from more politicized systems of local government, ones that held elections simultaneously with races for state and national office, that were partisan, that employed the mayor-council form rather than a city manager, and that used district instead of at-large elections in choosing council members.

Table 22 provides evidence largely consistent with our prestige or attractiveness proposition. Where there are four or fewer council positions on the ballot, there is a mild though not statistically significant tendency for blacks to attain more equitable candidacy rates. It seems likely that black resources may be less divided when fewer seats are voted on. Thus those resources may be directed toward converting interest in an office into actual candidacy. Given the limited financial resources of most blacks, the politically ambitious must rely on community support rather than on their own finances. When contributions can be funneled into few races, the result may be a somewhat higher level of black candidacy.

Table 22
Black Council Candidacy and Political and Election Rules

| Political and Election Rules | Black Candidate Representation | Black Candidate Equity |
|---|---|---|
| System of representation | | |
| District (59) | .49 | 2.08 |
| At large (198) | .38 | 1.49* |
| Partisanship | | |
| Partisan (85) | .33 | 1.22 |
| Nonpartisan (170) | .45 | 1.84* |
| Form of government | | |
| Commission (28) | .38 | 1.48 |
| Manager-council (115) | .40 | 1.74 |
| Mayor-council (114) | .43 | 1.55 |
| Term of office | | |
| Two years or less (78) | .25 | 1.16 |
| More than two years (168) | .50 | 1.92* |
| Council salary | | |
| Less than $1,000 (19) | .37 | 2.11 |
| $1,000–$4,999 (140) | .38 | 1.59 |
| $5,000–$9,999 (49) | .50 | 2.85 |
| $10,000 and over (27) | .54 | 1.55 |
| Number of Council seats | | |
| Fewer than 4 (82) | .49 | 2.08 |
| 4–6 (78) | .36 | 1.50 |
| 7–9 (50) | .40 | 1.46 |
| 10 and over (37) | .42 | 1.45 |
| Independence of elections | | |
| Simultaneous (104) | .36 | 1.76 |
| Independent (144) | .46 | 1.61 |

*$p \leq .05$. For explanation, see note to table 5.

Council income is weakly but positively related to black candidate representation but unrelated to candidate equity. One would expect that blacks would find more attractive and perhaps financially necessary those posts that pay more. Cities with council salaries of less than $5,000 have somewhat fewer black candidates. The highest rates are discovered in communities paying $10,000 and over. Again, since council income is not associated with candidate equity, we must be suspicious of its real effect. The regression analyses at the end of the chapter will help us sort out whether council income is actually related to black candidate representation.

Of even greater apparent importance is the length of the council's term of office. Where the term is more than two years, blacks have double the number of candidates per council seat (.50 compared with .25). Furthermore, the equity ratio was substantially higher in cities with longer council terms (1.92) than in those with briefer ones (1.16). Positions offering stability are probably considered more attractive and are accorded higher status than those of shorter duration. Short terms mean more frequent elections. And, for several reasons, frequent elections are less preferred by candidates. Short terms divert attention from the development of public policy, they afford less opportunity to plan initiatives, and, perhaps most critically, they require a more frequent commitment of financial resources. With a greater need to invest psychic, monetary, and physical resources in campaigns for reelection, shorter terms of offices are doubtless less attractive to most politicians, regardless of race.

There is, then, some preliminary support for our expectations about the positive role of council desirability in influencing the level of black candidacy. In analyzing actual election to council office, however, our hypothesis was the reverse. That is, we believed black council equity would decrease as the desirability of the council seats became greater. Our logic was founded on the general proposition that the more attractive positions would also trigger greater interest among whites, and thus blacks would do less well.

We found some support for the desirability hypothesis as it relates to council equity (table 23). Council equity does vary by term of office. In cities where the term is two years, blacks obtain .70 of the warranted rate, and and where the term of office is longer the rate is almost the same, .72. However, black council equity does not vary significantly with both the level of council pay and the number of seats on the city council. As we predicted, blacks do somewhat better in cities where the salaries are lowest. Black council equity is .87 in cities where council members are paid less than $1,000 a year. The equity figures descend as salary rises until blacks gain only .58 of their justified rate of council members, an underrepresentation of −10.8 percent, in cities offering council salaries of over $10,000 a year. This inverse pattern may result from the added competition spurred by higher remuneration for public service.

A still stronger relationship is evident when we look at the black council equity levels in cities with councils of different sizes. As council size increases, blacks do progressively better in acquiring proportional representation. Black council equity rates are intermediate in medium-sized councils, with between five and nine members. In these situations, blacks gain roughly the average for all cities, about .70 of the justified level, leaving somewhat more than 7 percent underrepresentation. The bleakest rates are found in cities employing the smallest councils, those with fewer than five members. On such councils, blacks win merely .42 of the expected rate.

Table 23
Black Council Equity and Political and Election Rules

| Political and Election Rules | Council Equity Ratio | Council Equity Score |
|---|---|---|
| System of representation | | |
| District (62) | .92 | −1.3% |
| At large (202) | .64* | −9.2%* |
| Partisanship | | |
| Partisan (88) | .79 | −5.1% |
| Nonpartisan (174) | .67 | −8.4%* |
| Form of government | | |
| Commission (28) | .29* | −18.0% |
| Manager-council (118) | .74 | −7.1% |
| Mayor-council (118) | .78 | −5.0% |
| Term of office | | |
| Two years or less (79) | .70 | −6.8% |
| More than two years (169) | .72 | −7.3% |
| Council salary | | |
| Less than $1,000 (20) | .87 | −3.9% |
| $1,000–4,999 (144) | .77 | −6.1% |
| $5,000–$9,999 (50) | .59 | −8.9% |
| $10,000 and over (28) | .58 | −10.8% |
| Number of council seats | | |
| Fewer than 5 (40) | .42 | −15.2% |
| 5–6 (73) | .69 | −7.6% |
| 7–9 (93) | .70 | −7.2% |
| 10 and over (58) | .94* | −1.9%* |
| Independence of elections | | |
| Simultaneous (106) | .75 | −5.5% |
| Independent (149) | .69 | −8.3% |

*$p \leqslant .05$. For explanation, see note to table 5.

Several possible reasons may be advanced for the evident influence of council size on the proportional representation of blacks. First, as we have noted, a seat on a large council tends to be less desirable than a seat on a small council because power, authority, and status on the larger council must be shared with more individuals. As the desirability decreases, fewer whites are interested in capturing the post. Hence blacks may do better when many council seats are available.

Second, as the number of positions increases, whites may be more willing to support the election of one or two black candidates to the city council. If the council is composed of only, say, four members, then the election of one or two blacks would mean that blacks are accorded 25 to 50 percent of the seats, and consequently 25 to 50 percent of the power and authority. Whites may be unwilling to allocate that much decision-making authority to the black population. In fact, the allocation of that share of council power may be numerically unjustified. If blacks constituted only 10 percent of the population, being accorded even one of the four seats would result in substantial overrepresentation. With four council posts and a 10 percent black population, there is no way for blacks to obtain representation roughly based on their percentage of the city population. With any representation, they are actually overrepresented numerically. The more likely effect is no representation at all. Conversely, in cities with ten or more council members, whites may vote for the black candidate, understanding that blacks deserve some representation and that electing one or two black candidates will not result in black power disproportionate to the black share of the overall population in the city.

Third, when council size is larger the black population may be better able to exert its electoral muscle. The principle of electoral power would operate somewhat differently in district elections than in at-large races. In the district case, an increase in the number of seats ordinarily means an increase in the number of districts. As the number of districts increases, the size of each district is reduced. Owing to the residential segregation of blacks in virtually every city of the nation, providing small districts means that blacks are likely to constitute population majorities in one or more of these districts. In cities with just a few large districts, it is possible that the black population will not be a majority in any given district.

Let us take two hypothetical cities, each with 10,000 blacks and 90,000 whites. One city has four council districts and the other has ten. In the first city, with four council posts, even if all 10,000 blacks were placed together, there would be 15,000 whites in the same district with them, thus decreasing the chances that any blacks will be elected to council office. In the second city, with ten districts, even if the black population was divided into two districts, blacks would likely constitute the majority in at least one district. Therefore in district races large council size probably promotes black council equity.

In at-large contests, increases in council size are likely to advance black representation in another fashion. Let us again take our two hypothetical cities, each with 10,000 blacks and 90,000 whites. Assume that one city has four at-large seats and the other has ten at-large seats. In either city election, blacks can "single-shot" vote—that is, cast ballots only for the black candidate and ignore others running for office. However, in the four-member election, since the white electorate's votes are split over just a few candidates, the black seeking office may fail to win. When ten seats are contested, on the other hand, black single-shot voting for the black candidate is likely to be more successful, because white votes are divided among more candidates. Thus, in at-large elections, increased council size may also advance black council equity.

Our original expectations were that simultaneous elections, mayor-council government, partisanship, and district elections would promote more black candidates and more proportional black representation on city councils. However, neither simultaneous elections nor mayor council government appears to affect black candidacy. Indeed, contrary to our hypotheses, candidate equity is a bit higher in city-manager systems than when there is a mayor-council government, and candidate representation is somewhat higher when council elections are independent of non-municipal races. These patterns do not approach statistical significance, and we should not be misled to believe that independent elections and manager-council government promote black candidacy. Yet these findings do show no advantage from simultaneous races and mayor-council political forms. And council equity is only slightly related to simultaneous elections. In cities that hold city elections simultaneously with non-municipal races, black council equity stands at .75. Where the election is held independently, the rate is .69. The respective underrepresentation rates are −5.5 percent for simultaneous elections and −8.3 percent for independent races. Further, as we had anticipated, mayor-council governments have the most equitable rates of black election to the city council (.78) and the least underrepresentation (−5.0). Still, these levels are not appreciably different from the rates obtained in their city-manager counterparts, where equity levels are .74 and underrepresentation is −7.1 percent. However, commission cities do provide profoundly lower equity, with only .29 of the expected level of black representation being met—a rate that is a mere one-third of the levels in mayor-council and manager cities. And underrepresentation in commission cities is an enormous −18.0 percent. This pattern was so dramatic that we checked the rates of black council equity in 1972 and 1975 in commission cities to see if the 1978 rates were simply an aberration. These analyses demonstrated parallel low equity levels in commission cities in years other than 1978.

Why do commission forms of government provide such incredibly poor black representation on city councils? There are at least three possible explanations. First, commission cities tend to be located disproportionately in the South, where representation is lower than in any other region. Second, commission governments tend to have smaller councils, and small councils have less equitable black representation. Third, commissioners—as council members in commission cities are called—not only serve as members of the legislature but also act as municipal department heads. In a typical commission city, one commissioner will be head of the police department, another the head of the fire department, and a third in charge of public works. White voters in commission cities may be less disposed to elect blacks who will act as executive officers and have considerable power over particular service agencies. In a sense, our logic here is related to our earlier discussion of desirability. As the office becomes more attractive and is given greater responsibility and pay—as commission posts are—there will be more competition from whites and the white electorate will be less prone to support black candidates.

As with other variables, the multiple regression analysis will allow us to probe more deeply into the relationships between commission government and black council equity. This analysis will include southern location, council size, and council income in addition to commission government and thus will permit some better assessment of why commission cities have such dismal records in providing black representation.

Some previous studies have urged that partisanship would increase election of blacks to office because political parties are more apt to take ethnicity into consideration and to reward groups based upon their size and the extent of their electoral participation. Nonpartisan systems are said to favor the wealthy and the civic notables and therefore to harm the opportunities of blacks seeking office. Others have argued that political parties are irrelevant in local politics and that in any case they tend to be racist. Such arguments suggest that political parties are detrimental to the interests of blacks. One study of New Jersey cities in 1972, which attempted to ascertain the role of partisanship in the election of blacks, could find no strong pattern favoring either kind of municipality. In our own examination, we can test these competing views by determining whether blacks are more often candidates and are more proportionally represented in partisan or nonpartisan cities.

Nonpartisan systems appear to have more black candidates. In these systems, candidate representation (.45) and equity (1.84) are considerably higher than are representation (.33) and equity (1.22) in partisan cities. It is possible, of course, that in nonpartisan systems black candidates have less chance of winning than in partisan ones. Therefore nonpartisanship might not increase the actual representation of blacks on city councils. Our data appear to support this view. Partisan cities actually have *higher* equity rates. The association is just short of statistical significance for the equity ratio. We cannot at this point conclude that partisanship promotes the election blacks to city councils, but these findings do appear to contradict the view that partisanship impedes black opportunities. Political parties, then, probably do not harm the electoral chances of blacks and may actually promote their chances of winning council seats.

The final political condition to be examined, whether the city has district or at-large elections, has attracted widespread attention, and numerous court cases have considered the issue. Most prior research on the topic has concluded that district elections provide considerably richer opportunities for blacks seeking council office.

In fact, district elections are positively associated with black candidacy among our cities. The fifty-nine pure district cities have a candidate representation score of .49, whereas cities with at-large elections have a score of .38. District cities have equity rates of 2.08, while the equity for at-large communities is significantly lower (1.49). This finding is consistent with past observations that district races are related to higher black representation. The reasons district elections promote black candidate equity probably are that, in cities with elections by district, blacks are likely to constitute population majorities in at least some districts because of residential segregation.

Table 24
Black Council Candidacy and Black Resources

| Black Resources | Black Candidate Representation | Black Candidate Equity |
|---|---|---|
| *Socioeconomic resources* | | |
| Black/white income ratio | | |
| Less than .60 (125) | .35 | 1.32 |
| .60–799 (110) | .40 | 1.72 |
| .80 and over (22) | .79* | 2.91* |
| Median black education | | |
| Less than 9 years (61) | .36 | 1.13 |
| 9–10.9 years (155) | .37 | 1.57 |
| 11 years and over (39) | .57 | 2.38* |
| *Population resources* | | |
| Percentage black in city | | |
| 10–19.9 (119) | .24 | 1.72 |
| 20–34.9 (90) | .41 | 1.56 |
| 35–49.9 (41) | .48 | 1.14 |
| 50 and over (12) | 1.68 | 2.92 |
| *Organizational resources* | | |
| Black banks or savings and loans | | |
| Present (43) | .51 | 1.48 |
| Absent (214) | .39 | 1.65 |
| Black media outlets | | |
| 0 (147) | .37 | 1.73 |
| Radio *or* newspaper (69) | .40 | 1.31 |
| Radio *and* newspaper (41) | .54 | 1.75 |
| Number of civil rights groups | | |
| 0 (61) | .29 | 1.28 |
| 1 (76) | .33 | 1.37 |
| 2 or more (93) | .52* | 1.79 |
| *Protest resources* | | |
| Number of racial disturbances, 1961–68 | | |
| 0 (175) | .40 | 1.55 |
| 1 (56) | .41 | 1.92 |
| 2 or more (24) | .47 | 1.45 |

*$p \leq .05$. For explanation, see note to table 5.

Blacks are minorities in the electorate in all but a few at-large cities. When blacks constitute population majorities, as they do in many districts, blacks are more likely to become candidates. Furthermore, districts are often small enough that blacks need not expend as many resources as they would in attempts to become candidates at large, and blacks in district races are likely to have a greater measure of name recognition than they would in a citywide attempt to gain candidacy.

The evidence on council equity is consistent with that on candidacy. Those cities with pure district elections have almost one-third more equitable representation (.92) than cities with an at-large component (.64). Moreover, district cities have hardly any underrepresentation of blacks (−1.3 percent), whereas at-large cities underrepresent blacks by −9.2 percent. These relationships are both strong and statistically significant.

The same logic underlying the facilitation of black candidacies by district systems probably explains the greater black council equity. District races are less expensive than citywide contests. The sheer cost of running a successful at-large race, with the extra expenses for media advertising, are probably more prohibitive to blacks than to white candidates, given the financial gulf between the races. Candidates in district elections need rely less heavily on name recognition through the city. In at-large elections, the lack of name recognition may be more of a problem for blacks than for whites. Endorsements by newspapers and civic groups, perhaps more easily obtained by whites, are less crucial in district elections. Last, in district races blacks can take advantage of residential segregation Because of segregation, blacks are very likely to constitute population majorities in one or more districts. Blacks are more prone to vote for black candidates (Murray and Vedlitz 1978), just as whites are more likely to support white candidates for office. The evidence at this juncture indicates that district elections do enhance the likelihood that blacks will gain representation in numbers closely proportionate to their share of the population. Indeed, in district elections blacks obtain more than 90 percent of the number of black council seats that would be expected on the basis of their percentage in the city's population.

*Black Resources*

The final cluster of variables refers to attributes of the black population. We believed that blacks would gain more equitable candidacy and representation rates in cities that had experienced serious racial disturbances in the past; had a greater number of civil rights organizations; had black financial institutions; had black communications media; and had more affluent and better-educated black citizens. Further, we believed that, while candidacy representation would be directly related to black population, black council and candidate equity would show a curvilinear relationship with the percentage of the population that is black. That is, we believed blacks would obtain more proportional representation in cities with smaller black populations—which would be less threatening to the white majority—and in cities that were more than 50 percent black. In these latter communities, blacks can control who wins elections. In cities with intermediate black populations, between 20 and 49.9 percent, we predicted the lowest equity.

We found no preliminary evidence attesting to the importance of the hypotheses concerning racial disturbances, civil rights groups, financial institutions, and communications (tables 24 and 25). Of course, the reader should not conclude that factors such as these are irrelevant to the election of black candidates. We will again discuss these variables when we present our multivariate analysis.

We did uncover powerful support for the socioeconomic resources hypotheses. In fact, the indicators of black income and black education both evince a strong link with the incidence of black candidates and their election. Where black education is over eleven years, the representation and equity rates are .57 and 2.38. Where median black education is less than eleven years, black candidacy per seat ranges from .36 to .37, and black equity ranges from 1.13 to 1.57.

Differences in black income seem to result in even more pronounced variations in black candidacy. The narrower the difference between white income and black income, the greater the black candidacy levels. The strongest socioeconomic factor is this black/white income ratio. In cities where black income is at least 80 percent of that of whites, the rate of black candidate representation (.79) and equity (2.91) is more than twice as high as candidate representation (.35) and equity (1.32) in cities where blacks receive less than 60 percent of the income of whites.

Similarly, in examining council equity, there is .89 council equity in cities where blacks have a median education of at least eleven years. In cities where blacks have between nine and eleven years of median education, the respective equity value is less favorable (.73). Where blacks have a median education of less than nine years, the equity score drops quickly to just .49, and underrepresentation burgeons to −15.6 percent. The level of black education, then, appears to be strongly associated with the proportionality of black representation.

Again consistent with its relationship with candidacy, indicators of black economic status appear to have a strong association with black council equity. For example, where black income is less than 60 percent that of whites, blacks gain barely half (.54) of their justified representation, leaving −12.1 percent underrepresentation. Where blacks make between 60 percent and 80 percent of the income of whites, the equitability values improve to .78 and −4.0 percent. In the cities in which black income is at least 80 percent that of whites, blacks do so well politically that they are actually overrepresented on city councils, with black council equity reaching 1.21, resulting in +1.6 percent overrepresentation.

These findings clearly suggest the critical nature of socioeconomic resources. Historical factors rooted in racism have produced enormous poverty in the black population and, though recent years have witnessed some progress, marked by growth in the black middle class, still the black/white income ratio hovered around 60 percent in 1978, as it did in 1968. If every act of racial discrimination were to vanish at once, blacks would still be faced with social class barriers posed by less education and lower income. Successful electoral activity ordinarily requires basic middle-class skills and interests. Such skills produce the pool of middle-class blacks whom the electorate may find acceptable for public service and provide the cumulative resources necessary to wage political campaigns.

As our data suggest, where blacks have attained better educational

Table 25
Black Council Equity and Black Resources

| Black Resources | Council Equity Ratio | Council Equity Score |
|---|---|---|
| *Socioeconomic resources* | | |
| Black/white income ratio | | |
| Less than .60 (126) | .54 | −12.1% |
| .60–.799 (114) | .78 | −4.0 |
| .80 and over (24) | 1.21* | +1.6 |
| Median black education | | |
| Less than 9 years (61) | .49 | −15.6 |
| 9–10.9 years (158) | .73 | −5.7 |
| 11 years and over (43) | .89* | −2.3* |
| *Population resources* | | |
| Percentage blacks in city | | |
| 10–19.9 (120) | .76 | −3.6 |
| 20–34.9 (90) | .60 | −11.1 |
| 35–49.9 (42) | .71 | −11.6 |
| 50 and over (12) | .95 | −2.4 |
| *Organizational resources* | | |
| Black banks or savings and loans | | |
| Present (44) | .62 | −10.8 |
| Absent (220) | .73 | −6.7 |
| Black media outlets | | |
| 0 (152) | .72 | −6.9 |
| Radio *or* newspaper (54) | .68 | −7.7 |
| Radio *and* newspaper (58) | .74 | −8.4 |
| Number of civil rights groups | | |
| 0 (61) | .71 | −7.7 |
| 1 (77) | .65 | −8.0 |
| 2–4 (152) | .68 | −7.7 |
| *Protest resources* | | |
| Number of racial disturbances, 1961–68 | | |
| 0 (180) | .72 | −8.0 |
| 1 (57) | .69 | −6.2 |
| 2 or more (25) | .66 | −5.2 |

*$p \leq .05$. For explanation, see note to table 5.

levels, their representation is close to proportional. Moreover, in those cities where black income is at least 80 percent of white income, blacks are very successful in competing for public sector representation. Indeed, in these kinds of communities, blacks even obtain a mild degree of numerical overrepresentation on city councils. The fairer the share of private-sector resources in the possession of blacks, the greater are their chances of obtaining a fair share of public-sector representation.

The final black resource variable is the percentage black in the city. We expected a powerful relationship between black candidate representation and percentage black. And that is precisely what we found. In cities that are less than 20 percent black, the black candidate representation score is .24. This ratio grows to .41 in cities that are 20 to 34.9 percent black. In communities that are 35 to 49.9 percent black, the ratio is larger (.48). Last, in black majority cities the representation score leaps to 1.68 (i.e., there are 1.68 black candidates for each council seat being voted upon). Clearly, population concentration can act as a unique resource for blacks. As the black population increases, we should expect more and more black candidates for office. This principle is especially operative in cities in which blacks achieve majority status.

We expected that black candidate and council equity would be negatively associated with percentage black up to the point where blacks became a majority. In other words, blacks would gain fewer council candidacies relative to their population as the percentage black rose to just short of 50 percent. At 50 percent and higher, we expected the equity rate to increase again. Our expectation was based on past studies reporting that discrimination against blacks was most prevalent where they composed a larger segment of the population and apparently were more threatening to whites.

The curvilinear effect we predicted is mirrored by the figures reported in table 24. Cities that are less than 20 percent black afford black candidate equity of 1.72. This score drops to 1.56 in cities that are 20 to 34.9 percent black. The equity ratio plummets to 1.14 in communities that are 35 to 49.9 percent black. When blacks constitute majorities of the population, however, the candidate equitability ratio soars to 2.92. In these latter cities, blacks actually may be the most threatening to whites. But once they have gained majority status blacks are, in a critical sense, in control of their own electoral destinies. Our finding, then, is that there a curvilinear relationship between black candidate equity and percentage black. As blacks become a progressively larger segment of the population, they obtain progressively less desirable results—until the point at which they are transformed from a minority of the population to a majority. Once that transition is made, blacks obtain the very best candidacy results of all.

The same relationship is found with council equity (see table 25). Cities with the smallest percentage of blacks in our sample, between 10 percent and 19.9 percent, have comparatively better black council equity ratios (.76) and comparatively less underrepresentation (−3.6 percent). For cities with intermediate black populations, between 20 percent and 49.9 percent, the range of council equity is a little lower (.60 to .71) and under-representation is highest (−11.1 percent to −11.6 percent). Once blacks become a majority of the municipal citizenry, the equity rates increase to just short of virtual equality (.95), and there is only minimal under-representation (−2.4 percent). Thus, blacks not only contest many more seats when they are majorities, they also gain representation at a far more equitable rate.

Multivariate Analysis

The tabular material displayed above has permitted us to determine the kinds of communities where blacks tend to have the most equitable candidate and council representation. We have examined the implications of a wide array of white population and demographic characteristics, federal antipoverty efforts, political and election rules, and black resources. These tables, while giving us some initial hints about what conditions encourage black representation and candidacy, need to be supplemented with additional information before we can draw confident generalizations.

The next step is to compare the relative importance of our clusters of variables to determine which general types of factors best account for black candidacy rates. For instance, how much of the variation in black candidacy is explained by our black resources measures? And are black resources more important than, say, political and election rules? To obtain this information, we performed multiple regression analyses using each cluster of variables. Table 26 reports the findings for our four measures of council and candidate representation.

With respect to candidate equity, none of the clusters is dramatically useful. The federal antipoverty efforts have the least value, accounting for less than 1 percent of differences in candidate equity. Black resources explain another 6.6 percent of the variation, and white population and demographic features contribute 7.6 percent. The political and election rules account for the greatest amount of variation in black candidate equity, 9.5 percent.

For black candidate representation, federal antipoverty efforts explain 3.2 percent of the variation, white population and demographic characteristics account for 6.8 percent, and political and election rules contribute 9.2 percent. Black resources are the most powerful explanatory factors, accounting for 34.7 percent of the variance in black candidate representation, far more than all the other factors combined.

Table 26
Variation in Black Council Candidacy Explained by Variable Clusters

| Variable Clusters | Black Candidate Representation | Black Candidate Equity | Council Equity Ratio | Council Equity Score (Subtractive) |
|---|---|---|---|---|
| Black resources | 34.7% | 6.6% | 15.0% | 20.0% |
| Political and election rules | 9.2 | 9.5 | 9.6 | 13.4 |
| White population and demographic characteristics | 6.8 | 7.6 | 10.5 | 15.8 |
| Federal antipoverty efforts | 3.2 | 0.7 | 3.3 | 3.0 |

The ordering of the relative importance of the clusters is similar for the council equity scores and the candidacy rates in that black resources explain the most variation and poverty efforts explain the least. Black resources account for a substantial proportion of the variation in equity measures—15 percent in the ratio measures and 20 percent in the subtractive measures.

White population and demographic factors are the second most important in determining equity, slightly more important than for the candidacy measures. Political and electoral rules follow as a close third, with about the same effect as on the candidacy scores. Finally, antipoverty efforts appear to have minimal effect.

These findings suggest that variables from each cluster, possibly excepting the antipoverty measures, are likely of some importance in understanding the reasons underlying the rates of black candidacy and council representation. This evidence is consistent with information uncovered in the earlier tables, which recorded significant bivariate relationships. However, as we noted in chapter 3, placing too great an emphasis on these tables could lead to unjustified conclusions. As with virtually all social science data, numerous interrelationships exist between variables in different clusters—for example, region and form of government—and within variable clusters—for example, percentage black and the presence of black media. As a consequence, to improve our confidence in the effect of given variables, it is essential that we undertake a single comprehensive analysis of all significant variables.

As in chapter 3, the additional step we shall take is a multiple regression analysis using all variables that are significantly related to either of our candidacy or black council equity measures in (1) the bivariate case, that is, without controls; (2) the regressions using the other variables in the cluster; or (3) a large, preliminary regression employing every independent variable explored in the chapter.

Table 27, presenting the results of our final candidacy regressions, indicates which white population and demographic factors, antipoverty programs, political and election rules, and black resources have a significant effect on the level of black candidate representation and equity.

In all, nine of the variables were significantly associated with candidate representation at some stage of the research. These nine factors account for a substantial 42 percent of the variation in candidate representation. Of the total, five retained their significant effects: percentage black, the black/white income ratio, partisanship, Model Cities participation, and western locale. Of the four that are no longer significant, civil rights group development and southern locale are wholly unrelated to candidate representation. Longer terms of office and higher council pay are associated in the predicted fashion with candidate representation. But these relationships are relatively weak and not quite significant.

Table 27
Multiple Regression of Black Council Candidacy Rates on Previously Significant Factors

| Independent Variables | Black Candidate Representation | Black Candidate Equity |
|---|---|---|
| Percentage black | .55 | — |
| Black/white income ratio | .25 | .30 |
| Partisanship | −.14 | −.19 |
| Western locale | .12 | — |
| Model Cities participation | .09 | — |
| District elections | — | .16 |
| Term of office | — | .15 |
| | $R^2 = .42$[a] | $R^2 = .15$[b] |

*Note*: All variables are significant at $p \leqslant .05$.
[a]Council income, civil rights mobilization, and southern locale were not significantly related in this final regression.
[b]Southern locale, civil rights mobilization, and western or midwestern locale were not significantly related in this final analysis.

Percentage black is clearly the chief determinant of candidate representation. Indeed, percentage black alone accounts for 31 ($.55^2$) percent of the variation in representation, more than all the other factors combined. As blacks constitute greater proportions of the municipal population, we can expect more blacks to seek election and gain candidacy. The second most important variable is also a black resource, the black/white income ratio, adding another 5 percent of explained variation in candidate representation. This suggests that factors internal to the black community are the most critical determining how many blacks seek office. Where the black population is larger and the socioeconomic resources more closely match those of whites, we can expect to see a greater number of black office seekers.

Nonetheless, the evidence suggests that factors outside the black community also have implications for black candidacy rates. Location in the West, with its presumably more open, egalitarian social system and its absence of long-standing racial antagonism, appears to favor black candidate representation. Furthermore, in the only finding that was opposite to our expectation, partisanship evidently depresses black candidate representation, though we cannot yet determine whether the lower rate of black candidacy means that there will be fewer black elected officials in partisan cities. Participation in the Model Cities program is also slightly positively related to black candidate representation.

Turning to candidate equity, table 27 shows that, of the seven variables we included in the examination, four have a significant influence on candidate equitability. None, however, has an effect approaching the powerful role played by percentage black on candidate representation. In total, the seven variables account for roughly 15 percent of the variance in candidate equity. The regional and civil rights development measures are not significantly associated with equity. On the other hand, one black resource and three different kinds of election rules do bear significantly on the rate of black candidate equity.

The black/white income ratio has the strongest influence on black candidate equity, once more demonstrating that as blacks obtain more private-sector resources, they can become more competitive with whites in seeking public-sector representation on city councils. With enhanced socioeconomic resources, blacks have more money available and probably have more talent and political interest that can be converted into candidacy for city council office.

Though black socioeconomic resources are the single most important measure, explaining 5 percent of the variation in candidate equitability, the election rules that are significantly related to black candidacy—partisanship, district elections, and term of office—collectively contribute more explained variance (9 percent). Therefore we should carefully note that election rules are not necessarily neutral. Rather, they can impede or promote the opportunities of particular groups in obtaining candidacy and eventual election to public office. Partisanship once more displays a negative effect on black candidate equity. The term of office is positively related to equity, presumably because longer terms of office make city council posts more attractive to potential black candidates. Finally, district races are significantly related to more equitable black candidacy rates.

More factors are significantly associated with council equity than with candidacy rates (see table 28). Region is one white population and demographic variable consistently and significantly associated with council equity. Northeastern locale has a significant and negative relationship with both the ratio and the subtractive indicators. Southern and midwestern location are almost significantly and negatively related to the ratio measure as well ($p \leq .10$).

Recall that we encountered a similar pattern in chapter 3. In the multiple regression, we are introducing controls for numerous factors, asking whether each region has higher or lower equity rates than would be predicted on the basis of its other characteristics. To use a specific example, the South has the poorest black socioeconomic resources. In the Northeast, blacks tend to be better off financially and educationally. Therefore, since black council equity is strongly related to black socioeconomic resources, the association between equity and southern locale will be reduced once black socioeconomic resources are entered into the regression. The relationship between equity and southern locale found in the bivariate analysis is largely indirect. In the South, blacks have lower income ($r = -.71$) and median educational levels ($r = -.67$), and it is these conditions, rather than southern locale per se, that produce most of the low black council equity. Southern location does have a small direct effect, too, since in both equations the betas are relatively large (−.19 and −.13) and are negative. However, most of the variation explained by southern locale is accounted for by other factors in the regression, and thus the South is not strongly related to black council equity in a direct fashion.

Table 28
Multiple Regression of Black Council Equity on Previously Significant Factors

| Independent Variables | Equity Ratio (Beta) | Equity Score (Beta) |
|---|---|---|
| Black/white income ratio | .46 | .29 |
| Black media outlets | .23 | .18 |
| Northeastern locale | −.22 | −.22 |
| Racial disorders | −.20 | −.13 |
| Per capita federal antipoverty funds | .16 | .12 |
| District elections | .15 | .18 |
| Commission government | −.14 | −.15 |
| Black financial institutions | −.12 | −.15 |
| Median black education | n.s. | .19* |
| | $R^2 = .30$ | $R^2 = .34$ |

Note: All variables shown are significant at $p \leqslant .05$. Variables entered into the final equation but found not to be significant include southern and midwestern locale, percentage white ethnic, council size, percentage in educational services, mayor-council government, partisan elections, percentage black, and median white income.

A parallel phenomenon, but opposite in its effect, is at work with respect to the Northeast, where black council equity levels are about the same as those for the nation as a whole. But the black resource levels in these cities are considerably higher than average. Consequently, the level of black council equity is significantly lower than would be predicted on the basis of black resources and other factors. There are, then, some unmeasured environmental circumstances in northeastern cities that determine black representation but that were not included in our examination. We can only guess what these factors might be. It is possible that the pressures of population and economic decline, in the Northeast especially but in the Midwest too, have made whites reluctant to support black candidates. At the very least, we can conclude that the level of black council equity in the Northeast is not as high as it "should be" given the presence of factors that ordinarily increase the proportion of black representation on city councils.

We began the analysis with five indicators of federal antipoverty efforts. Of the five measures, only one, per capita federal funds, was significantly related to either equity measure at any step of the analysis. Therefore it was the only one included in the final regression analysis. As table 28 shows, total antipoverty spending was positively and significantly related to both measures of council equity in these regressions. This finding supports the view that, though there was a considerable degree of mismanagement of funds, antipoverty programs during the 1960s probably had some of the desired effects on target black communities. That particular programs—such as Community Action programs—did not affect council representation leads us to believe that the particular type of program was less important than the overall amount of funds gained by the city. The higher level of financial resources flowing to black communities could trigger the development of black organization, the identification and socialization of viable political activists, and the organizational base for further political activities such as successful campaigns to win city council seats.

In this chapter we examined seven political and election rules. Two of these factors, council term of office and council salary, were not significant at any point in the research. One might assume that longer terms of office and higher council pay would harm the chances of black electoral success because more whites would then seek office. But there is no proof of such an effect in this study. Manipulating the length of council terms and the salaries accorded council members is unlikely to affect the rate of black representation.

In our final analysis, council size demonstrates a surprisingly small and nonsignificant relationship with both indicators of black council equity, with beta values ranging between .08 and .10. However, in both regressions, council size is significant or nearly significant at $p \leqslant .10$.

Given the findings of others, the nearly significant associations, and the fact that we are examining virtually the universe of cities over 25,000 that are at least 10 percent black, we can say that increasing the number of council posts will have a mildly beneficial effect on blacks' chances of winning council seats more in line with their numbers in the population. Yet our findings do show that simply increasing council size, without taking additional steps, will not dramatically alter the numerical fairness of black representation on city councils.

Partisanship appears unrelated to black council equity. This further suggests that the role of local parties may have been exaggerated in recent literature. On the one side, basing their conclusions on Tammany and other political machines at the turn of the century or on idiosyncratic machine organizations of the near past—such as in Albany, New York, and East Saint Louis, Illinois—critics have argued that cities with political parties tend to be corrupt, inefficient, and often racist. On the other side, recently there has been a nostalgia for what some believe were the responsive local political parties of the past. To be sure, parties may act as effective recruiting mechanisms that allocate council posts according to the racial makeup of the electorate (or at least the racial makeup of the party's constituency), such as in Chicago, where the city council's racial composition is relatively equitable for blacks. But parties may also act as "old boy networks" that exclude minorities as well as women from candidacy. Moreover, even in partisan cities, as we indicated earlier, recruitment is frequently a choice made by individuals or interest groups rather than by a tight party hierarchy.

That partisanship is positively associated with black council equity in both equations, and actually is significantly related at $p \leqslant .10$ in the regression using the subtractive score, should somewhat allay the concerns of reformers who fear that political parties will exclude minorities from elected service. The weak but positive relationships may, in fact, give some comfort to scholars, such as Willis Hawley, who advocate the re-emergence of parties in local politics. Hawley's argument for political parties active in local elections is intended to mean parties with the power to recruit candidates, reward voting blocs, and provide organizational as well as financial support to candidates. And it may be that this kind of partisan organization—like the one in Chicago—may advance black chances of election. The simple partisanship/nonpartisanship indicator reflects only whether political parties are allowed to place their names on local ballots, and it therefore fails to capture important variation in the organization and power of political parties in different cities. Because candidates are not permitted to place the party name on the ballot, the nation's most partisan large city, Chicago, is classified as nonpartisan; hence, our test of the effect of partisanship is weak. Nevertheless, our data do indicate that the simple designation of a local system as partisan or nonpartisan has no strong effect on the proportionality of black council representation though it does seem to weakly promote black representation.

We could find no evidence that mayor-council government increased black election to city councils. It is also true that manager governments have no significant effect on black representation. In other words, there is no real difference between the rates of black representation in mayor-council and manager cities. However, there is abundant difference between the effect of these government forms and the effect of commission government on black proportional representation.

From the earlier tables, we discovered that commission cities provided the least equitable levels of black election to councils. Commission government is one of the two political and election rules that have a strong and significant effect on the dependent variables. In both regressions, commission government is negatively associated with black council equity. We indicated above that the role of commission government may be spurious, and we speculated that perhaps the pattern was due to the disproportionate concentration of commission government in the South, the small number of commission seats, and the at-large nature of commission elections. But all of these factors are controlled for in the regression, and still commission government negatively affects blacks electoral chances. The reason probably is rooted in the desirability and importance of commission seats mentioned before. Not only is intense competition for such important positions more apt to come from whites, but the white electorate probably will be less willing to elect a black to such a major office. Of course, since blacks are, with few exceptions, population minorities, white support is essential because commission elections are at large.

The political and election rule that has stirred the greatest recent interest is that of district and at-large elections. Our findings clearly attest to the favorable influence of district races in promoting black proportional representation. In both regressions, district races have a significant positive effect—in fact, district elections have the highest $F$ value in the regression employing the subtractive measure of black council equity. This information tends to reinforce the arguments of activists who have brought court challenges against the use of at-large elections, claiming that they discriminate against blacks. The provision of district elections is evidently the most important variable that can be politically manipulated to improve the opportunity for equitable black representation on city councils.

With district elections, blacks can exercise greater control, more blacks become candidates, campaigning is less expensive, media attention is less critical, the need for name recognition throughout the city is reduced, and the necessity of newspaper and civic group endorsement is diminished. All these conditions are advantageous to blacks seeking to win proportional representation on city councils. In fact, table 23 indicates that, on the average, the black council equity rates are quite close to perfect proportionality in district cities: .92 and $-1.3$ percent. Of course, with the cooperation of whites or with single-shot voting, blacks can achieve respectable council equity levels in certain at-large elections. But the data do indicate that even with multiple controls introduced, the likelihood of proportional black representation is significantly greater in cities that use district elections in their races for city council positions.

We began with seven indicators of black resources. One of these measures, the number of national civil rights groups, did not have a significant relationship with black council equity in any stage of the analysis and consequently was not included in the last regressions. This does not mean that civil rights groups play little or no role in the election of blacks. Many case studies of local elections have pointed to the prominent influence of organizations on the election of black candidates. The absence of a relationship probably reflects the limitations of our indicators of civil rights group mobilization. The variable we used simply indexed the number of national civil rights associations organized in the city in the early 1970s. Our measure takes no account of local civil rights organizations. Also, the number of civil rights association does not indicate the commitment, influence, or activities of the groups. And our information may be outdated. Research using the same variable did find that civil rights mobilization had a strong favorable effect on black council equity in 1972 (Karnig 1979b). Owing to developments in the intervening six years, particular organizations may have been phased out in many cities. This was a period in which CORE chapters virtually vanished, SCLC lost much of its influence, and a trend developed toward purely local groups. In sum, we believe that this variable was of interest because of the importance of the concept and the absence of other information on the location and activities of civil rights groups in various cities. But the lack of significant relationship should not lead to a firm conclusion that civil rights groups have no effect on electoral success of blacks.

Only one of the six black measures entered into the regression failed to record a significant relationship with black council equity. The percentage black in the city is totally unrelated to the ratio level, though it has a negative but not significant association with the subtractive score $(p \leqslant .10)$.[1] The lack of a significant relationship is due to the curvilinear effect of percentage black, a pattern we discussed above. All the other five black resource variables were significantly associated with the proportionality of black representation on city councils.

The extent of racial disturbances in the 1960s does have a significant effect on black representation, and so does the presence of black financial institutions. But in both instances the regressions show relationships contrary to the ones we predicted. The incidence of racial disorders and the presence of black banks or savings and loan associations are inversely related to the proportionality of black council representation.

We expected that cities that had racial protests in the 1960s would funnel the political content of these protests into more traditional activities like electoral politics in the 1970s. Further, we expected that the protests would have impressed whites with the need for black representation. These propositions were *dis*confirmed. It may be that the riots engendered further racial hostility, so that whites in these cities are now even more reluctant to consider black candidates. Perhaps, also, the riots reflected an extreme disillusionment with traditional politics that would lead to a deemphasis on electoral activity. At any rate, experience with riots in the 1960s has a significant and depressing effect on equitable black representation on city councils in the 1970s.

It is more difficult to interpret why the presence of black financial institutions in the city would reduce the proportionality of black electoral success. Possibly the very presence of black-owned and black-run financial institutions makes political representation seem less important. More likely our information, similar to our information on civil rights groups, is outdated, since it was gathered in the early 1970s. Black banks and savings and loans associations have sprung up in a number of communities during the past decade. The financial information we used probably does not adequately mirror the changes that have taken place.

We have less difficulty in interpreting why the presence of black newspapers and of radio programming for blacks has a positive effect on black council equity and why increases in black socioeconomic achievement similarly favor more proportional black council representation. Both black communications and socioeconomic resources are strongly, positively, and significantly related to each of the equity rates in the regression analysis. We earlier outlined the reasons why we expected such an outcome.

Where available, black media outlets provide the black candidate with the most critical item of all—an audience. With a ready-made audience of fellow blacks, the candidate has at hand a forum that, by nature of its audience and its own interests, will focus heavily on black candidates for office. Black candidates, as a result, will have a channel for communicating ideas, stating policy concerns, gaining exposure, advertising, and stimulating electoral activity. Where such media are present, blacks do in fact gain representation more proportional to their share of the population.

In a parallel manner, increased black socioeconomic resources promote black council equity. Indeed, in both regressions the difference in black and white income is the single most important explanatory variable. It has the highest zero-order correlations and the highest beta values. Black median education is not significantly related to the ratio indicator, but it does have a significant positive association with the subtractive measure of black council equity. Actually, given the strong positive correlation between the two socioeconomic measures ($r = .67$), it is surprising that both variables display a significant effect on black equity. If either of the economic and educational indicators was used alone, its relationship would be even higher than what we display. Employed apart from black median education, the black/white income ratio would remain the strongest predictor in either equation. And, if employed without the income variable, black median education would become the strongest single predictor in the two regressions.

The evidence seems to imply that income has a somewhat more potent effect on black council equity than does education. However, education is critical to the unfolding of equitable black penetration of city councils in two ways. First, black education is powerfully linked to black income. Without substantial educational attainment, blacks are unlikely to develop the economic resources necessary for successful election to city councils. In this sense black education probably has a strong indirect influence on black representation because black education helps determine the level of black economic resources. Second, at least for the subtractive score, black education has a significant and strong effect separate from that of black income. Such a finding is consistent with an abundance of research reports that consistently uncover a link between education and participation in politics: educated groups participate more often in electoral politics and vote more often than those with less educational achievement.

Income, for its part, is critical too. Economic resources are key instruments in gaining fair representation. Political activism and success in American electoral politics have long been wedded to economic status. Money is necessary for fruitful campaigns, and middle-class status is needed for the candidate to appear "legitimate." When their resources are competitive with those of whites, blacks gain council seats roughly as warranted by the black share of the city population. Where economic resources are lower, so too is the proportion of black council representation. Private-sector resources, then, can be converted into public-sector representation directed as redressing injustices in the private sector.

In sum, in this section we have concentrated on (1) black candidate representation rates (number of black candidates per council seat up for election); (2) black candidate equity rates (number of black candidates per council seat divided by black population size in the city; and (3) black council equity rates. The representation rate is important because it indicates roughly the proportion of council posts blacks are contesting; and in general the greater the proportion of positions for which blacks are candidates, the greater the number of positions they can potentially win. As we mentioned, black candidate representation is in fact strongly related to the percentage of council offices that blacks do gain. The equity rate is important in its own right because it indicates the "fairness" of the number of black candidates who are seeking office.

The most important variables affecting black candidate representation were black resources. The most critical factors underlying black candidate equity were election rules. White population and demographic characteristics, as well as federal antipoverty programs, have lesser effects on black candidacy.

The percentage black in the city is without doubt the primary factor determining the rate of black candidacy for the city council. In addition, black socioeconomic resources, partisanship, and western location significantly affect the representation rate. Black socioeconomic resources and partisanship once more appear as significant factors affecting candidate equity. District elections and the term of council office also have some influence here.

Candidacy rates are in fact strongly related to actual rates of black election to city councils. Thus, as we might expect, most of our explanatory variables show similar effects on candidacy and on council equitability. Black resources, in particular, are crucial to council equitability. Most previous literature has concentrated on election rules and characteristics of the white population in explaining the electoral success of blacks. Of course these are salient phenomena that do affect the opportunities of blacks. Indeed, among our chief findings are those that indicate that district elections do strongly advance the proportionality of black service on city councils. This suggests that political and election rules are not necessarily neutral in their effect on the representation of different groups in society. Consequently, at-large cities that do not now afford reasonably fair proportional representation of blacks might well consider adopting district elections as a mechanism to improve the rate of black election to city councils. Similarly, to advance the chances of equitable black council representation, cities with commission governments might consider shifting to a mayor-council or manager form of government.

But characteristics of the black population are salient, too. Blacks with greater resources do have the capacity to deal with the political environment and obtain representation more in line with their share of the citizenry. There is truth in the old saw, "Them that has, gets!"

Yet getting more equitable—or even perfectly proportional—representation does not mean that blacks obtain council power. Council power depends not on mere equitability of representation, but on the percentage of council posts allocated to blacks regardless of their share of the population. The issue of power is rooted not in how numerically "fair" the share of decision-making authority is, but in what the overall share is.

In the next section, therefore, we investigate the conditions that promote black council power, and in chapters 5 and 6, we ask whether black council power makes any difference in influencing municipal public policy choices.

## Black Council Representation

In examining the determinants of black council equity, we concentrated on two indicators of the proportionality of black representation on city councils. The equity question is obviously a key one. Whether discrimination is overt and malicious or so institutionalized that no one seems responsible, its core is that particular individuals or groups receive less than their warranted share. But since blacks are a distinct minority in most United States cities, even if they should obtain representation proportional to their numbers (their warranted share)—or even if blacks should receive somewhat more than their "fair share"—they nevertheless would constitute a small minority of elected decision-makers. For blacks, proportionality is an important step toward gaining power, but it is no guarantee that a substantial degree of power will be forthcoming.

To explore the issue of black power on city councils in greater depth, this brief section will focus on the share of council posts that blacks have won, irrespective of the percentage blacks in the city population. If a city that is 10 percent black has one black on a council of ten, blacks would have obtained precisely proportional representation, or 100 percent of the warranted rate. But we would say that blacks have obtained only 10 percent of the decision-making authority on that council. On the other hand, in another city blacks may constitute 40 percent of the population but receive only 20 percent of the council posts. In this community blacks would have gained only 50 percent of their proportional rate of representation, but they would have obtained 20 percent of the decision-making authority. In sum, proportional representation and decision-making authority are distinguishable concepts. It is possible for blacks to win equitable representation but still have little decision-making authority; it is also possible for blacks to be underrepresented yet possess considerable decision-making authority.

In this section we will shift our attention from council equity to the correlates of black decision-making authority on city councils. On the average, blacks have gained roughly 17.3 percent of the council positions in cities over 25,000 with at least 10 percent blacks in the population. This figure compares quite favorably with the 11.2 percent of council seats won by blacks in 1975 and the mere 6.6 percent of seats won in 1970. Moreover, the 17.3 percent of council posts is substantially higher than the 10 percent rate of mayorships blacks obtained. Still, council seats are not as influential or as prestigious positions as the mayoralty. And, on city councils, blacks remain rather small minorities, even in cities with considerable black concentrations (recall that the median black percentage in these cities was 24.3 percent).

As we found in chapter 3, the probability of a black's being chosen mayor is greater where the percentage black in the city is higher. We felt that percentage black would also be the single best predictor of black council authority. The larger the black population, the larger the proportion of council seats gained by blacks.

We also wished to ascertain what other environmental factors influenced the degree of council representation afforded to blacks. Based on our findings in the previous section, we could predict with virtual precision the variables that would be significantly related to black council representation. All the measures that were significantly associated with black council equity also would be significantly related to black council representation in the regression analysis. We could predict with high certainty because of the statistical similarity in the different regression equations. In the equity analysis, we standardized—that is, divided—the percentage of black council seats by the percentage of blacks in the city. In the regression presented below, one of the independent variables is percentage black. Therefore, both examinations control for the percentage black—one by using it to divide the dependent variable, and the other by using it as a separate independent variable.

From the bivariate relationships, the results of entering clusters of variables into regression analyses, and the findings of a large regression employing all variables in the study, we selected variables that were significantly associated with black council representation in at least one step of the research. In all, seventeen independent variables were chosen. The list is almost exactly the same as the list of indicators used in the council equity regressions. Two variables were not used here but were used in the council equity final regression—the percentage of the population in education and median white income. However, neither of these two measures was significantly associated with council equity in the final regressions. Similarly, one variable—the presence of a Model Cities program—was not included in the equity regressions but was included in the regression focused on council representation. Again, however, in the final regression Model Cities programs had no significant effect on black council representation.

Indeed, as table 29 reports, except for the percentage black variable, the nine indicators that were significantly related to council equity in the regressions are the same nine variables that are significantly related to council representation. The direction of the relationships, of course, also remains the same. Commission government, northeastern locale, the presence of black financial institutions, and experience with racial disorders all have a depressing effect on black council representation. On the other hand, district elections, higher per capita antipoverty efforts, and increasing black education and income favor black council representation.

With percentage black in the equation, the seventeen variables account for a very substantial 57 percent of the variance in black council representation. However, nearly 38 percent of the overall variation—or about two-thirds of the explained variance—can be accounted for by percentage black alone. And the simple addition of the black/white income ratio contributes another 8 percent of explained variance. Hence, percentage black and the black/white income ratio together explain 46 percent of the variation. The two political and election rules also are important. District elections contribute 4 percent of explained variance, and commission government adds 2 percent more. This latter information suggests that adopting district elections and shifting from commission government to either mayor-council or manager political institutions could significantly improve the levels of black council representation.

Table 29
Multiple Regression of Black Council Representation on Previously Significant Factors

| Independent Variables | Black Council Representation |
| --- | --- |
| Percentage black | .67 |
| Black/white income ratio | .26 |
| Northeastern locale | −.18 |
| District elections | .14 |
| Black media outlets | .14 |
| Black financial institutions | −.12 |
| Median black education | .12 |
| Commission government | −.11 |
| Per capita antipoverty funds | .10 |
| Racial disorders | −.10 |
| | $R^2 = .57$ |

*Note:* All variables shown are significant at $p \leqslant .05$. Variables entered into the equation that were not significant include partisanship, council size, mayor-council government, southern and midwestern locale, and percentage white ethnic.

Moreover, these findings highlight the critical nature of black resources in the unfolding of black council power. As table 30 shows, the different types of black resources can explain a total of 52 percent of the variance in black council representation, whereas the next most important set of factors—political and election rules—can account for just 11.7 percent. Clearly, then, though certain steps can be taken that are likely to promote the level of black council power—for example, adopting district elections—most of the factors that strongly affect black council representation are difficult to manipulate.

Table 30
Effects of Variable Clusters on Black Council Representation

| Variable Clusters | Total Explained Variances |
| --- | --- |
| Black resources (including percentage black) | 52.0% |
| Percentage black (alone) | 37.6 |
| Political and election rules | 11.7 |
| White population and demographic factors | 5.2 |
| Federal antipoverty programs | 2.7 |

The key factor, as we have noted, is the relative size of the black population. Simply stated, owing to patterns of racial voting by blacks and whites alike, the more blacks there are, the greater the number of citizens apt to vote for black candidates. Of course, such a finding is hardly surprising. Black leaders have long understood that political power would be forthcoming mainly in cities with large black populations. As a result, they have been consistent in opposing metropolitan government proposals that would combine the populations of the largely black central city and the overwhelmingly white suburbs and thus reduce the percentage of blacks within the new boundaries of the district. However, any strategy directed at gaining greater political power by producing or maintaining high black proportions in the population is fraught with difficulties. Given black/white income differences, there is a powerful tendency for income levels to fall as the percentage black in any community rises. Therefore, cities with large black concentrations have fewer financial resources for the management of municipal affairs.

Does the availability of economic resources affect whether blacks can influence public policy? More centrally, does black council equity, black council representation, or the election of a black mayor make any difference to the types of public policies adopted in various cities? Is the election of blacks to mayoral and council seats simply of symbolic importance? Or does such election have demonstrable effects on public policy? And for which kinds of policy might the election of blacks make a difference? It is to these and related questions that we turn our attention in chapters 5 and 6.

# 5 The Effect of
## Black Officials
## *A Review*

In chapters 3 and 4 we have explored the extent to which several characteristics of the urban community favor or impede black representation. We have seen that the probabilities of black election to both the mayoralty and the city council are substantially increased when the resources of the black community are greater, especially in terms of black population size and socioeconomic factors. Some political characteristics, too, aid in increasing black representation: for city councils, characteristics such as district rather than at-large elections; for the mayoralty, shorter terms of office and lower salaries. Regional locale also has an effect; there are fewer black officeholders in the Northeast than one might expect on the basis of other community characteristics.

Knowing what factors underlie black election to office is interesting in itself. Indeed, given the history of discrimination, black proportional representation is a highly desirable outcome. But perhaps the larger question is, What difference does black representation make? Once elected to office, do these black officials influence changes in urban policy? It is to this crucial issue that we turn in this and the next chapter.

## Black Officials and Black Representation

The implicit assumption of studies that attempt to assess the effect of black municipal officials is that blacks elected to office will work toward policies favorable to blacks. We too will make this assumption, which we feel is justified. However, both the reasons for adopting the assumption and the pitfalls it involves are worth exploring in a bit more detail.

The notion of representation is complex, involving definitions and discussions of the rights and responsibilities of both the represented (the public) and the representative (the elected official). Pitkin's (1972) discussion of representation is elegant and well developed; we shall not attempt to summarize it here. If we use as a starting point her definition of representation as "acting in the interest of the represented, in a manner responsive to them," several points are relevant. Pitkin distinguishes between "descriptive" and "substantive" representation. The former refers to the racial, social class, religious, and other attributes of the representative and the public, which may or may not be matched. Substantive representation deals with the congruence between the policy wishes of the representative and the public. Clearly, a black elected to office provides descriptive representation for the black population. But if the elected official does not share the policy viewpoints of the black community, there would be no substantive representation. The election of blacks, then, is no guarantee that the policy needs or preferences of the black community will be reflected in the officeholder's behavior. Moreover, even when black officials are substantively representative of the black public, the actions of these officials may not be effective in securing policies favorable to blacks.

Even under those conditions, however, the election of a black official might benefit the black community by promoting knowledge and awareness of local government, providing symbolic reassurance of blacks' capability to serve in public office, stimulating more black participation in government, and increasing the affect of blacks toward government, though this last may be, at best, a mixed blessing if the government is not producing benefits for the black community. Several studies demonstrate that the election of black officeholders favorably influences the perceptions and behavior of the black community; however, it is currently impossible to determine the extent to which these changes are caused by positive perceptions of the policy goals of black officeholders rather than simply by the fact that the officeholder is black.

Empirical evidence of improved black images and knowledge of government has been discovered in previous examinations. Leonard Cole's New Jersey study found that, in cities with black mayors, 87 percent of the black community could identify this official by name compared with 72 percent of blacks in cities with white mayors (Cole 1976, p. 109). Foster (1978) also found that more black schoolchildren knew their mayor and had positive images of the mayor's role when the mayor was black.

Moreover, in Cole's sample of black New Jersey residents, only 15 percent disagreed with a statement that it is important that blacks hold elective office (Cole 1976, p. 111). And Conyers and Wallace (1976) found that their sample of black officials felt that heightened black confidence in government would be one of their main contributions. This is fragmentary evidence, to be sure, but it does suggest that electing black public officials may help stem the tide of alienation toward government displayed among blacks (e.g., Miller 1974).

Evidence about the effect a black officeholder has on black political participation is sketchier still. However, it seems reasonable to expect that when blacks see that their participation can have some payoff in electing a fellow black, then their interest and activity in the electoral process may be raised. Further, an increase in voting participation might also spring indirectly from diminished alienation and heightened interest in political life at the urban level. In one study that looked at black participation as a function of black candidates or officeholders, Abney (1974) found that black turnout in Mississippi was modestly related to the presence of black candidates for office. The strongest two-variable relationship between voter turnout and the sociopolitical variables he examined was with the number of black candidates. When other factors were controlled, this association was somewhat reduced, but black candidacy still retained a favorable relationship with voter turnout. Given the evidence of black voting solidarity found so far (see Feagin and Hahn 1970; Walton 1976; Hahn, Klingman, and Pachon 1976), this pattern could generate a mutually reinforcing cycle of participation and candidate success. Exploration of the effect of black candidates and officeholders on black political participation is a very fruitful avenue for future research. Unfortunately, we did not have the data to undertake the inquiry here.

In the long run, black affect toward government and participation in government will probably not be stimulated by black officeholders unless these officials are representative of the black community in more than just a symbolic or "descriptive" manner. Hence we would expect that the most important long-term benefit to the black community of black elected officeholders would be a consequence, at least in part, of their ability to represent the interests of the black population in the policymaking process.

Policy ties between the public and their representatives have frequently been studied, yet we do not know as much as we would like about these linkages. We know that among state legislators, for example, many see themselves as "delegates," acting largely in response to directives from their constituents. Others view themselves as "trustees," acting on behalf of constituents but using their own best judgment. And still others say that their role is a mixture of both the trustee and the delegate functions (Wahlke, Eulau, Buchanan, and Ferguson 1962). Prewitt and Eulau (1969) found that among eighty-two city councils in the San Francisco area, members of thirty-six claimed *not* to act in response to any organized public view, thus presumably conceiving of themselves as trustees. Regardless of whether a representative perceives himself as a delegate or a trustee, we know that in general there is a correspondence between what a representative thinks on most important issues and what his or her constituency thinks (Miller and Stokes 1966; Achen 1978; Erickson 1978). It is unclear whether this convergence is due to representatives' taking cues from constituents in order to gain reelection or whether the representative is elected because of an initial similarity of views arising from parallel needs, similar socializing experiences, group identification, and the like. Nevertheless, normally there is some convergence of perspectives between the elected and the electorate. Thus, if black representatives are similar to other representatives, their views should parallel those of their constituents—not in all cases, of course, but on the main issues.

We have some limited evidence to confirm this. Indeed, Mann (1974) has suggested that blacks on school boards are more likely than whites to adopt decision-making roles conducive to policy directives from the electorate. Further, Thompson (1963), Ippolito, Donaldson, and Bowman (1968), and Kronus (1971) have found that there is a basic congruence between policy orientations of blacks of various social classes. If this is true, then a basic policy congruence could be expected between black elected officials and their constituents. This congruence can result even though socioeconomic disparities are larger between black school board members and the black population than between parallel white groups (Wirth 1975). We would expect these differences to be similarly acute when comparing other types of black officeholders with their black constituents. For example, Cole (1976) discovered a greater gap between the educational attainments of black municipal officials and the black public than among white officeholders and the white community. Browning, Marshall, and Tabb (1978, p. 15), in their study of California cities, suggest that a disproportionate number of minority elected officials come from ''relatively prestigious occupations.''

Overall, then, there is cause to believe that black officials are generally sympathetic to the policy concerns of the black public and therefore constitute more than mere symbols of black representation. At the very least, the policy viewpoints of black officials are apt to agree generally with those of the black community.

What are these policy areas with which the black public is primarily concerned? The major black urban policy concerns are rooted largely in the living conditions of urban blacks; that is, inequalities of housing, health care, employment, and income, as well as the quality of education in the city. It seems reasonable to assume that blacks tend to be less committed to downtown beautification and new city amenities, for example. This assessment is supported by data found in surveys of blacks in major cities after the urban riots of the 1960s. Along with police practices, most blacks ranked unemployment, housing, and education as serious concerns. Inadequate recreation was also seen as a problem (Kerner 1968). To whatever extent large segments of the black population are troubled primarily by issues other than this core of socioeconomic issues, our assumptions about policy are in error.

### Previous Research on the Effect of Black Elected Officials

Earlier, highly optimistic expectations about the dramatic influence black officials might have on urban policy were unrealistic (Nelson 1972; Bullock 1975). There should have been little reason to believe that profound policy shifts would quickly follow the election of some black men and women to office. Nonetheless, we may assume that blacks place confidence in black officials because they expect these elective officers to understand their plight and to help adopt policies aimed at improving conditions. Therefore, it is appropriate to examine whether policy changes have been made in cities with black officials.

Black mayors and council members have special problems: they must act swiftly to asssure the black electorate that they are committed to redressing long-standing grievances, but there are also powerful counter-forces from the white community pressing for only cautious movement (see Persons 1977; Nelson 1972; Davis and Van Horne 1975; Levine and Kaufman 1974; Levin 1974). Given their usual control over business, finance, newspapers, and other key local institutions—which are necessary for success in proposed redevelopment, reform, or other plans—the desires of these whites must be carefully considered. Efforts to strike some balance among these competing pressures triggers psychological strain for the official and also may cause a loss of confidence by blacks, by whites, or by both communities (see Nelson and Van Horne 1974).

Clearly then, black officials encounter special limitations and problems. Beyond the factors we have mentioned, there are additional reasons for skepticism about the policy influence of black elected leaders. For example, even where blacks are elected as mayors or council members, they ordinarily constitute a decided minority of municipal policymakers. Hence they do not usually have the power to make unilateral decisions. And when they do capture control, as Friesma (1969) suggested, it may be a "hollow prize." According to this logic, black majority cities tend to be so depleted of resources that injections of federal and state funds are required. Yet, once a city is under black control, federal and state legislatures—composed of whites—may fail to provide adequate monetary transfers. Jones (1971, p. 72), arguing that the critical decisions are made in the private sector, contends that "the keys to black liberation lie somewhere external to electoral politics."

In an often-quoted comment, Keech (1968) concluded that, at least in southern cities, "the vote is a far more potent instrument for achieving legal justice than social justice." Again with regard to the South, because of the economic dependence of blacks, Matthews and Prothro (1916, p. 481) viewed as "political hyperbole" the arguments predicting racial equality as a result of black electoral participation. And given the shortfall of black economic resources in both the North and the South, Wilson (1966) saw little cause for optimism.

These observations come closer to political reality than those of commentators who anticipated that remarkable changes in the social fabric would follow increases in black voting and the election of black officeholders. We should be circumspect about the degree of change that is possible within the American social and political systems, especially at the local level, where redistributive changes are least apt to occur. However, we can also become unduly pessimistic about the possibility of improved conditions. The unique constraints operating on black elected officials do not mean that black representation is ineffectual. In fact, some studies have suggested that black officials have already had an effect. Browning, Marshall, and Tabb (1978) concluded that minority municipal employment in 1977 was highly related to minority representation on city councils in 10 California cities. Cole (1976, chap. 7) has documented at least partial success by black officials in getting their policy preferences adopted by city councils in New Jersey. And Campbell and Feagin (1975) have pointed to a number of communities, even very poor ones, where the election of black officials has brought about major changes in policies affecting blacks: jobs, street-paving, education, and other public services. Feagin's (1970) survey of forty-two black officials in the South in 1969 showed that almost all (83 percent) felt they had as much or more in-fluence in office as they had anticipated before being elected. This is supported by Paulson's (1979) more recent finding that a similar 83 per-cent of black mayors believed they had ''sufficient power'' to do their jobs.

Most analyses of the effect of leadership have been case studies (Nel-son 1972; Nelson and Meranto 1977; Greer 1971; Weinberg 1968; Masotti and Corsi 1969; Stone 1970; Poinsett 1970; Stokes 1973; Levine 1974; Persons 1977; Coombs et al. 1977). These investigations, all but two focusing on the mayoral leadership of Carl B. Stokes of Cleveland or Richard G. Hatcher of Gary, Indiana, detail the political problems that the black mayor or representative faces in trying to achieve policy objectives. Although the experiences of the two men were different, and in some ways it can be argued that Mayor Hatcher was the more successful, some generalizations can be drawn from their experiences. First of all, each man was successful in bringing to his municipality federal and private funds to help in rehabilitating the inner city. With these revenues, as well as with ordinary city revenues, new housing was built, job training and employment centers were run, and other social/economic programs were enhanced (Nelson and Meranto 1977; Levine 1974; Levine and Kaufman 1974). Further, both mayors dramatically increased black employment in the city; by 1969, for example, fourteen of Gary's twenty-seven de-partments were headed by members of black and Hispanic groups (Levine 1974, p. 79), and Davis and Van Horne (1975) report that Stokes hired or promoted 274 minority individuals to supervisory positions in the Cleve-land government. Hatcher, in particular, was able to take giant strides in professionalizing city government, reducing corruption in government, and combating organized crime within and outside the governmental structure.

However, both mayors were unable to achieve a substantial portion of their goals. They were hampered by the grave financial condition of their cities; in both cases the tax base was insufficient to provide decent salaries for city employees and to finance new and expanded programs for the poor community.[1] In Cleveland, because of municipal financial problems, Mayor Stokes at one point fired fifteen hundred city employees, including many low-paid workers such as garbage collectors. Another black mayor, Maynard Jackson of Atlanta, fired one thousand sanitation workers who had gone on strike illegally (Persons 1977). Hatcher and Stokes also could not overcome the formidable political constraints posed by the city council; in neither case did the mayor have a supportive council, though this changed somewhat in Hatcher's second term. In both instances, the council was racially divided, and in Gary part of the council was under the control of a machine antagonistic to Hatcher's programs. Stokes could never make peace with the Cleveland police force, which was adamantly opposed to him, and in both Gary and Cleveland the white community was largely hostile to the black mayor. According to Persons (1977), Mayor Jackson also encountered difficulty with the white community and police, and he nearly had to fire his newly recruited black police chief. In addition, Jackson did dismiss a popular black administrator who was resented by the white business community of Atlanta for aggressively requiring "firms doing business with the city to enter joint-ventures with black firms whenever possible" (p. 15). All these factors, then, can operate as severe constraints on a black official attempting to implement an activist policy that will cost money and require considerable community support.

In investigating the policy influence of black mayors, Keller (1978) went slightly beyond the case study approach and compared three cities that had black mayors (Gary, Cleveland, and Newark) with three somewhat similar cities having white mayors (Indianapolis, Cincinnati, and Trenton). He compared city spending in these cities from 1965 to 1973, looking particularly at expenditures on police, fire, roads, public welfare, parks and recreation, and housing and urban development. Keller's initial hypothesis was that black mayors emphasize social welfare programs and spend more in that area than do cities with white mayors. He found, however, that black-run cities spent *more* than white-run cities on police; in fact, as the black population increased, each city spent more on fire and police protection. Expenditures on roads did not differ in the two groups of cities. Cities with black mayors did *not* spend more on social welfare programs, contrary to Keller's proposition. He argued that these results may be a consequence of a variety of constraints, such as those we have discussed above. Keller's approach was an improvement over single-city examinations. Unfortunately, however, because of the small number of cases, Keller could not take into account a host of factors, such as the racial composition of the city council, that might influence city expenditures.

In an extremely interesting study, Coombs et al. (1977) compared

Greene County, Alabama, where blacks control the county government, with two white-controlled Alabama counties. The authors found that in Greene County government employment grew faster, federal grants rose substantially more, and personal income increased more rapidly than in the two other counties. This account, as well as others we have noted, indicates that the election of blacks can make a difference in public policy outcomes.

## Problems in Studying the Influence of Black Elected Officials

Studying the influence of black elected officials on public policy is a difficult chore at best. Such an analysis is fraught with methodological and conceptual difficulties. First, the presence or absence of policy changes may not be due at all to mayoral activity or inactivity. As we have seen, the political environment sharply limits the ability of black mayors to translate their policy initiatives into policy. Therefore, policy developments during a mayor's term of office cannot necessarily be attributed to his goals and work. At a minimum, the fiscal condition of the city, the views of the city council, public opinion, and the willingness of the state and federal governments and private foundations to support city undertakings all play a role in policy formation and implementation. Solanik and Pfeffer (1977) suggest that the mayor (whether black or white) has relatively little influence on expenditure patterns in cities.

As we argued in the previous section, the position of a black mayor is often much weaker than that of white mayors. Not only are there political constraints, but we can expect that blacks will most often be elected in cities where blacks are a majority or close to a majority of the population. These are the very cities that tend to be in the poorest financial condition, with middle-class whites fleeing the central city for the suburbs and industry deserting the area to locate in suburbia or the "sunbelt." These cities are marked by rising public needs that far outrun exhausted resources. Thus, many of the nation's black mayors have won election in cities that have been in the decay spiral so long (e.g., Newark, Gary, East Saint Louis) that it is difficult to imagine how the trend could be reversed. For a mayor operating under these conditions, success may mean simply holding on to the status quo. Dramatic improvement is out of reach, at least in the short run.

A black mayor may also expect that a majority of the white public will oppose any attempt to significantly alter the distribution of resources (Nelson and Van Horne 1974). Whites in the least affluent cities might be the most hostile to changes. Consequently, attempts to mobilize public support, except in cities where the black population is a substantial majority, will be highly difficult, if not impossible, for the black mayor.

Measuring the influence of black city council members is even more complex than assessing the effect of black mayors. Unlike the mayoralty, where black control of the office is easily discernible, the proportion of city council seats held by blacks is highly variable. Black influence on the council is not, however, necessarily proportional to number—it may be greater or less. In a racially torn city, for example, blacks may be a strong numerical minority on the council but be outvoted on every issue. On the other hand, it is possible that in some cases a single black council member may have several allies among sympathetic whites and be able to achieve several of his or her policy goals. An equitable proportion on the city council is probably less important to meeting policy objectives than is the absolute representation that blacks possess on the council. That is, we would expect blacks to have greater influence where they hold 60 percent of the council seats, even if that is only 80 percent of the equitable rate, than where they hold one-quarter of the seats and this reflects an equity ratio 1.5 times their share of the population.

In evaluating the effect of black leadership, one must also take into account an "interaction effect" between the mayor and the council. One would suppose that black mayors will obtain more of their policy goals, other things being equal, if they have a black majority on the council. Mayor Stokes, for instance, faced a hostile, white-dominated council that refused to approve many of his major policy initiatives, whereas Maynard Jackson of Atlanta had a council evenly divided between blacks and whites, thus giving him more room to bargain and negotiate (Persons 1977). In any event, one must consider whether blacks control mayorships and hold a dominant voice on the council or have gained just one of these power positions.

The intergovernmental context also may have a negative influence on the mayor's ability to act (see Preston 1976). Not only are many city problems really national problems (unemployment, for example), but many cities do not control the most important "city" services. Housing policy may be controlled by a county housing authority, education by the school board of an independent school district. Welfare regulations are largely made in and monitored by the federal government and state welfare agencies. The discretion and resources that the city, let alone the mayor and council, can use to deal with these and other problems are in many cases minimal.

Moreover, the mayor may well lack the political influence necessary to enlist the aid of other political institutions and decision-makers. County services may be under the control of a countywide political organization not responsive to either a black mayor or the black community. Similarly, the city's representatives in the state legislature and the United States Congress may not be allies of the mayor.

In negotiations with other levels of government, the black mayor's political resources may fail to match the demands made of the other governments. When bargaining from a position of weakness, the mayor is unlikely to be successful in negotiations.

An additional problem in assessing the influence of black officials concerns expectations about black leadership. What kinds of policy changes might one logically predict? We have seen from the investigations on Stokes and Hatcher that jobs and housing were high on their priority lists, and these factors might be nearly universal desires of black populations in large cities. Generally, we would join Keller (1978) in hypothesizing greater emphasis on social welfare expenditures over physical plant expenditures. However, in some communities a major benefit to the black community would be spending for physical improvements in black neighborhoods—for street and road paving and improvement, for better sanitary facilities, for more playgrounds and recreation areas, and so forth. It is only realistic to recognize that the perceived needs in one black community are not identical to those in other black communities, any more than all white neighborhoods and communities are alike. In one city, increased expenditures in welfare could be meeting black community needs, whereas in another community more money for the sanitation system could be helping to resolve equally pressing problems. Still, to assess the effect of black leadership across a large number of cities, we do have to make some assumptions about which kinds of city services are the highest priorities of most black populations.

A further set of problems concerns method. How does one find an appropriate cluster of policy variables in order to measure the effect of black officials? In a case study or modified case study approach, one can look at internal shifts in resources, for example, to see if urban renewal money is shifted from new downtown retail establishments to new housing for the poor and the lower-middle income groups. Redirected educational expenditures from neighborhood to neighborhood and program to program can also be gauged. In aggregate data analysis these kinds of shifts are much harder to discern and to compare over a large number of cities.

It became essential, then, to employ indicators of overall spending trends rather than within-city shifts of expenditures. The most comparable intercity data are those collected by the United States Bureau of the Census. The bureau's *Government Finance* series records city expenditure in several functional areas: police, fire, highways, sewage, sanitation, public welfare, education, hospitals, health, libraries, parks, and housing and urban renewal. City revenue is also reported and classified by standard categories: for example, tax revenue from property, sales, and other taxes, and intergovernmental revenue, categorized by federal, state, and other. While these data do let us compare cities, they also raise certain problems. One is that functional responsibilities are not the same across cities; that is, some city governments organize and finance city schools, but in most cities the schools are run and financed by autonomous school districts. Likewise, not every city has responsibilities in the area of welfare, roads, sanitation, and other functions (see Liebert 1974). These discrepancies are most apparent in the areas of welfare and education. Therefore one might compare two cities with entirely different legal responsibilities for financing these functional areas. As Liebert (1974) has shown, this divergence in functional responsibilities can make a difference in the cross-sectional analysis of comparative urban data.[2]

Another obstacle to determining the effect of black officials on public policy is the time span. It is fruitless to analyze the policy correlates of black leadership at only one point in time. Too many extraneous variables affect the policy output; black leadership is only one of the many factors. Then, too, one must allow for some lead time. Blacks coming into office in January 1978, for example, probably would not have an effect on the budget until at least January 1979, and perhaps later if the fiscal cycle is July to July or September to September. Therefore an appropriate method is a study over time (longitudinal). Such an examination would utilize a baseline established before black leadership to serve as a "control" for many of the other factors affecting a city's budget pattern. But what lead time is optimal? If it is too short, no effects will be apparent; if it is too long, it is possible that any short-term influences will no longer be ascertainable. Ideally, perhaps, a time-series analysis could be utilized, with many readings taken over a period of years. But because relatively few blacks are elected in any particular year, and because only recently have blacks won election to municipal office, it is too early to employ a time-series analysis.

## Research Design

The brief inventory of problems mentioned above is imposing, and we have designed our research to avoid or reduce each of them. We will use multiple regression and an over-time design to test for the effect of black representation on city budgetary allocations. In total, twelve separate spending indicators are included. To organize the numerous expenditure variables under analysis, we categorized them into four groups. The first, *social welfare* expenditures, includes spending on health, housing, welfare, and education. A second category, *protective services,* consists of spending for fire and police services. Park and library expenditures constitute our third category, which we refer to as *amenities*. Finally, a fourth category consisting of expenditures for streets and highways, sanitation, sewage, and hospitals is labeled *physical facilities*. In addition to analyzing each individual expenditure category, we also summed spending within each cluster to analyze the effect of black officials on the four aggregate scales. Additionally, we utilized revenue totals for federal revenue, state revenue, and total intergovernmental revenue received by the city. These data were obtained from the City Finance section of the *Government Finance* publication of the Bureau of the Census.

Our basic hypotheses were that the presence of a black mayor and greater council representation would lead to:

1. more of an increase in spending for social welfare;
2. less of an increase in spending for amenities;
3. less of an increase in spending for physical facilities;
4. less of an increase in protective services, especially fire;
5. more of an increase in intergovernmental revenue, especially federal revenue.

We utilized three measures of black representation as independent variables. First, we computed the mean absolute black representation in 1970 and 1972:

$$\frac{1970 \text{ representation} + 1972 \text{ representation}}{2} \ .$$

Second, we computed the mean proportional representation in those two years:

$$\frac{1970 \text{ representation} + 1972 \text{ representation}}{2 \times \text{ the proportion blacks in the population}} \ .$$

And finally we summed the presence of a black mayor in either of those two years. Since the absolute and proportional representation measures were highly correlated, however, we ran separate regressions for each, using the same dependent and other independent variables.

Our baseline year is 1968/69, a time when there were few black mayors in any of these cities. Our end year is 1974/75. In addition to being the most recent year available when the data were collected in 1977, use of this information allows for a two- to four-year lag between mayoral incidence in 1970 and 1972 and the time of measurement for expenditure. This time period should be long enough to capture an effect without being so long that short-term influences are washed out. Of course, ideally we would follow these measures over another three to four years as data became available.

Using a longitudinal design eliminates the need for many control variables. We will, however, control for black population change between 1960 and 1970 as one measure of change. We assume that cities that had a bigger increase in black population between 1960 and 1970 will continue to have a bigger change over 1970–74, thus possibly affecting the budgetary allocations. We also control for percentage black in the city, mean income and education levels, and total population change between 1960 and 1970. To control for region, we have computed regressions for the North and South separately.

We ameliorate in two ways the problem of different functional responsibilities for the cities in our sample. First, we utilized over-time design. The rationale is that legal changes in city functional responsibilities in these six years are negligible (e.g., few cities gained or lost the power to spend for fire protection, education, etc.), and those changes that did occur were random with respect to the other variables under consideration. Second, in our examination of expenditures in each functional category, we eliminate from the analysis cities that had no expenditures in either the earlier or the later period. We assume that if a city did not spend anything in a particular functional area in either of the years, then that city did not have the authority to do so. One disadvantage of this procedure, of course, is that it reduces the number of cases under analysis. With the exception of hospital expenditures ($N=27$), however, there are at least forty-five cities in each expenditure category.[3]

In this analysis we include only cities of more than 50,000 population, since that is the only class of municipalities for which the census reports yearly budgetary data. This reduces the sample size to 139 cities for which we have data for both 1968/69 and 1974/75.

Two types of regression equations are used. For each of our expenditure and revenue categories, we initially constructed gain scores—1974/75 amounts less those of 1968/69. These gain scores were then used as dependent variables for multiple regression. The regression weights of the black representation variables, then, tell us whether cities with black mayors (and/or council members) increase their expenditures in a given category more than cities without black representation. This is a straightforward procedure and is widely used. However, Bohrnstedt (1969) has pointed out that gain scores are usually highly correlated with the baseline score; given the tendency for regression toward the mean, those with higher initial scores are likely to have lower gain scores than those with lower initial scores. To correct this problem, Bohrnstedt suggested regressing the time-two score on the time-one score. The regression weights of the other independent variables allow us to assess their effects on the time-two score (the dependent variable), controlling for the initial score. Frequently, however, the correlation between time-one and time-two scores is very high. This leaves little variation to be explained by the other independent variables. This is of course a virtue of the procedure, for if the time-one score explains all the variation in the time-two score, then it is obvious that black representation or any other independent variable could not have determined the time-two score. For comparison, we will use both the gain score and the Bohrnstedt approach in our analysis.

Our dependent variables are presented in two ways. We have computed per capita expenditure scores (expenditure/population) to assess the level of per capita resources invested in each functional area. An analysis of these scores aids in determining whether the absolute per capita amount spent on education, for example, increased more in cities with black mayors. However, one drawback of using per capita scores in this kind of analysis is that black mayors and council members might be found disproportionately in cities with the most severe budget problems. This may mean that budgets in these cities did not increase overall at the same pace as budgets in other cities. Thus, despite the priorities of black representatives, it is possible that expenditures could not increase as fast as in wealthier cities. We used another measure, the proportion of the budget devoted to each expenditure category (education expenditure/total expenditure), as one way of dealing with that problem. This measure permits us to see if a city increased the proportion of its resources devoted to a particular functional area, regardless of the absolute dollars it had available. Thus, for each budget category, we have four dependent variables: per capita expenditures, gain in per capita expenditures, proportional expenditures, and gain in proportional expenditures.

In chapter 6 we present the results of this analysis.

# 6 The Effect of Black Elected Officials
## *Some Preliminary Findings*

Despite the imposing difficulties in undertaking a large-scale analysis of the policy effects of black elected officials, the issue is of considerable importance. Here we assess the kinds of policy upon which black elected officials have influence, the direction of that influence, and whether black mayors or black council members have greater effects on spending outcomes. Our focus is on spending patterns, because budgetary decisions reflect the commitments of decisions-makers and are thus a concrete reflection of the priorities of the particular city.[1]

## Some Descriptive Data

Table 31 presents some descriptive information concerning per capita general expenditures; expenditures on social welfare, amenities, physical facilities, and protective services; and revenues from federal, state and combined federal and state sources.[2] The data on these spending measures are categorized by year of expenditure and by degree of black representation. Some general trends are apparent in this table. First, cities with black mayors and higher black council representation increased their total expenditures and social welfare expenditures more than did other municipalities. As one would expect, then, cities with black mayors or city council members or both tend to spend more both overall and particularly in the social welfare area. This provides some support for the most important propositions we formulated.

Further, these cities with black mayors and black council representation increased their state, federal, and total intergovernmental revenue substantially more than cities without black mayors and with a smaller black share of the city council. In contrast, gains in protective services and amenities expenditures were about the same for cities with and without black mayors and were reasonably consistent across cities with different levels of black council representation. Gains in spending on physical facilities showed a curvilinear relationship with black representation on the city council. Communities with an intermediate level of black council representation had the greatest expenditures in this area; those with the most black representation spent least on physical facilities. Increases in physical facilities expenditures were negatively related to the presence of black mayors; cities without black mayors raised their physical facilities

Table 31
Selected Revenue and Spending Variables, 1968–69 and 1974–75 in per Capita Dollars

| Revenue and Expenditure Variables | | No Black Mayor | Black Mayor[a] | No Black Council Representation[a] | 1 to 19.9% Black Council Representation[b] | Over 20% Black Council Representation |
|---|---|---|---|---|---|---|
| General expenditure | 1968–69 | $205 | $201 | $163 | $227 | $212 |
| | 1974–75 | 385 | 399 | 313 | 418 | 418 |
| | Gain | 181 | 198 | 150 | 191 | 206 |
| Social welfare | 1968–69 | 57 | 54 | 35 | 70 | 53 |
| | 1974–75 | 93 | 110 | 62 | 112 | 97 |
| | Gain | 36 | 56 | 27 | 42 | 44 |
| Physical facilities | 1968–69 | 44 | 41 | 41 | 45 | 45 |
| | 1974–75 | 85 | 60 | 70 | 95 | 67 |
| | Gain | 41 | 19 | 29 | 50 | 22* |
| Amenities | 1968–69 | 15 | 13 | 12 | 13 | 16 |
| | 1974–75 | 26 | 23 | 24 | 25 | 28 |
| | Gain | 11 | 10 | 12 | 12 | 12 |
| Protective services | 1968–69 | 37 | 43 | 32 | 38 | 46* |
| | 1974–75 | 72 | 75 | 63 | 73 | 84* |
| | Gain | 35 | 32 | 31 | 35 | 38 |
| State revenue | 1968–69 | 34 | 30 | 20 | 41 | 32 |
| | 1974–75 | 80 | 104 | 48 | 91 | 118* |
| | Gain | 54 | 74 | 28 | 50 | 86* |
| Federal revenue | 1968–69 | 15 | 11 | 9 | 12 | 13 |
| | 1974–75 | 33 | 47 | 28 | 36 | 39 |
| | Gain | 18 | 36 | 19 | 24 | 26 |
| Total intergovernmental revenue | 1968–69 | 55 | 55 | 33 | 68 | 49 |
| | 1974–75 | 132 | 174 | 102 | 150 | 153 |
| | Gain | 87 | 119 | 69 | 82 | 104 |

[a]In either 1970 or 1972.  [b]Mean level 1970, 1972.
*Differences among cities significant at $p \leq .05$.

expenditures twice as much as cities with black mayors, even though they started from similar base points.

An examination of the descriptive data in table 31 also helps to explain why, in seeking to determine the effect of black representation on expenditures, it is necessary to control in some way for the initial level of expenditures (or revenues). In 1968, for example, cities that would later elect a black mayor and those that would not, both budgeted roughly the same level of per capita general expenditures ($201 and $205). However, cities that subsequently displayed divergent rates of black election to city councils had very different levels of per capita general expenditures in 1968, ranging from $163 to $227. The explanation for these differences is, of course, that demographic, socioeconomic, and other municipal characteristics were not randomly distributed among cities with different levels of black council representation in the 1970s. Rather, as we have seen, certain characteristics are more common in cities with higher black representation—most notably, large, relatively affluent, and better-educated black populations. Thus expenditure and revenue rates are influenced by a number of factors, and any plan of analysis must be sure the effects of these factors are taken into consideration.

We now turn to the multivariate analysis, where we establish controls for a number of potentially salient city factors already reviewed in chapter 5: percentage black, median educational and income level, population change, and black population change. Our baseline year is 1968/69, and the change-score year is 1974/75. By observing the pattern of shifting expenditures, we can assess whether the incidence of black elected officials is related to spending configurations. Procedurally, by regressing 1974/75 expenditures on those of 1968/69, we are in effect controlling for the battery of factors influencing the 1968/69 expenditures. As we noted in chapter 5, the same is not true when we simply use gain scores as dependent variables. The findings presented in tables 32 through 40 reflect the policy effect of black representation after the variables above have been controlled.

## Multivariate Analysis

We had hypothesized that cities with black mayors and council members would increase their social welfare spending more than cities with no black mayor and fewer blacks on the council. Of course, the distribution of gain scores (displayed in table 31) gave initial support for the policy influence of both black mayors and blacks serving on city councils. Tables 32 and 33 indicate, however, that this proposition is only partly confirmed in the multivariate analysis.

In general, the regression weights (betas) for the presence of a black

Table 32
Effect of Black Representation on per Capita Social Welfare Expenditures

| Dependent Expenditure Variables (N) | $R^2$ | Black Mayor[a] | Mean Council Representation[a] | $R^2$ | Black Mayor[a] | Proportional Representation |
|---|---|---|---|---|---|---|
| General expenditure (135) | .85 | .00[b] | .06* | .85 | .03 | .00 |
| Gain | .16 | .04 | .02 | .16 | .02 | .03 |
| Total social welfare (119) | .88 | .05 | .05 | .87 | .07* | .01 |
| Gain | .28 | .16* | -.01 | .28 | .17* | -.05 |
| Health (90) | .71 | .01 | .07 | .71 | .01 | .07 |
| Gain | .27 | .13 | .08 | .28 | .13 | .10 |
| Housing (89) | .24 | .06 | -.08 | .25 | .06 | -.12 |
| Gain | .04 | .06 | -.08 | .05 | .06 | -.12 |
| Education (45) | .79 | .08 | .04 | .79 | .09 | -.01 |
| Gain | .16 | .31* | -.05 | .16 | .32* | -.06 |
| Welfare (45) | .75 | -.08 | .06 | .75 | -.07 | .06 |
| Gain | .22 | -.05 | -.03 | .22 | -.06 | -.01 |

[a]Includes controls for black population proportion, mean income and education levels, population change, and black population change.
[b]Figures are standardized regression weights (betas).
*$p \leq .05$.

mayor are positive, both for the per capita measures and for the proportion of budget measures. Cities with black mayors demonstrated a significantly higher gain in educational expenditures and in overall social spending than did cities without black mayors. Indeed, in each of the social spending categories except the one specifically dealing with welfare benefits, black mayors are associated with higher than average per capita expenditure gains. Accordingly, this set of findings is consistent with our expectations about the areas black mayors are apt to influence. Welfare spending is an exception in large part because welfare levels are generally set by the state, as are the amounts that cities themselves must contribute to total welfare payments. Hence the city has relatively little autonomy in this particular form of expenditure; and, though the issue is worthy of testing, there is little reason to believe black mayors could affect welfare spending, since the policy is established at government levels above the municipality.

The pattern of relationships for the proportional measures of public policy is similar to that found for the per capita indicators. The presence of black mayors is associated with a slightly greater than average rise in the proportion of the budget allocated to social welfare expenditures, with public welfare again being the lone exception. Only one of these positive relationships is statistically significant, however, reinforcing the interpretation that the effect of black mayors on city spending patterns is small. Nevertheless, the general consistency of the signs gives us confidence in concluding that these effects are not spurious and that the pattern of mayoral influence is far from random. Apparently, black mayors can affect the course of municipal policy and can do so in a manner congruent with our expectations.

Black representation on the city council is another matter, however. Here the signs of relationships between council representation and policy measures are almost as likely to be negative as positive, and in the case of per capita indicators they are not statistically significant at all. Therefore a reasonable interpretation is that expanding black representation on the city council alone, absolutely or proportionately, will not result in a consistent shift toward committing more funds to social policy programs. The one exception is that the proportion of expenditures devoted to health policy seems to increase with black representation on the council, both proportional and absolute. This relationship holds to a somewhat lesser extent when per capita expenditures are examined.

Thus, overall, we can tentatively conclude that, though black mayors appear to bring about a greater increase in social welfare expenditures than do white mayors, the effect is neither large nor completely consistent. Further, even that small effect does not seem to hold for black city council members.

In the 1970s, many cities had reached either the financial or the political

Table 33
Effect of Black Representation on Budget Proportions of Social Welfare Expenditures

| Dependent Expenditure Variables (N) | R² | Black Mayor | Mean Council Representation[a] | R² | Black Mayor[a] | Proportional Council Representation |
|---|---|---|---|---|---|---|
| Health (91) | .54 | .01 | .12 | .55 | .01 | .16* |
| Gain | .22 | .05 | .17 | .24 | .04 | .23* |
| Housing (89) | .20 | .11 | -.00 | .20 | .12 | -.09 |
| Gain | .02 | .07 | -.09 | .03 | .07 | -.12 |
| Education (45) | .75 | .07 | -.06 | .76 | .07 | -.07 |
| Gain | .12 | .06 | -.11 | .13 | .07 | -.13 |
| Welfare (45) | .67 | -.11 | .05 | .67 | -.10 | .03 |
| Gain | .43 | -.18 | .14 | .43 | .10 | -.15 |
| Total Scale (118) | .79 | .08* | -.01 | .79 | .09* | -.03 |
| Gain | .09 | .09 | -.01 | .09 | .10 | -.05 |

[a]Includes controls for black population proportion, mean income and education levels, population change, and black population change.
[b]Figures are standardized regression weights (betas).
*$p \leq .05$.

limits of taxation. In these cities at least—and probably in most others as well—if there were to be budgetary "winners," there had to be budgetary "losers." If cities are to increase the proportion of their budgets spent on social welfare, then that gain is likely to be at the expense of other types of budgetary allocations. Consequently, we hypothesized that the remaining expenditure categories—protective services, amenities, and physical facilities—would grow less in cities with black mayors and more black council representation. Note that this proposition does not predict a decline in these areas, but rather relatively less growth under black elected officials.

Tables 34 and 35 reveal that the presence of a black mayor results in a significantly lower increase in per capita protective services expenditures, particularly spending on fire protection. The inverse relationships are not as strong with police expenditures, whether we look at per capita or proportional scores. The signs for the relationships between the presence of a black mayor and protective expenditures are all negative in both the per capita and the proportion of budget analyses. However, spending on police evidently fares better than spending on fire protection in cities with black mayors.

Again, the effect of black council members is less clear. None of the associations are statistically significant; moreover, the sizes of the regression coefficients are almost uniformly small, and the signs are mixed. Hence, no evidence of clear effect emerges from this analysis. The numerical strength of black council members, absolutely or proportionately, seems little related to increases or decreases in protective services expenditures. Again, therefore, our hypothesis is partially confirmed. The presence of a black mayor appears to make a difference in reducing the size of the protective service budget relative to other cities; and, as we noted, this is especially true of that portion allotted to fire protection. On the other hand, enhanced black council representation does not have a clear effect on any of these expenditures.

For amenities spending the evidence is again more definite for mayors than for council members (tables 36 and 37). The presence of black mayors is modestly and negatively associated with per capita spending increases for amenities. The relationships are rather small, and none is quite statistically significant. The same pattern is observed when proportions of the budget are examined. Here, the gain in library budget proportions is related with black mayors in a statistically significant and negative direction. The effect of black council members on amenities spending appears more positive, though the signs are somewhat mixed. Sixteen of the twenty-four signs are positive, indicating that perhaps black council members support this portion of the city budget. It may be that for the black council member, getting a new library branch or community park in one's neighborhood is a substantial and desirable goal, even

Table 34
Effect of Black Representation on per Capita Protective Expenditures

| Dependent Expenditure Variables (N) | R² | Black Mayor[a] | Mean Council Representation[a] | R² | Black Mayor | Proportional Council Representation |
|---|---|---|---|---|---|---|
| Total scale (135) | .71 | −.09* | −.00 | .69 | −.08* | −.02 |
| Gain | .11 | −.12 | .08 | .11 | −.11 | .06 |
| Police (135) | .65 | −.03 | .00 | .65 | −.02 | −.01 |
| Gain | .11 | −.04 | .08 | .11 | −.03 | .05 |
| Fire (135) | .71 | −.17* | −.01 | .71 | −.17* | −.02 |
| Gain | .13 | −.22* | .05 | .12 | −.22* | .05 |

[a]Includes controls for black population proportion, mean income and education levels, population change, and black population change.
*$p \leq .05$.

Table 35
Effect of Black Representation on Budget Proportions of Protective Expenditures

| Dependent Expenditure Variables (N) | $R^2$ | Black Mayor[a] | Mean Council Representation[a] | $R^2$ | Black Mayor | Proportional Council Representation |
|---|---|---|---|---|---|---|
| Total scale (135) | .49 | −.04 | −.04 | .49 | −.06 | .03 |
| Gain | .07 | −.05 | −.08 | .07 | −.08 | .03 |
| Police (135) | .47 | −.02 | −.04 | .47 | −.03 | .03 |
| Gain | 06 | −.01 | −.09 | .06 | −.04 | .02 |
| Fire (135) | .51 | −.06 | −.04 | .51 | −.08 | .03 |
| Gain | .08 | −.13 | .04 | .08 | −.10 | −.07 |

[a]Includes controls for black population proportion, mean income and education levels, population change, and black population change.

though these services might be seen by some as less basic than spending on education and housing.

Our last set of expenditures are those we have called "physical facilities"—which includes such items as highways and streets, hospitals, sanitation, and sewers. It may be that, in very poor communities, blacks see these basic physical structures as primary needs, but we hypothesized that, by and large, these types of expenditures would be a lower priority for black officials than would social services. Our hypothesis is largely supported with respect to black mayors. Cities with black mayors gained less in expenditures for sewers and sanitation and streets and highways. Several of these relationships were statistically significant, particularly those referring to per capita expenditures. In contrast, hospital spending grew faster in cities with black mayors than in other cities. This finding cannot be generalized too far, since there were only twenty-seven cities spending for hospitals and only one had a black mayor.

Overall, black council members once more had an inconsistent influence on expenditures for physical facilities. Their effect on sanitation expenditures and on per capita highway expenditure gains seems to be very positive, but on most of the other expenditure categories their effect is negative. Again, the link between black council members and public policy is less clear-cut than that between black mayors and policy. Some reasons for this pattern of ambiguity will be discussed below, in this and the following chapter.

Finally, we examined per capita revenues from all intergovernmental sources and from the federal and state governments individually. One of the most frequently mentioned accomplishments of both Mayor Stokes and Mayor Hatcher was their ability to attract outside funding, particularly federal funds. Was this a common pattern, or were these two exceptional cases? Table 40 indicates that black mayors do in fact obtain more intergovermental revenue than do other mayors. Each of the signs is positive, though only the relationship with gains in total intergovernmental revenues is statistically significant. Black council representation bears a consistently negative relationship with the inflow of intergovernmental funds. It is difficult to discern a reason for this inverse linkage because high levels of absolute black council representation are associated with a high percentage of blacks in the population, and consequently with need factors that in part determine some state and federal funding. Nevertheless, neither proportional nor absolute council representation is favorably related to the inflow of federal funds.

Thus far our data indicate that black mayors have affected the direction of municipal public expenditures. With some deviations, expenditures have grown faster in social services and increased more slowly in other areas of city life—amenities, protective services, and physical facilities—in municipalities that had black mayors during the measurement period. On the other hand, black council representation seems to

Table 36
Effect of Black Representation on per Capita Amenities Expenditures

| Dependent Expenditure Variables (N) | R² | Black Mayor[a] | Mean Council Representation | R² | Black Mayor[a] | Proportional Council Representation |
|---|---|---|---|---|---|---|
| Total scale (133) | .35 | −.08 | .02 | .29 | −.10 | .09 |
| Gain | .14 | −.09 | .03 | .14 | −.11 | .10 |
| Libraries (96) | .25 | −.02 | −.12 | .24 | −.04 | −.05 |
| Gain | .05 | −.03 | −.14 | .04 | −.05 | −.06 |
| Parks (128) | .27 | −.08 | .06 | .28 | −.09 | .10 |
| Gain | .06 | −.04 | .03 | .06 | −.04 | .05 |

[a]Includes controls for black population proportion, mean income and education levels, population change, and black population change.

Table 37
Effect of Black Representation on Budget Proportions of Amenities Expenditures

| Dependent Expenditure Variables (N) | $R^2$ | Black Mayor[a] | Mean Council Representation | $R^2$ | Black Mayor[a] | Proportional Council Representation |
|---|---|---|---|---|---|---|
| Total scale (133) | .37 | −.01 | .00 | .38 | −.03 | .11* |
| Gain | .09 | −.01 | .09 | .09 | .02 | −.03 |
| Libraries (96) | .42 | −.01 | −.06 | .42 | −.05 | .04 |
| Gain | .07 | −.17 | −.07 | .07 | −.20* | .06 |
| Parks (128) | .33 | .01 | .01 | .34 | −.02 | .11 |
| Gain | .10 | .02 | −.01 | .10 | −.01 | .08 |

[a]Includes controls for black population proportion, mean income and education levels, population change, and black population change.
*$p \leq .05$.

Table 38
Effect of Black Representation on per Capita Physical Facilities Expenditures

| Dependent Expenditure Variables (N) | R² | Black Mayor[a] | Mean Council Representation | R² | Black Mayor[a] | Proportional Council Representation |
|---|---|---|---|---|---|---|
| Total scale (133) | .54 | -.09 | .01 | .54 | -.08 | -.03 |
| Gain | .04 | -.13 | .00 | .04 | -.12 | -.03 |
| Highways (134) | .32 | -.04 | .03 | .32 | -.04 | .02 |
| Gain | .11 | -.04 | .10 | .13 | -.06 | .16* |
| Hospitals (27) | .94 | .04 | .05 | .94 | .05 | .01 |
| Gain | .35 | .28* | -.49* | .36 | .25* | -.36 |
| Sanitation (139) | .42 | -.17* | .09 | .43 | -.17* | .12* |
| Gain | .15 | -.18* | .11 | .16 | -.19 | .14* |
| Sewers (128) | .10 | -.13 | -.03 | .10 | -.13 | -.04 |
| Gain | .06 | -.14* | -.07 | .06 | -.14* | -.05 |

[a]Includes control for black population proportion, mean income and education levels, population change, and black population change.
*$p \leq .05$.

Table 39
Effect of Black Representation on Budget Proportions of Physical Facilities Expenditures

| Dependent Expenditure Variables (N) | $R^2$ | Black Mayor[a] | Mean Council Representation | $R^2$ | Black Mayor[a] | Proportional Council Representation |
|---|---|---|---|---|---|---|
| Total scale (133) | .56 | −.10 | −.05 | .56 | −.10* | −.05 |
| Gain | .03 | −.09 | −.05 | .04 | −.09 | −.07 |
| Highways (134) | .41 | −.03 | −.05 | .41 | −.04 | −.02 |
| Gain | .06 | −.06 | −.03 | .06 | −.06 | −.02 |
| Hospitals (27) | .97 | .04 | −.05 | .97 | .05 | −.06 |
| Gain | .35 | .21 | −.29 | .40 | .21 | −.33* |
| Santitation (139) | .38 | −.14* | .12 | .40 | −.15* | .18* |
| Gain | .04 | .02 | .14 | .06 | .02 | .17* |
| Sewers (128) | .17 | −.11 | −.06 | .17 | −.12 | −.08 |
| Gain | .08 | −.12 | −.15* | .09 | −.12 | −.16* |

[a]Includes controls for black population proportion, mean income and education levels, population change, and black population change.
*$p \leq .05$.

make much less of a consistent difference. Within every category of expenditure, the effect of black council representation is mixed.

Yet, before we accept these findings, we need to undertake some further explorations. Several questions immediately come to mind. For example, perhaps by entering both black mayoral presence and black council representation into the equation at the same time, their effects cancel each other out. Or, more likely, because of the correlation between black mayors and black council members, the effects of black mayors cause council influence to appear smaller than if it were entered into the regression without black mayoral presence.

Table 41 shows the results of separate regressions run for each expenditure and revenue category. In each analysis, only the control variables—percentage black, median education and income, black and citywide population change—plus one of the black representation variables were entered. The findings largely confirm the interpretations derived from tables 32–40. The signs for absolute black council representation appear a bit more consistent than before, but the coefficients are very small, except for the social welfare expenditures. The directions of signs for the proportional council measure continue to be mixed. And a scale incorporating both black council and mayoral representation largely mirrors the mayoral representation variable in its effect. In sum, even employing these additional approaches in order to provide opportunities for observing the relative policy consequences of black mayors and city council officeholders, the effects are essentially the same as before. The linkages between black mayors and policy continue to be evident and in the hypothesized directions, whereas associations between policy and council officials are again smaller and are inconsistent in the direction of influence.

A second question one might raise is whether the effect of black representation, particularly mayoral representation, might be different depending on what kind of political power the mayor can wield. For example, it is logical to expect that a black mayor would have more influence in a strong-mayor system than a weak-mayor system, a mayor-council government rather than a council-manager one. Unfortunately, the number of black mayors ($N=13$) remains too small to realistically test such hypotheses. However, when the number of black mayors increases, or when a longer time period can be analyzed, these would certainly be fruitful to explore. Surely it is important to understand the ways institutional arrangements condition the influence of black officials.

A further avenue of exploration concerns possible differences in the effect of black officeholders in the North and the South. Unfortunately, all the black mayors in this subset of cities are from the North. Recall that the latest expenditure data available to us at the outset of the study pertain to cities over 50,000 in 1974/75. To leave satisfactory lead time for black

Table 40
Effect of Black Representation on per Capita Intergovernmental Revenue

| Dependent Revenue Variables (N) | R² | Black Mayor[a] | Mean Council Representation | R² | Black Mayor[a] | Proportional Council Representation |
|---|---|---|---|---|---|---|
| Total intergovernmental | | | | | | |
| revenue (132) | .53 | .10 | −.06 | .53 | .10 | −.06 |
| Gain | .18 | .13 | −.08 | .18 | .13* | −.09 |
| Total federal | | | | | | |
| revenue (135) | .15 | .10 | −.07 | .15 | .11 | −.10 |
| Gain | .11 | .07 | −.10 | .12 | .07 | −.08 |
| Total state | | | | | | |
| revenue (132) | .64 | .05 | .02 | .64 | .06 | −.00 |
| Gain | .21 | .09 | −.03 | .21 | .10 | −.05 |

[a]Includes controls for black population proportion, mean income and education levels, population change, and black population change.
*$p \leq .05$.

Table 41
Black Representation and Major Categories of Expenditures and Revenue (per Capita)

| Expenditures and Revenue | Mayoral Presence | Council Representation | Proportional Council Representation | Representation Scale |
|---|---|---|---|---|
| General expenditure | .03[b] | .06* | .01 | .05 |
| Gain | .05 | .04 | −.01 | .06 |
| Social welfare | .07* | .08* | .03 | .08* |
| Gain | .16* | .05 | −.01 | .16* |
| Physical facilities | −.09 | −.03 | −.05 | −.09 |
| Gain | −.13 | −.05 | −.06 | −.13 |
| Amenities | −.08 | −.01 | −.06 | −.07 |
| Gain | −.08 | −.01 | .08 | −.08 |
| Protective services | −.09* | −.04 | −.04 | −.09* |
| Gain | −.10 | .04 | .03 | −.08 |
| State revenue | .06 | .05 | .01 | .07 |
| Gain | .08 | .01 | −.03 | .08 |
| Federal revenue | .08 | −.06 | −.05 | .06 |
| Gain | .04 | −.08 | −.07 | .02 |
| Total intergovernmental revenue | .08 | −.02 | −.04 | .07 |
| Gain | .11 | −.03 | −.06 | .09 |

[a]A simple additive scale where O = no council or mayoral representation 2= 100% council representation plus black mayor. The presence of a black mayor = 1 in the scale, council representation was a simple proportion of blacks in the council 0 to 1.0.
[b]The beta for each representation variable was calculated in a separate regression.
*p ≤ .05.

elected officials to effect policy change, the black representation information refers to 1970 and 1972. Although Maynard Jackson of Atlanta, Dutch Morial of New Orleans, and other blacks have since been elected mayors of southern cities, in 1970 and 1972 there were no black mayors in southern cities of over 50,000 population. Therefore we could make no comparison of the effects of northern and southern black mayors. We could, however, compare the black council representatives from these two regions. It is possible, for example, that council members from one of the regions were behaving as expected while those from the other region were acting in a less patterned manner. To test this possibility, we probed the effect of both northern and southern proportional and absolute black council representation on the major categories of municipal expenditures and revenues. More detailed breakdowns were impossible owing to the small number of cases that would result in each regional subcategory. Regression coefficients were computed with mayors and council members entered both together (for the North) and separately. The mayoral variable was, of course, not entered into the southern equation.

Electing southern black council members seems to have a small positive influence on all expenditure categories except amenities and protective services. In no case, however, is this influence statistically significant. Rather, we see a pattern in which the strength of the black delegation of southern city councils is positively related, but usually in a very small way, to total expenditures and to social welfare and physical facilities expenditures. Southern black council representation is also associated in a reasonably strong way with state revenue gains, and still favorably, though less closely, with gains in federal revenue and total intergovernmental revenue. Northern council representation, in contrast, has a mixed relationship with both revenues and expenditures. The strongest linkages that northern black council representation displays are with state and total intergovernmental revenue, and there the relationships are in the opposite direction from that hypothesized: larger black council representation actually is linked to smaller gains in state revenue and total intergovernmental revenue.

These findings are mildly surprising. We see that it is southern council representation whose effect more closely conforms to our expectations. Where the relationships are clearest, northern council representation has an effect opposite to what we predicted.

We might consider briefly why black council representation could be negatively related to the inflow of intergovernmental funds. A logical possibility is that these cities with large black representation also have a very high proportion of blacks. In the North, cities with high proportions of blacks tend to be in the states that are suffering acute economic decline marked by higher unemployment, higher taxes, faltering services, population losses, and other aspects of financial disruption. Under these conditions, it is plausible that state aid to cities would not be increasing as

Table 42
Effect of Black Council on Major Categories of per Capita City Spending by Region

| Expenditures and Revenue | Absolute Representation | | | Proportional Representation | | |
|---|---|---|---|---|---|---|
| | North | North[a] | South | North | North[a] | South |
| General expenditure | .12* | .12* | .02 | .03 | .05 | .01 |
| Gain | -.09 | -.02 | .17 | -.08* | -.05 | .10 |
| Social welfare | .05 | .11* | .05 | .00 | .05 | .02 |
| Gain | -.01 | .11 | .14 | -.09 | -.04 | .11 |
| Physical facilities | .08 | .06 | .05 | .03 | .03 | -.04 |
| Gain | -.02 | -.04 | .02 | .00 | -.01 | -.07 |
| Amenities | .16 | .15 | -.04 | .20* | .20* | -.01 |
| Gain | .19 | .19 | -.04 | .25* | .25* | -.00 |
| Protective services | -.00 | -.03 | -.01 | -.00 | -.02 | -.03 |
| Gain | -.02 | -.01 | .09 | .04 | .03 | .05 |
| State revenue | .02 | .00 | .18 | -.17* | -.01 | .07 |
| Gain | -.05 | -.07 | .18 | -.20* | -.07 | .08 |
| Federal revenue | .34 | -.33* | .03 | -.02 | -.14 | .04 |
| Gain | -.33 | -.33* | .02 | -.09 | -.16 | .04 |
| Total intergovernmental revenue | -.21* | -.16 | .04 | -.15* | -.13 | .02 |
| Gain | -.19 | -.15 | .06 | -.13 | -.12 | .02 |

*Note*: Controlling for all factors controlled for in previous tables.
[a] Also controlling for the presence of a black mayor: North $72 \leqslant n \leqslant 78$; South $47 \leqslant n \leqslant 50$.
*$p \leqslant .05$.

rapidly as in states without these economic problems. Until the mid-1970s, at least, federal aid also had been shifting away from these states toward the states of the "sunbelt," especially in the South and Southwest, where there was marked economic and population growth during this period.

## Conclusions

In this chapter we have explored the effect of black representation on city revenues and expenditures. We have found that black mayors do have the anticipated effect: their presence is positively related to spending on social welfare and to the inflow of intergovernmental revenue but negatively related to spending for amenities, protective services, and physical facilities except hospitals. Black council representation, on the other hand, has a mixed effect. There appears to be no consistent influence of black council representation on these expenditures and revenues. A closer look at the effects of council representation in the North and in the South reveals that black representation has more of the anticipated influence in the South than in the North. However, on the whole, council representation in neither region conforms to our hypotheses as well as does black mayoral presence.

We believe these findings do indicate that electing black officials can and does affect urban public policy, at least as measured by urban expenditures. The implications of these findings and some of the reasons stronger relationships were not evident will be discussed in the next, concluding chapter.

# 7 Conclusions

Representation: A Look at the Past

Historically, blacks in the United States have suffered so much discrimination that it is difficult to know what equal opportunity would mean. Clearly, the situation has improved immeasurably in recent decades. However, the problem of assessing inequalities is rooted in the fact that the inequalities have not only additive effects, but interactive effects as well. For example, as is often noted, inequities in education affect income opportunities, which in turn have implications for housing decisions, which affect educational and income choices, ad infinitum. Of course, not the least of historical inequities that have shackled the black population is inequality in political representation. For the greater part of the more than two hundred years since America's independence, blacks have been accorded virtually no representation. This absence of political representation was of enormous symbolic importance; it demonstrated to black and white alike that blacks were both inferior and impotent. This situation also prevented blacks from having their preferences effectively expressed in policy-making bodies. The freedom to participate in the process of change was firmly closed to the black population.

In recent times, however, a number of societal trends have coalesced to promote the chances of black representation. Among the key trends we discussed in chapter 1 are:

1. Geographical shifts in black and white population that have led to a rapid expansion in the black proportion of numerous American cities.

2. Legislative, judicial, and administrative decisions by the federal government that collectively constitute rather formidable protections for the black community. Most notable among the legislative actions were the 1964 Civil Rights Act and the 1965 and 1975 Voting Rights Acts.

3. Shifting black attitudes have been marked by greater militancy, racial pride, and politicization, all factors that tend to advance the prospects of black candidates for municipal office.

4. White attitudes have also undergone change, in this instance moving considerably toward positions less prejudiced against blacks, and many whites are now more inclined to support blacks who seek political office.

These trends have helped make the election of blacks possible. In and of themselves, they do not ensure that an equitable number of blacks will gain elective posts. What the changes have ensured, however, is that blacks will win at least some representation in many cities and have, at a minimum, the opportunity for representation in other communities across the country.

It is patently unrealistic to contend that these changes, including landmark civil rights legislation, have produced racial equality. That simply is not the case. Gross racial inequalities still permeate social, economic, cultural, and political life. In this book the focus has been on politics, and the evidence is overwhelming that blacks are clearly underrepresented in both mayoral and city council offices. The point is inescapable—blacks have far to go before they achieve representation in line with their share of the population. Nevertheless, the data presented in chapters 3 and 4 demonstrate profound improvement in the rate of black election to municipal office during the 1970s.


Representation: A Look at the Present

The improvement in black representation during the past decade has been dramatic. In 1970 blacks had won only 4 percent of mayoral seats. By 1978 this figure had grown to 10 percent—a 250 percent improvement. Similarly, in 1970 blacks had gained barely 7 percent of council seats. By 1978 this election rate had burgeoned to 17 percent of the city council members. We do not wish to minimize the underrepresentation of blacks. Indeed, even with this remarkable growth, since blacks constitute 25 percent of the population in these cities, they are represented in mayoral and council seats respectively at only 40 percent and 71 percent of the equitable rates. Yet this progress ought not to be ignored. Whether we look at rises in black representation rates, percentage of cities with equitable rates, percentage of cities with at least some black representation or other measures of change, we see a substantial net increase in black municipal officeholders during the 1970s.

The recent overall successes of blacks notwithstanding, there are abundant differences in the degrees of black representation in various American cities. Some cities elect black mayors, others do not. Certain communities actually overrepresent blacks on city council, whereas many cities never elect even a single black council member. To explore more deeply the factors underlying these differences in black representation, we developed several interrelated measures of black candidacy and success. These included: (1) the presence of black mayoral candidates; (2) black candidate victory rates; (3) black mayoral representation in 1978; (4) black mayoral representation in 1970 through 1978; (5) black city council candidacy; (6) black city council equity (gauged by ratio and subtractive scores); and (7) overall black council representation. We then examined the effect on black representation of nearly thirty indicators of white population and demographic characteristics, political and election rules, federal antipoverty funds, and black resources.

Far and away the most critical variables were black resources. Almost without exception, this cluster accounted for the most variation in the black candidacy and representation rates. However, each of the other kinds of factors was also influential for some of the representation measures. The effects of each of the indicators have been discussed in previous chapters, and we will not attempt to review each of our findings here. Nevertheless, several variables—at least one from each cluster—deserve additional brief attention because of their relationships with black representation.

In general, the influence of federal antipoverty efforts was disappointing. In most instances this was the least important set of factors in patterning black representation rates. Community Action and other OEO programs appeared to have had no discernible effect on the presence of black candidates or on the election of blacks to municipal office. Model Cities efforts did affect black candidacy for mayor and city council, but their influence was limited to the candidacy stage. Communities with Model Cities programs did not have a higher yield of black mayors or council members. The only antipoverty measure that was linked to the election of blacks was the per capita amount of antipoverty funds, suggesting that federal government monies injected into black communities can promote black organizational development that results in electing blacks to office. But even here it should be noted that the linkage between antipoverty spending and black council representation was comparatively weak and just barely statistically significant. The quality and emphasis of particular antipoverty programs may have stimulated black electoral activity and therefore the election of blacks in some cities; but the "quantity" or the amount of funding had little apparent effect on black election rates.

Demographic and white population characteristics also demonstrated rather limited effect on the fate of black political aspirants. Indeed, white social class characteristics were not related to any of the seven types of black candidacy and representation measures. It is unclear whether the white middle class is actually more sympathetic than other classes to the need for black representation; even if it is, there is no evidence here that such a set of attitudes translates into more equitable black representation in communities comprising greater numbers of the white middle class. The only demographic factor displaying an effect on both black mayoral and council rates was region. Both northeastern and southern cities tended to have roughly the same low proportion of black mayors —much lower than in the Midwest and the West. Further, the South had the least equitable black council representation and the Northeast the second least equitable level; again, these were considerably lower than in the Midwest and West. In all the multiple regression equations examining black mayoral and council representation, it was Northeastern location that showed a significant and *un*favorable influence. Of course, this finding does not mean that northeastern cities have less black representation than southern communities; to the contrary, as we have seen, northeastern municipalities have a bit more equitable black council level (.73) than do southern cities (.54). Rather, the findings suggest that, by virtue of other variables in the analysis, we can explain why southern representation is poor, but we cannot account in a similar manner for the low northeastern rates.

In the South, black representation is low primarily because blacks have fewer resources. The gaps between blacks and whites in economic and educational attainment are so great that blacks have difficulty competing politically. The shortage of essential socioeconomic resources (to be discussed below) constrains black political fortunes in the South and thus helps explain the poor representation level. In the Northeast, black socioeconomic resources are not lower than elsewhere, but they are not being converted as readily into black electoral success. Since our independent variables do not explain the poor black representation in the Northeast, we must look elsewhere for an explanation. As we noted, it is more likely that depressed black representation there is embedded in the economic and financial dislocation that the region has suffered in the recent past. In the spiraling economic decline, racial and class tensions become exacerbated, and it is possible that whites in the Northeast behave as though they are threatened by possible growth in black political power. Neither the West nor the Midwest has encountered the same degree of economic stagnation, and, of course, neither has the same generally high percentage of blacks in its cities. We attribute the uncharacteristically low black representation in the Northeast, then, to the belief by whites that expanding black political power is threatening; this belief is based on the confluence of two trends: large black population size and recent economic decline.

Of the political and electoral factors, several had little apparent influence on black representation. Contrary to our expectations, salary levels, terms of office, and elections simultaneous with state or national races were virtually unrelated to black representation. Similarly, there was little difference in black electoral outcomes between mayor-council and council-manager cities, though the handful of communities with commission government did have somewhat lower rates of blacks winning election to office. Blacks are somewhat more likely to gain the mayor's seat in cities that do not elect their mayors directly, suggesting that members of the council are more sensitive to the need for black mayors than is the electorate generally. Of course it must be emphasized that the link between indirect election to office and black mayoral representation is rather weak, and only forty-seven of our sample cities employed other than direct election.

Two of the political and election rules have particularly interesting connections with black representation. The first, partisanship, was unfavorably associated with all the measures of black mayoral and council candidacy. This group of findings indicates that blacks confront greater difficulty in becoming candidates for municipal offices when party labels appear on the ballot. Blacks have long complained about being excluded by local parties, and our evidence may be interpreted to provide some indirect support for that complaint. It may be strategically "rational" for political parties to encourage black candidacy and thereby enlist black electoral support for other candidates of the party (Banfield and Wilson 1963); but our data reveal that this does not generally occur. It is simply more likely that blacks will become candidates by gathering sufficient numbers of signatures or by winning primaries in nonpartisan systems. Whether we look at mayoral or council candidacy rates, the result is the same. Partisanship reduces the number and proportionality of black candidacies. These preliminary findings support the reformist view that nonpartisan elections are more open to the public generally.

However, before we conclude that partisanship has dire consequences for black representation, we need to stress a few other points. Partisanship was not significantly related to black council equity scores, council representation, or mayoral presence in 1978. Indeed, the only measure of black electoral success associated with partisanship was the incidence of black mayors in the overall period 1970–78. Even here, partisanship was one of the very weakest predictors of black mayors, and the relationship was only just statistically significant at $p \leq .05$. Hence, there is little reason to conclude that partisan systems dramatically impede black representation at the municipal level.

Actually, our data suggest that partisanship may favor the chances of black candidates, since, though partisanship reduces black candidacy, it generally has no effect on black representation. Pomper (1966), Gordon (1970), and Pettigrew (1976) have found there is more "ethnic" voting— that is, voting for members of one's own ethnic group—in nonpartisan races. In partisan systems, the party is said to "bridge" ethnic differences, with the result that numbers of a given ethnic group are more likely to vote for party candidates, regardless of ethnicity, than simply for candidates of their own group. Since there are fewer black candidacies in partisan cities, but not fewer winners, we would guess that, once on the ballot, blacks benefit from the partisan system. Although the mechanisms here are not clear, they probably include the "bridging" effect of parties as well as the increased costs and media influence in nonpartisan elections. In any event, these findings suggest that, if blacks gain more equitable candidacy rates in party systems, they may win election to office at an even more rapid pace. Obviously, at this juncture, the findings indicate that partisanship has a weak but negative effect on black representation. This pattern perhaps should lead to reconsideration of unqualified endorsements of partisanship because of its presumed advantages for minority representation. Even in Chicago, with its presumed party emphasis on winning, Grimshaw (1979) found considerable underfunding and understaffing of black ward organizations. On the other hand, if more blacks gain candidacy for partisan posts, theorists such as Willis Hawley (1973) may be correct in surmising that partisanship would advance the interests of the black community by helping blacks win political representation at the local level. Indeed, gaining candidacy in a nonpartisanship election may be a shallow victory if the black candidate has a disproportionately slim chance of winning in the general election.

The other political and election rule meriting some additional consideration concerns district elections. The consequences of this particular rule are reasonably clear, and there is little comfort in our findings for civic reformers who contend that at-large systems are as favorable to minorities as they are to whites. Whether we look to council candidacy, equity, or overall representation, the relationships show that district races favor black political interests. To be sure, there are at-large cities that provide blacks with fair numerical representation on city councils, and there are district communities that greatly underrepresent blacks. Indeed, there is no inevitable causality between election type and black council penetration. But the evidence is persuasive that, for the most part, district races promote and at-large races impede black council representation.

Moreover, although we have not presented the analysis, additional research reported elsewhere indicates that there is little improvement even when at-large elections call for district residence requirements, that is, systems in which candidates for council seats must live in particular districts of the city but are elected by a citywide electorate (Karnig and Welch 1978). At-large races with or without district residence requirements are quite similar in their levels of black representation—and both produce significantly less equitable black representation than do systems using pure district contests. The at-large nature of both types of contests evidently is the critical dimension in depressing the chances of blacks winning election to city councils. Cottrell and Fleischmann (1979) also have concluded that minority representation has grown substantially in cities that have shifted from at-large to district elections—for example, San Antonio, Fort Worth, Waco, and El Paso, Texas. And Karnig and Welch (1978), in an examination of black representation in "mixed" cities—those with both a district and an at-large component—demonstrated that blacks gain far greater representation from the district races.

Several characteristics of pure district systems probably contribute to the positive influence in advancing the electability of blacks. The district system stresses shoe-leather, door-to-door neighborhood political organization rather than the media politics necessary in citywide elections. With limited funds for buying media time, blacks are more apt to succeed at the neighborhood level than at the citywide level. In a parallel-manner, district contests are advantageous to blacks not merely because the costs are lower, but also because there is less need for citywide name recognition or for endorsements by the media and civic groups. Probably of more formidable effect, blacks running in district contests can often avoid direct competition with whites. District elections allow blacks to take advantage of residential segregation to increase black representation, though the beneficiaries are black men, not black women (Karnig and Welch 1979).

District elections favor the election of blacks because most contemporary American cities are composed of white majorities, and whites are simply less likely to support black candidates. If we define racial orientation loosely as behavior based on racial motivation—whether conscious or unconscious—then America is indeed racially oriented. This is, of course, not a novel point. However, the research on which this book is based does provide some hints about the degree of racial motivation demonstrated in city elections. Where blacks are population minorities, they have little chance of electing a black mayor. On the basis of numbers alone, for example, we would expect more than a third of the cities with 35–49.9 percent black to have black mayors. Actually, only 10 percent do. We surmise that whites, at least in part, use racial criteria in choosing to elect white candidates.

But there is evident racial motivation among the black electorate too. Once blacks obtain majority status, there is a greatly disproportionate chance that a black will be elected mayor. Of the dozen-odd cities with black majorities, fewer than 20 percent had white mayors in 1978. A marked trend during the decade showed the proportion of black mayors increasing in black majority cities from a low of one-third in 1970, to 58 percent in 1972, to three-quarters in 1975, to an overrepresented 83 percent in 1978. The same pattern holds true for city councils. And, in cities with white majorities, blacks are generally more underrepresented on at-large than on district city councils. Put differently, whites tend to be overrepresented in most at-large cities. Yet, consistent with our overall discussion, blacks themselves gain overrepresentation in at-large communities that have black electoral majorities. In sum, where blacks constitute more than 50 percent of the population and the election is citywide—either a mayoralty race or an at-large council election—whites receive a lower share of the city council seats and have less chance of gaining the mayoralty than their share of the population would justify.

The stress on electing blacks in these white minority cities is understandable, since underrepresentation of blacks has been a stark historical fact. And, in several of these communities, blacks in the past were not even permitted to become candidates for office. In the short run, then, blacks voting for fellow blacks may be seen as a healthy affirmation of black competence to run municipal affairs and an expectation among black voters that black candidates will better comprehend pressing racial problems and act more decisively to improve the situation.

There is little short of exhortation that can be done to help ensure that representative numbers of whites will be elected mayors in black majority cities and representative numbers of blacks elected mayors in white majority cities. The practice of racial voting will probably continue to guarantee that mayors, elected citywide, ordinarily will belong to the racial group with the most voters. Though not a perfect mechanism, district elections increase the chances that minorities, black or white, can gain representation roughly in line with their numerical share of the city population. In council elections, if rigorous attention is given to the fair development of district lines, it is less likely that significant segments of the population will be excluded by a racially motivated majority electorate. In most instances, the primary beneficiaries of such a policy would be blacks, because American cities will for some time probably contain mostly whites. Yet, in the growing number of cities with black majorities, the white minorities would benefit from district elections as well. Our research indicates that district elections provide unambiguous advantage to minorities, whether black or white. Adopting district races is the single most important institutional change that can help foster the proportional representation of racial groups in American cities.

This research also shows unambiguously that the chief conditions in determining the level of black council representation or the likelihood of electing a black mayor, however, are neither political and election rules, characteristics of the white population, nor antipoverty efforts. To the contrary, the principal factors are characteristics of the black population—what we have referred to as black resources, including socioeconomic characteristics and organizational, media, and other resources. Among these black resources, indicators of black population and socioeconomic resources are the most powerful in their influence. We have already noted the profound effect of black population size. Where blacks are a population minority, they are usually underrepresented. As the black percentage grows, black election to executive and legislative office also progresses. And once a black majority exists, there is a sudden and enormous tipping of representation. The reason is simple enough. Given the pattern of racial voting in the United States, where there are more blacks there are also more black candidates and more blacks elected to office. Indeed, black population size is the very best predictor of whether blacks win the mayoralty or gain a large portion of city council posts.

Black socioeconomic resources, both educational and economic, have a strong influence on black representation. If black population size is the single most critical variable in molding the absolute amount of black representation, black socioeconomic resources are an important second. Further, if we turn to the equitability of black council representation, socioeconomic resources are far and away the most salient conditions. Comparatively well-educated and affluent black communities evidently have the wherewithal to seek and obtain candidacy and election. Social-class characteristics, especially education, underlie conventional political behavior such as voting. The middle class votes and otherwise participates in elections at a considerably higher rate than does the lower class. Both education and some measure of affluence are important precursors to securing candidacy and electoral victory. Private-sector resources can be converted into public-sector representation. Characteristics of the black population, then, appear to have substantial influence on levels of black representation in municipal executive and legislative seats. One clear implication of this finding is that black success in winning elections is in part attributable to the black population rather than merely a result of factors external to the black community.

Policy Effect

Clearly, winning local political office is only half the battle—perhaps the lesser half at that. The election of blacks satisfies what some may view as symbolic goals, by incorporating the group into the overall political system and ostensibly letting blacks give input into decisions. Yet input does not necessarily mean influence. Obtaining a few council seats or even the mayoralty does not necessarily bring power to make decisions. Indeed, even where blacks are represented in numbers matching their share of the population, they will generally constitute only a small segment of all decision-makers in the city. Without question, there are many obstacles to translating black representation into policy change. These barriers extend beyond the basic problem that blacks will ordinarily constitute only a minority of city decision-makers.

Five sets of factors are particularly salient in restricting the likelihood that black representation will have substantial influence on public policy. One set of restricting conditions is lodged in the attitudes and talents of black elected officials themselves. Though evidence suggests that black officials normally articulate the same political views as the black population, there are doubtless numerous exceptions to this. Where the black representative has policy preferences similar to those of whites, or where a black representative is serving in place of a white who had policy views congruent with those of the black population, we surmise that black representation makes little policy difference. Some have suggested that black council members elected at large need to appeal to whites as well as blacks to win and retain office and are therefore less committed to social change. Also, the political abilities to negotiate, compromise, and deal play a role. Just as many white politicians are largely ineffective as legislators and executives, it is highly likely that many black mayors and council members will be of limited effectiveness in obtaining desired policy outcomes.

A second obstacle to black success in achieving policy change involves the cooperation of white officials. Where sympathetic white decision-makers are supportive of the policies sought by blacks elected to office, the chances of policy shifts improve. Certainly, when we speak of sympathetic white decision-makers, we mean not only mayors and council members, but bureaucrats and private-sector elites, too. In Gary, Mayor Hatcher not only struggled with an antagonistic white city council but was opposed at nearly every step by a recalcitrant white bureaucracy as well. Mayor Stokes of Cleveland fought prolonged battles with the white police department, as has Detroit's Mayor Young. And, more recently, events in Cleveland have shown how a large black council contingent may be at loggerheads with the white mayor and how private-sector elites—in this instance, the leading banks—can narrow the policy choices of elected officials. Black officeholders clearly need the assistance of other decision-makers if they are to succeed in their policy initiatives.

The neccessity of cooperation is further highlighted by the limited role of local government in the United States, which is a third dimension constraining the influence of black representatives. Municipalities are, according to Judge Dillon's rule, "creatures of the state." As such, they must operate in accord with state laws. Hence cities encounter frequent limitations on borrowing, spending, and permissible functions. In addition, many programs, such as public welfare and education, are either basically state and national programs or are frequently administered by a special district government independent of the municipality. It might be added, too, that, despite the attention showered on them by political scientists, sociologists, and others interested in social change, most cities—except New York and a few others—have a rather dismal record in passing innovative policies directed at social change. Their policies tend to be distributive, not redistributive; and even in the political heyday before the reform movement, the primary benefits of cities to the poor and immigrants were patronage and favors rather than comprehensive attempts to alter social conditions. If anything, this disinclination to treat existing social problems may have increased recently because of the nationalization of public policy and because of the success of the civic reform movement, which has stressed that city government ought to be run on a low-cost, efficient, businesslike basis, providing for street maintenance, protective services, and perhaps some amenities. Questions of social equality are to be left to the more "political" agencies at the state and national levels.

A fourth primary obstacle to converting black representation into policy shifts is the limited tax base available to many American cities. Given the generally lower incomes of blacks—on the average only 60 percent that of whites—cities with large black populations tend to be among the nation's poorest. Limited funds means limited policy options for black officials, thus forestalling policy options that might be implemented under other financial conditions.

A fifth and final factor making unlikely a strong relationship between black representation and policy is time. It is only recently that blacks have begun to win office in appreciable numbers. Substantial lead time is necessary for new officials to enact changes. Even our use of 1970 and 1972 data on representation and 1974/75 information on policy may not have allowed enough time for black officials, many first elected in 1970 or 1972, to initiate policy shifts.

There are, then, a series of overriding reasons why at best the effect of black municipal officials to this point can only have been small. Elected blacks may not be representative of the black public; and, if they are, they may not have skill enough to effectuate their preferences. Even when such officials are representative and skilled, they may encounter opposition from other key decision-makers. The limited role of most local governments and the fragmentation of local policymaking also creates problems. Moreover, even where black officials have sufficient authority or the cooperation of others, where they reflect the views of the black public and are skilled politicians, and where they govern in a city disposed toward policy changes, black officials nonetheless encounter the debilitating effects of scarce municipal resources and, in any case, may not have been in office long enough to bring about favored policies. With these constraints on black officeholders, dramatic new policy innovations and new spending programs may be hopelessly romantic goals. Simply clinging to the status quo may be the best attainable objective at least in the short run.

In this matrix of crisscrossing obstacles, it is perhaps surprising that our analysis indicates that black mayoral representation does result in some changes in the level of municipal expenditures. Black council representation makes little consistent difference, but cities with black mayors made greater gains in educational spending and in the social welfare areas generally. Such cities also increased spending significantly less for fire protection, sanitation services, and sewers. For the most part, there were small gains in spending in areas with a social welfare function and a lower rate of gain in services aimed at physical maintenance.

To be sure, the gain scores uncovered in cities with black mayors are not great, and the relationships, though often statistically significant, are not powerful. But, given the barriers, it is somewhat remarkable that even weak, significant relationships exist. Also, the test we employed is among the most severe. It is quite possible, owing to financial straits as well as the difficulty of changing policy in other than an incremental fashion, that the emphasis of black officials may be on shifting program benefits from white to black neighborhoods. For example, the stress may be on more police protection in black neighborhoods, more spending on black schools, improved paving and repair of streets in black areas, and so forth. All of this may occur without changing the distribution of expenditures in the overall policy categories. An analysis like ours would have wholly missed transfers of this kind. It is therefore possible that, even where we find no influence of black officials, a rather important set of effects may have actually taken place. Only intensive examination of one or a few cities could discover consistent shifts of this kind.

## Representation and Policy Effect: A Look at the Future

Overall, our analysis demonstrates that during the 1970s blacks made rather sharp progress in gaining elective posts in city government. And, as far as the mayorship is concerned, the election of blacks has made at least some modest policy difference. But what of the future? Is there reason to expect continued growth in the number of black decision-makers? Will black elected officials have a greater effect on policy? We have no crystal ball, but our data, coupled with our understanding of recent trends and events, do provide some clues.

Let us consider first the question of black election to office. For the next several years, we anticipate continued expansion in the number of black council members. The trend during the 1970s has been uni-directional improvement. Blacks began the decade in 1970 with barely a quarter of the proportional rate of council seats; the representation level grew to about half in 1975 and nearly three-quarters of the proportional rate in 1978. This trend shows no signs of ending, though we would not expect black representation to achieve perfect equity in the near future. Beyond simple extrapolation of the trend line, a number of other developments contribute to our optimism. Blacks are most inclined to support black candidates. As cities enlarge the black proportion of their populations, more blacks are likely to secure election. This progress is most apt to occur below the Mason-Dixon line, owing to the reported shift in black population movement back to the South. But, in all regions of the nation, as blacks become majorities, they can win control of city councils regardless of whether district or at-large races are the rule.

The renewed tendency toward district elections also augurs well for the election of blacks, especially where they are minorities. Several cities, such as Charlotte, North Carolina, have recently voted to institute district races. Other cities, such as San Antonio, Texas, have provided for district elections because of federal pressure. And still more municipalities have been forced by federal judges to provide district contests for the city council in order to provide blacks with numerically fair representation. Again, most of these changes have occurred in the South, the area most laggard in providing proportional representation for blacks. Some cities will doubtless attempt to respond to black demands for representation by expanding the number of at-large seats. Our analysis demonstrates that such a shift is unlikely to foster significant change from the present level of black city council representation. Also a favorable portent of continuing progress is the rapid increase in educational attainment by blacks. More blacks now graduate from high school and college than ever before. Moreover, there has been meaningful growth of the black middle class. We have dwelt heavily on the importance of black education and affluence in raising the level of black representation on city councils; the notable growth of black socioeconomic resources is advantageous for the rate of blacks winning council seats. With a large black middle class, there are apt to be more viable black candidacies, greater financial and organizational support for candidates, and higher black electoral participation and activity. All these factors are likely to increase the number of blacks sitting on city councils.

Our expectation about black success in gaining mayorships is less rosy. The trend line shows growth in the number of black mayors from 1970 through 1975. However, in both 1975 and 1978, an equal number of cities (10 percent) had black mayors. In these three years, the black share of city council memberships increased steeply, but there has been no progress in the proportion of black mayors elected. The reason here, we believe, lies in the racial voting patterns of most Americans. With notable exceptions, such as Tom Bradley of Los Angeles, blacks win mayoral elections only when blacks constitute at least a near majority of the population. Of course, in those cities that will soon develop black majorities, there will probably be black mayors; but in the overwhelming majority of cities, despite expansion in the size of the black middle class, blacks will remain a minority, and their chances of winning the mayor's seat may be slim indeed. Consequently, we would expect only very limited improvement in the number of black mayors in the cities we have examined.

The last question concerns the effect of black elected officials on public policy. There are reasons for optimism here; unfortunately, there is also cause for pessimism. On the optimistic side is the dimension of time, which works in several ways that may favorably affect the ability of black officials to alter public policy.

In the American political system, at nearly all levels of government, policy changes slowly. Many policy commitments and patterns of expenditure are established years in advance. Changes in spending patterns frequently come only after protracted opposition by personnel and clients who stand to lose by redirected policy. Additionally, alterations in policy priorities ordinarily must be negotiated with other officials, both elected and appointed, before final decisions are rendered. In this complex situation, more time will permit black officials further opportunity to work for policy shifts.

As time elapses, black officeholders, as individuals and collectively, should gain experience and skills in formulating public policy and working for its enactment. It is naive, we believe, to expect all black officials to be effective. Personal and environmental limitations limit their skills, just as they do for whites. Yet one would anticipate greater effectiveness and sharpened policymaking ability among black officials as they increase the length of their municipal service.

Finally, time may work to the advantage of black effectiveness as more blacks are elected at the municipal level. If we are correct in our earlier prediction, a greater number of blacks will become city council members. And in cities that attain black majorities, it is probable that blacks will secure the mayoralty and more than 50 percent of the council posts. In those communities blacks will have greater authority to foster changes in policy.

On the negative side, some conditions are likely to counteract these developments. First of all, we anticipate growth in the number of black council members but not in the incidence of black mayors, except in municipalities with black majorities. As we have discovered, black council representation therefore will probably be concentrated in that group of elected officials less likely to affect public policy.

In general, the economic picture of the nation is not encouraging. At this time, most economists consider an economic downturn inevitable. In a recessionary period, with even more unemployment and a decreased gross national product, it is probable that satisfactory funding will not be available to cities. A recession would affect cities in three primary ways. First, more people would need social services. Second, less money could be raised internally through sales, property, and income taxes. Third, if state and federal governments have diminished revenues, less money will be forthcoming to cities through intergovernmental transfers.

Furthermore, the problem of intergovernmental revenues will not be resolved merely by avoiding an economic recession. Events in the late 1970s have made it apparent that the early 1980s, at least, will be a time of economic retrenchment. The federal government is committed to decreasing budget deficits and has already pared both Comprehensive

Employment Training Act (CETA) and Community Development Block Grant (CDBG) programs. Further cuts in CETA and drastic decreases in revenue-sharing are part of the 1981 budget proposals. The funds lost by reductions in these programs may not be offset by municipal sources, especially with the spirit of California's Proposition 13 pervading the nation. Local politicians are fearful of a taxpayer revolt, and the political limits of taxation, if not the financial limits, have evidently been reached in many cities. Even in the absence of legislation mandating spending or taxing limits, the lack of a firm financial base will plague many cities in the near future. And the problem may well be most acute in cities with substantial numbers of black decision-makers. Recall that black representation is greatest in cities with large black populations. Recall, too, that blacks tend to be far less prosperous than whites.

Of all cities, then, those with the largest black representation are apt to be the most distressed financially, as are Detroit, Newark, East Saint Louis, Cleveland, and other cities with black mayors or hefty black city council contingents. To further complicate matters, the black middle class may waver in its commitment to social programs. In times of economic instability, members of the black middle class may feel themselves threatened: on the one hand, they are buffeted by economic recession; on the other hand, they live in cities with great social problems but with a limited tax base. It is possible, in these circumstances, that they may feel they are being asked to shoulder a unique burden in financing programs for the black poor. If this occurs, members of the black middle class may begin to make demands parallel to those of whites: for protective services, low taxes, and efficient government rather than for shifting spending into areas of social welfare. On the other hand, this increasing conservatism is not now evident. Caldwell (1978) quotes a study by Charles V. Hamilton showing that the black middle class not only is more liberal in policy voting than the middle class of some other ethnic groups, but is also more liberal than the black lower class. Thus, firm predictions of a more conservative posture on the part of the black middle class are certainly premature to say the least.

While we have some limited confidence about progress toward additional black representation in American cities, we are somewhat less sanguine about the prospects of increasing black influence over urban policy. In particular, we are not especially optimistic about shifting funds into social welfare categories. However, unexpected events can occur. It may be, for example, that the federal government will enact new social programs—for example, health insurance and income maintenance—that will shift the burden for major social services from the hard-pressed cities to the federal government. Although this prospect does not now seem imminent, predicting the future can be risky and embarrassing. Indeed, a competent social observer of the 1940s and early 1950s would probably have predicted continued exclusion of blacks from the political system, a forecast proved false by subsequent developments. Social and political events have an intriguing way of playing havoc with predictions, and we hope ours are no exception.

# Notes

## Preface

1. A few states with small black populations have no black elected officials (Idaho, Montana, North and South Dakota, Vermont, and Wyoming). Louisiana had more (333) than any other state, and Mississippi (303), Illinois (279), and Michigan (256) ranked next. Because of the larger base of black officials, the rate of increase has slowed from 22–27 percent a year over 1970 to 1972 to 8 percent in 1977 and only 4 percent in 1978.

2. It is still rare for a black to win a statewide office. While there has recently been one black United States senator (Edward Brooke, Republican, of Massachusetts), no blacks have been elected governor; some do hold minor statewide offices such as lieutenant governor and secretary of state.

3. For example, in 1969 Howard Lee, a black mayor of Chapel Hill, North Carolina, wrote that "in the near future no black man will be able to sit in the U.S. House of Representatives from a Southern district" (Lee in Dymally 1971). Yet in 1972 two black southern members of Congress were elected, and in 1974 a third.

## Chapter 1

1. Some of these tactics will be dealt with in greater detail in chapter 4. Wilson (1960) attributes the greater number of black officials in Chicago than in New York in part to the smaller election districts in Chicago.

2. At this time the one exception is Peter Rodino of New Jersey, whose district is about 51 percent black.

3. It is worth noting that, in almost every district, the percentage of blacks in the voting-age population is slightly lower than their percentage of the total population, owing to the different age distributions of urban black and white populations. Three black members of Congress represent districts where blacks are 40–49 percent of the voting-age population, even though they are more than 50 percent of the population—Augustus Hawkins and Julian C. Dixon (formerly Yvonne Burke's seat) of California, and William Clay of Missouri (Joint Center 1973). Patterson (1974, p. 254) shows that in every city of more than 500,000 the number of blacks of voting age is two to five percentage points less than the total proportion black.

4. Devices such as the "grandfather clause," where only those whose ancestors were eligible to vote could register, and the white primary had earlier been declared unconstitutional by the United States Supreme Court. See *Guinn* v. *United States*, 238 U.S. 347 (1915); *Lane* v. *Wilson*, 307 U.S. 268 (1939); *Nixon* v. *Herndon*, 273 U.S. 536 (1927); *Nixon* v. *Condon*, 286 U.S. 73 (1932); *Grovey* v. *Townsend*, 295 U.S. 45 (1935); *Smith* v. *Allwright*, 321 U.S. 649 (1944). See Lawson (1976) for a history of the fight against black disfranchisement in the South.

5. In South Carolina, however, this requirement could be waived upon proof of payment of taxes on property of more than $300 value (*CQA* 1965, p. 539).

6. That is, the registrars had to prove the candidate illiterate if he had a sixth-grade education, rather than the candidate having to prove himself literate.

7. The northern counties were able to demonstrate to the attorney general that they were not discriminating and thus did not receive the federal examiners.

8. Of course this white support may later cause problems for the black official who tries to balance his actions between doing something for the black masses and not moving too fast for his white supporters. See Nelson and Van Horne (1974) for a discussion of some of these problems.

9. However, a substantial minority did feel that demonstrations were "somewhat important."

10. A good discussion of the special problems of the black official is found in Nelson and Van Horne (1974).

## Chapter 2

1. 437 F. Supp. 137, 1971 (U.S. District Court, M.D. Georgia); 374 F. Supp. 363, 1974 (U.S. District Court, D.C.); 71 F.R.D. 623, 1976 (U.S. District Court, W.D. Louisiana, Shreveport Division); 423 F. Supp. 384, 1976 (U.S. District Court, S.D. Alabama); and on appeal 571 F. 2d 238, 1978 (U.S. Court of Appeals, 5th Circuit).

2. See Zimmer v. McKeithen 485 F. 2d 1297, 1973 (U.S. Court of Appeals, 5th Circuit, and Turner v. McKeithen 490 F. 2d 191, 1973 (U.S. Court of Appeals, 5th Circuit), where courts ruled that at-large districting for county school boards and police juries in East Carroll and Ouachita parishes in Louisiana deprived blacks of their right to representation. In both cases a history of discrimination and a failure of any blacks to be elected was shown.

3. See Nevett v. Sides 571 F. 2d 209, 1978 (3Q U.S.Court of Appeals, 5th Circuit), where the court ruled that black residents of Fairfield, Alabama, who had challenged at-large city council elections failed to show intent to discriminate. The Supreme Court in Whitcomb v. Chavis 403 U.S. 124, 1971, issued a similar ruling concerning a challenge to Marion County, Indiana's, multimember state legislative district. The court refused to overturn the multimember plan because there was no evidence that the intent was to dilute the black vote.

4. In White v. Regester 412 U.S. 755, 1973, the Supreme Court upheld generally the Texas reapportionment plan for the state legislature but invalidated that part dealing with Dallas County—a multimember district plan that they held to be discriminatory to blacks and Hispanics.

5. This may be a pattern peculiar to the United States. That is, in some systems low socioeconomic status may not lead to lower levels of political participation. This is obviously the most true in systems where participation is strongly encouraged or even required (as, for example, socialist systems) or where general levels of at least some kinds of participation are higher than in the United States and thus class differences in participation are not so apparent (for example, in Western Europe).

6. It is fallacious to assume that all Hispanic groups are similar. Mexican Americans, Cubans, and Puerto Ricans have different demographic profiles as well as different political orientations (Newman 1978).

7. For example, in measuring black socioeconomic resources, we at one point examined such variables as the proportion of blacks with college educations, the proportion with less than an eighth-grade education, median black income, the dollar difference in the median white and black incomes, the proportion of blacks below the poverty line, and several others. The variables we finally chose in this category—median black education and the black/white income ratio—were selected because they captured two distinct though related aspects of black socioeconomic development and because they had a lesser degree of statistical interrelatedness (multicollinearity) than did some of the other variables we considered.

## Chapter 3

1. Readers wishing a full explanation of multiple regression should consult a text such as Blalock (1972).

2. This means that the black resource variables explained 21 percent when they were entered first into the equation, but 23 percent when they were entered after the other

controls, thus indicating they were related in a negative way to one of the control variables. Once that variable was entered as a control, the amount of variance that could be explained by the black resources increased. A simple example might help. Suppose, as is usually true in the U.S., that education was related to voting participation. Suppose, further, that education was strongly and negatively related to age. Assuming these correlations were high enough, the simple correlation of age and participation would be negative. Yet, if within each education group older adults participated more than younger adults, the beta for a regression of participation on age, controlling for education, should be positive. This negative bivariate relationship, which becomes positive once education is controlled, is a simple example of a suppressor relationship. The suppressor relationships revealed in table 16 are rather minor, however, in relation to the unique variation explained.

## Chapter 4
1. This is the statistical artifact of the measure we discussed earlier in the chapter.

## Chapter 5
1. Although United States Steel provided more than 40 percent of Gary's property tax revenue, it contributed greatly to the problems of the city because of its air and water pollution and its discriminatory hiring practices (Levine 1974; Greer 1971).

2. When Liebert took into account the limited functional responsibilities of some cities, he concluded, in contrast to Lineberry and Fowler's (1967) groundbreaking study, that government structure tends to play no intervening role in the relationship between population characteristics and expenditure rates.

3. When examining the overall expenditure variables, we controlled for whether the city had spending authority in the area of education and welfare. That is, we coded cities as 1 if they were in states where cities had legal responsibility for schools, 0 if not. We followed the same procedure concerning welfare.

## Chapter 6
1. Obviously this is somewhat oversimplified, because the levels of city expenditures are to some extent influenced by state and welfare regulations.

2. Though we present our basic findings (tables 32 through 40) for each individual expenditure, for the other analyses we present only the summary scales, to avoid having the chapter read like a computer printout.

# References

Aberbach, Joel D., and Walker, Jack L. 1970. Political trust and racial ideology. *American Political Science Review* 64 (December): 1199–1219.

———. 1973. *Race in the city*. Boston: Little, Brown.

Abney, Glenn F. 1974. Factors related to voter turnout in Mississippi. *Journal of Politics* 36 (November): 1057–63.

Achen, Christopher H. 1978. Measuring representation. *American Journal of Political Science* 22 (August): 475–510.

Alford, Robert, and Lee, Eugene. 1968. Voting turnout in American cities. *American Political Science Review* 62 (September): 796–813.

Altshuler, Alan. 1970. *Community control*. New York: Pegasus.

Antunes, George, and Plumlee, J. P. 1977. The distribution of an urban public service. *Urban Affairs Quarterly* 12 (March): 313–32.

Bachrach, Peter, and Baratz, Morton. 1970. *Power and poverty: Theory and practice*. New York: Oxford University Press.

Banfield, Edward, and Wilson, James Q. 1963. *City politics*. Cambridge: Harvard University Press.

Barker, Lucius J., and McCorry, Jesse J. 1976. *Black Americans and the political system*. Cambridge, Mass.: Winthrop Publishers.

Blackwell, James. 1975. *The black community: Diversity and unity*. New York: Dodd, Mead.

Blalock, Hubert M. 1967. *Toward a theory of minority group relations*. New York: Wiley.

———. 1972. *Social statistics*. New York: McGraw-Hill.

Bohrnstedt, George W. 1969. Observations on the measurement of change. In *Sociological methodology*, ed. Edgar F. Borgatta. San Francisco: Jossey-Bass.

Bond, Julian. 1969. *Black candidates: Southern campaign experiences*. Atlanta: Southern Regional Council.

Browning, Rufus, and Marshall, Dale Rogers. 1976. Implementation of model cities and revenue sharing in ten Bay Area cities: Design and first findings. In C. O. Jones and R. D. Thomas (eds) *Public Policy Making in a Federal System*. Beverly Hills: Sage Publications.

Browning, Rufus P.; Marshall, Dale Rogers; and Tabb, David H. 1978. Responsiveness to minorities: A theory of political change in cities. Paper presented at the 1978 annual meeting of the American Political Science Association, New York (September).

———. 1979a. Minorities and urban electoral change: A longitudinal study. *Urban Affairs Quarterly* 15 (December): 206–28.

———. 1979b. Minority mobilization and urban political change. Paper presented at the annual meeting of the American Political Science Association, Washington, D.C.

Bullock, Charles S., III. 1975. The election of blacks in the South: Preconditions and consequences. *American Journal of Political Science* 19 (November): 727–40.

Button, James W. 1978. *Black violence: Political impact of the 1960's riots.* Princeton, N.J.: Princeton University Press.

Button, James W.; Scher, Richard; and Berkson, Larry. 1978. The quest for equality: The impact of the civil rights movement on black public services in the South. Paper delivered at the annual meeting of the Midwest Political Science Association.

Caldwell, Earl. 1978. The rising status of commitment. *Black Enterprise* 9 (December): 38–42.

Campbell, Angus. 1971. *White attitudes toward black people.* Ann Arbor: Institute for Social Research.

Campbell, Angus, and Hatchett, Shirley. 1974. *Black racial attitudes: Trends and complexities.* Ann Arbor: Institute for Social Research.

Campbell, Angus, and Schuman, Howard. 1968. Racial attitudes in fifteen American cities. In *Supplemental studies for the National Advisory Commission on Civil Disorders.* New York: Praeger.

Campbell, David, and Feagin, Joe. 1975. Black politics in the South: A descriptive analysis. *Journal of Politics* 37 (February): 129–59.

Caplan, Nathan, and Paige, Jeffrey. 1968. A study of ghetto rioters. *Scientific American* 219 (August): 15–21.

Caputo, David A. 1976. *Urban America: The policy alternatives.* San Francisco: W. H. Freeman.

Clark, Kenneth B., and Hopkins, Jeannette. 1969. *A relevant war against poverty: A study of community programs and observable change.* New York: Harper and Row.

Clark, Terry. 1968*a*. *Community structure and decision making: Comparative analyses,* ed. Terry Clark. San Francisco: Chandler.

———. 1968*b*. Community structure, decision making, budget expenditures and urban renewal in fifty-one American cities. *American Sociological Review* 33 (August): 576–93.

Cole, Leonard. 1974. Electing blacks to municipal office. *Urban Affairs Quarterly* 10 (September): 17–39.

———. 1976. *Blacks in power.* Princeton, N.J.: Princeton University Press.

Coleman, James. 1971. *Resources for social change.* New York: John Wiley.

Congressional Caucus. 1973. A position on the mass communication media. Pp. 1–7.

*Congressional Quarterly.* 1967. Urban problems and civil disorders. Special report, 36 (September).

Congressional Quarterly Almanac. 1965. Voting Rights Act of 1965. *Congressional Quarterly Almanac* 21:533–71.

———. 1970. Congress lowers voting age, extends Voting Rights Act. *Congressional Quarterly Almanac* 26:192–99.

———. 1972. Voting rights enforcement. *Congressional Quarterly Almanac* 28:258.

Connolly, Harold X. 1973. Black movement into the suburbs. *Urban Affairs Quarterly* 9 (September): 91–112.

Conyers, James E., and Wallace, Walter L. 1976. *Black elected officials: A study of black Americans holding governmental offices.* New York: Russell Sage Foundation.

Coombs, David W.; Alsikafi, M. H.; Bryan, C. Hobson; and Webber, Irving L. 1977. Black political control in Greene County Alabama. *Rural Sociology* 42 (fall): 398–406.

Cottrell, Charles L., and Fleischmann, Arnold. 1979. The change from at-large to district representation and political participation of minority groups in Fort Worth and San Antonio, Texas. Paper presented at the annual meeting of the American Political Science Association, Washington, D.C.

Crain, Robert L., with the assistance of Morton Inger, Gerald A. McWorter, and James J. Vanecko. 1968. *The politics of school desegregation: Comparative case studies of community structure and policy-making.* Chicago: Aldine.

Cunningham, James V. 1970. *Urban leadership in the sixties.* Waltham, Mass.: Brandeis University, Lemberg Center for the Study of Violence.

Danigelis, Nicholas. 1978. Black political participation in the United States: Some recent evidence. *American Sociological Review* 43 (October): 756–71.

Davis, Lenwood G., and Van Horne, Winston. 1975. The city renewed: White dream—black nightmare. *Black Scholar* 7 (November): 2–9.

Diamond, Irene. 1977. *Sex roles in the State House.* New Haven: Yale University Press.

Downes, Bryan. 1970. A critical reexamination of the social and political characteristics of riot cities. *Social Science Quarterly* 51 (September): 349–60.

Dunlop, Burton. 1973. Minority resources and community improvements in model cities. Ph.D. diss., Department of Sociology, University of Illinois, Urbana.

Dye, Thomas. 1969*a*. Income inequality and American state politics. *American Political Science Review* 63 (March): 157–62.

———. 1969*b* Inequality and civil rights policy in the state. *Journal of Politics* 31 (November): 1080–97.

Dymally, Mervyn, with the assistance of Andrew B. Schmocker. 1971. *The black politician: His struggle for power.* Belmont, Calif.: Wadsworth.

*Ebony Handbook, The.* 1974. Doris E. Saunders, ed. Chicago: Johnson.

Eisinger, Peter. 1978. The community action program and the development of black political leadership. Paper delivered at the annual meeting of the American Political Science Association, New York (September).

Erickson, Robert S. 1978. Constituency opinion and congressional behavior: A reexamination of the Miller Stokes representation data. *American Journal of Political Science* 22 (August): 511–35.

Feagin, Joe R. 1970. Black elected officials in the South: An explanatory analysis. In *Black conflict with white America,* ed. Jack R. Van der Slik, pp. 107–22. Columbus, Ohio: Charles E. Merrill.

Feagin, Joe R., and Hahn, Harlan. 1970. The second reconstruction: Black political strength in the South. *Social Science Quarterly* 51 (June): 42–56.

———. 1973. *Ghetto revolts.* New York: Macmillan.

Fischer, Claude. 1976. *The urban experience.* New York: Harcourt, Brace and Jovanovich.

Fleming, James G. 1966. The Negro in American politics: The past. In *The American Negro reference book,* ed. John P. Davis. Englewood Cliffs, N.J.: Prentice-Hall.

Foster, Lorn S. 1978. Black perceptions of the mayor: An empirical test. *Urban Affairs Quarterly* 14 (December): 245–52.

Friesma, Paul. 1969. Black control of central cities: The hollow prize. *Journal of the American Institute of Planners* 35 (March): 75–79.

Garret, B. E. 1970. How soulful is "soul" radio. Race Relations Information Center, Nashville, Tenn. March, pp. 1–42.

Gelb, Joyce. 1970. Blacks, blocs, and ballots. *Polity* 3 (fall): 45–69.

———. 1974. Black power in electoral politics: A case study and comparative analysis. *Polity* 6 (summer): 500–527.

Gilbert, Claire. 1968. Community power and decision-making: A quantitative examination of previous research. In *Community structure and decision-making: Comparative analyses,* ed. Terry Clark, pp. 139–56. San Francisco: Chandler.

Giles, Michael W. 1977. Percent black and racial hostility: An old assumption reexamined. *Social Science Quarterly* 58 (December); 412–17.

Glenn, Noval, and Simmons, John L. 1967. Are regional cultural differences diminishing? *Public Opinion Quarterly* 31 (summer): 176–93.

Gordon, Daniel. 1970. Immigrants and municipal voting turnout: Implications for the changing ethnic impact on urban politics. *American Sociological Review* 35 (August): 665–81.

Gordon, Milton. 1964. *Assimilation in American life.* New York: Oxford University Press.

Greeley, Andrew M. 1976. *Ethnicity, denomination, and inequality.* Sage Research Papers in the Social Sciences (Studies in Race and Ethnicity), vol. 4, ser. 90-029. Beverly Hills and London: Sage Publications.

Greeley, Andrew M., and Sheatsley, Paul B. 1971. Attitudes toward racial integration. *Scientific American* 225 (December): 13–19.

Greenstone, J. David, and Peterson, Paul E. 1973. *Race and authority in urban politics: Community participation and the war on poverty.* New York: Russell Sage Foundation.

Greer, Edward. 1971. Richard Hatcher and the politics of Gary. *Social Policy* 2 (November–December): 23–28.

Grimshaw, William. 1979. The development and place of black political leadership in Chicago politics. Paper delivered at the Midwest Political Science Association meetings, Chicago, April.

Hahn, Harlan; Klingman, D. D.; and Pachon, H. 1976. Cleavages, coalitions, and the black candidate: The Los Angeles mayorality elections of 1969 and 1973. *Western Political Quarterly* 29 (December): 507–20.

Halley, Robert M.; Acock, Allen; and Greene, Thomas H. 1976. Ethnicity and social class: Voting in the 1973 Los Angeles municipal elections. *Western Political Quarterly* 29 (December): 521–30.

Hamilton, Charles. 1976. *The struggle for political equality.* New York: National Urban League.

———. 1979. The patron-recipient relationship and minority politics. *Political Science Quarterly* 95 (summer): 211–28.

Hansen, Susan. 1975. Participation, political structure and concurrence. *American Political Science Review* 69 (December): 1181–99.

Harris, Louis. 1973. *The anguish of change.* New York: W. W. Norton.

Hawkins, Brett. 1971. *Politics and urban policies.* Indianapolis: Bobbs-Merrill.

Hawley, Willis. 1973. *Nonpartisan elections and the case for party politics.* New York: John Wiley.

Heilig, Peggy. 1978. The abandonment of "reform" in southern city: Outcomes of a return to district elections. Paper presented at the Midwest Political Science Association meeting, Chicago.

Holloway, Harry. 1969. *The politics of the southern Negro: From exclusion to big city organization.* New York: Random House.

Howard, John. 1978. A framework for the analysis of urban black politics. *Annals* 439 (September): 1–15.

Hyman, Herbert, and Sheatsley, Paul B. 1956. Attitudes on integration. *Scientific American* 195 (December): 35–39.

———. 1964. Attitudes toward desegregation. *Scientific American* 221 (July): 16–23.

Ippolito, Dennis; Donaldson, William; and Bowman, Lewis. 1968. Political orientation among Negroes and white. *Social Science Quarterly* 49 (December): 548–56.

Jackman, Mary. 1978. General and applied tolerance: Does education increase commitment to racial integration? *American Journal of Political Science* 22 (May): 302–24.

Jackson, John E. 1972. Politics and the budgetary process. *Social Science Research* 1 (April): 35–60.

Joint Center for Political Studies. 1973. Congressional districts with more than 25% black population. *Newsletter* (March).

———. 1975a. National roster of black elected officials. Washington, D.C.: Joint Center for Political Studies.

———. 1975b. *Newsletter* (March): A–D.

———. 1977. *National roster of black elected officials.* Washington, D.C.: Joint Center for Political Studies.

———. 1978. Increase in black elected officials. *Crises* (February), p. 70.

Jones, Bryan D. 1977. Distributional considerations in models of government service provision. *Urban Affairs Quarterly* 2 (March): 291–312.

Jones, Clinton. 1976. The impact of local election systems on black political representation. *Urban Affairs Quarterly* 11 (March): 345–54.

———. 1978. A comparative study of regional differences in black political, social, and economic status. *Western Journal of Black Studies* 2 (summer): 102–10.

Jones, Mack. 1971. Black officeholders in local government of the South. *Politics* 2 (March): 64–72.

———. 1978. Black political empowerment in Atlanta: Myth and reality. *Annals* 439 (September): 90–117.

Karnig, Albert K. 1975. "Private-regarding" policy, civil rights groups and the mediating impact of municipal reforms. *American Journal of Political Science* 19 (February): 91–206.

———. 1976. Black representation on city councils. *Urban Affairs Quarterly* 12

(December): 223–42.

———. 1979a Black economic political and cultural development. *Social Forces* 57 (June): 1194–1211.

———. 1979b. Black resources and city council representation. *Journal of Politics* 41 (February): 134–49.

Karnig, Albert K., and Walter, Oliver. 1974. Voter turnout in municipal elections: A multivariate analysis. *Rocky Mountain Social Science Journal* 11 (April): 55–72.

———. 1977. Municipal elections: Registration, incumbent success, voter participation. In *Municipal Yearbook* (1977), May–October 1975, pp. 65–72. Washington, D.C.: International City Management Association.

Karnig, Albert K., and Welch, Susan. 1978. Electoral structure and black representation on city councils: An updated examination. Paper presented at the annual meeting of the Midwest Political Science Association, Chicago, April.

———. 1979. Sex and ethnic differences in municipal representation. *Social Science Quarterly* 60 (December): 465–81.

Keech, William. 1968. *The impact of Negro voting: The role of the vote in the quest for equality.* Chicago: Rand McNally.

Keller, Edmund J. 1978. The impact of black mayors on urban policy. *Annals* 439 (September): 40–52.

Kelley, John. 1974. The politics of school busing. *Public Opinion Quarterly* 38 (Spring): 29–36.

Kerner, Otto. 1968. *National Advisory Commission on Civil Disorder.* Washington, D.C.: Government Printing Office.

Key, V. O., Jr. 1949. *Southern politics.* New York: Knopf.

———. 1964. *Politics: Parties and pressure groups.* 5th ed. New York: Crowell.

Kramer, John. 1971. The election of blacks to city councils: A 1970 status report and a prolegomenon. *Journal of Black Studies* 1 (June): 443–76.

Kramer, Ralph M. 1969. *Participation of the poor.* Englewood Cliffs, N.J.: Prentice-Hall.

Kronus, Sidney. 1971. *The black middle class.* Columbus: Charles Merrill.

Lamb, Gerald. 1971. The uncommon man. In *The black politician: His struggle for power,* ed. Mervyn M. Dymally, pp. 36–39, 100–102. Belmont, Calif.: Wadsworth.

Lane, Robert E. 1959. *Political life: Why people get involved in politics.* Glencoe, Ill.: Free Press.

Lawson, Steven F. 1976. *Black ballots.* New York: Columbia University Press.

Lemberg Center for the Study of Violence. 1968. *Riot data review,* nos. 1 and 2 (Brandeis University).

Levine, Charles H. 1974. *Racial conflict and the American mayor.* Lexington, Mass.: Lexington Books.

Levine, Charles H., and Kaufman, Clifford. 1974. Urban conflict as a constraint on mayoral leadership: Lessons from Cleveland and Gary. *American Politics Quarterly* 2 (January): 78–106.

Levy, Frank S.; Meltzner, A. J.; and Wildavsky, A. 1974. *Urban outcomes.* Berkeley: University of California Press.

Lewinson, Paul. 1932. *Race, class and party: A history of Negro suffrage and white politics in the South.* New York: Grosset.

169     References

Liebert, Roland J. 1974. Municipal functions, structure and expenditures: A re-analysis of recent research. *Social Science Quarterly* 54 (March): 765–83.

Lineberry, Robert L. 1975. Equality, public policy, and public services: The underclass hypothesis and the limits to equality. Paper presented at the annual meeting of the American Political Science Association.

Lineberry, Robert L., and Fowler, Edmund. 1967. Reformism and public politics in American cities. *American Political Science Review* 61 (September): 701–16.

Lineberry, Robert L., and Welch, R. 1974. Measuring the distribution of urban public services. *Social Science Quarterly* 54 (March): 700–712.

Lipset, Seymour M. 1960. Political Man. New York: Doubleday.

Lyons, William. 1978. Reform and response in American cities: Structure and policy reconsidered. *Social Science Quarterly* 59 (June): 118–32.

McKinney, James, and Bourque, Linda. 1971. The changing South: National incorporation of a region. *American Sociological Review* 36 (June): 399–412.

MacManus, Susan A. 1978. City council election procedures and minority representation: Are they related? *Social Science Quarterly* 59 (June): 153–61.

Mann, Dale. 1974. The politics of representation in urban administration. *Education in Urban Society* 6 (May): 297–317.

Marshall, Harvey, and Meyer, Deborah. 1975. Assimilation and the election of minority candidates: The case of black mayors. *Sociology and Social Science Research* 60 (October): 1–21.

Martin, Melvin, ed. 1966. *The public welfare directory.* Chicago: American Public Welfare Association.

Masotti, Louis H., and Corsi, Jerome R. 1969. *Shoot-out in Cleveland: Black militants and the police, July 23, 1968.* New York: Praeger.

Matthews, Donald, and Prothro, James. 1966. *Negroes and the new southern politics.* New York: Harcourt, Brace and World.

Milbrath, Lester. 1965. *Political participation.* Chicago: Rand McNally.

Miller, Arthur. 1974. Political issues and trust in government: 1964–1970. *American Political Science Review* 68 (September): 951–72.

Miller, Warren E., and Stokes, Donald E. 1966. Constituency influence in Congress. In *Elections and the political order,* ed. Angus Campbell, Phillip Converse, Warren E. Miller, and Donald Stokes, pp. 351–73. New York: Wiley.

Mladenka, Kenneth R., and Hill, Kim Q. 1977. The distribution of benefits in an urban environment. *Urban Affairs Quarterly* 13 (September): 73–93.

Morgan, William R., and Clark, Terry N. 1978. The causes of racial disorders: A grievance-level explanation. *American Sociological Review* 38 (October): 611–24.

Morlock, Laura. 1973. Black power and black influence in ninety-one northern cities. Ph.D. diss., Department of Sociology, John Hopkins University.

Morris, Milton D. 1975. *The politics of black America.* New York: Harper and Row.

Moynihan, Daniel Patrick. 1969. *Maximum feasible misunderstanding: Community action in the war on poverty.* New York: Free Press.

Mundt, Robert J. 1979. Referenda in Charlotte and Raleigh, and court action in Richmond: Comparative studies in the revival of district representation. Paper presented at the annual meeting of the American Political Science Association, Washington, D.C.

Murray, Richard, and Vedlitz, Arthur. 1978. Racial voting patterns in the South: An analysis of major elections in five cities. *Annals* 439 (September): 29–39.

National Advisory Commission on Civil Disorder. 1968. *Report*. Washington, D.C.: Government Printing Office.

National Research Council. 1975. *Toward an understanding of metroplitan America*. San Francisco: Canfield Press.

Nelson, William E. 1972. *Black politics in Gary: Problems and prospects*. Washington, D.C.: Joint Center for Political Studies.

Nelson, William E., and Meranto, Philip J. 1977. *Electing black mayors*. Columbus: Ohio State University Press.

Nelson, William E., and Van Horne, Winston. 1974. Black elected administrators: The trials of office. *Public Administration Review* 34 (November–December): 526–33.

Newman, Morris. 1978. Profiles of Hispanics in the U.S. workforce. *Monthly Labor Review* 101 (December): 3–14.

Niemi, Albert. 1975. *Gross state product and productivity in the Southeast*. Chapel Hill: University of North Carolina Press.

Olson, Marvin. 1970. Social and political participation of blacks. *American Sociological Review* 35 (August): 695–96.

Orum, Anthony. 1966. A reappraisal of the social and political participation of Negroes. *American Journal of Sociology* 72 (July): 32–46.

Parenti, Michael. 1967. Ethnic politics and the persistence of ethnic identification. *American Political Science Review* 16 (September): 717–26.

Patterson, Ernest. 1974. *Black city politics*. New York: Dodd, Mead.

Paulson, Darryl. 1979. Political and policy differences between the southern and nonsouthern black mayor. Paper presented at the annual meeting of the American Political Science Association, Washington, D.C.

Perrotta, John A. 1977. Machine influence on a Community Action program: The case of Providence, Rhode Island. *Polity* 9 (summer): 481–502.

Persons, Georgia. 1977. Black mayoral leadership: Changing issues and shifting coalitions. A paper presented at the annual meeting of the American Political Science Association, Washington, D.C. (September).

Pettigrew, Thomas F. 1976. Black mayoral campaigns. In *Urban governance and minorities*, ed. Herrington J. Bryce. New York: Praeger.

Pitkin, Hanna Fenichel. 1972. *The concept of representation*. Berkeley: University of California Press.

Piven, Frances Fox, and Cloward, Richard. 1971. *Regulating the poor*. New York: Vintage.

Ploski, Harry A., and Kaiser, Ernest, eds. 1971. *The Negro almanac*. 2d ed. New York: Bellwether.

Poinsett, Alex. 1970. *Black power Gary style: The making of Mayor Richard Gordon Hatcher*. Chicago: Johnson.

Pomper, Gerald. 1966. Ethnic group voting in nonpartisan municipal elections. *Public Opinion Quarterly* 30 (spring): 79–97.

Pressman, Jeffrey. 1972. Preconditions of mayoral leadership. *American Political Science Review* 66 (June): 511–24.

———. 1975. *Federal programs and city politics*. Berkeley: University of California Press.

Preston, Michael. 1976. Limitations of black urban power: The case of black mayors. In *The new urban politics*, ed. Louis Masotti and Robert Lineberry, pp. 111–34. Cambridge, Mass.: Ballinger.

Prewitt, Kenneth, and Eulau, Heinz. 1969. Political matrix and political representation. Prolegomenon to a new departure from an old problem. *American Political Science Review* 63 (June): 427–41.

Robinson, T., and Dye, Thomas. 1978. Reformism and black representation on city councils. *Social Science Quarterly* 59 (June): 133–41.

Rogers, Chester B., and Arman, Harold D. 1971. Nonpartisanship and election to city office. *Social Science Quarterly* 51 (March): 941–45.

Rustin, Bayard. 1965. From protest to politics: The future of the civil rights movement. *Commentary* 39 (February): 25–31.

Salamon, Lester. 1973. Leadership and modernization: The emerging black political elite in the American South. *Journal of Politics* 35 (August): 641.

Schoenberger, Robert A., and Segal, David R. 1971. The ecology of dissent: The southern Wallace vote in 1968. *American Journal of Political Science* 15 (August): 583–86.

Sears, David O. 1969. Black attitudes toward the political system in the aftermath of the Watts insurrection. *Midwest Journal of Political Science* 13 (November): 515–44.

Sears, David O., and McConahay, John B. 1973. *The politics of violence.* Boston: Houghton Mifflin.

Seligman, Lester; with King, Michael R.; Kim, Chong Lim; and Smith, Roland E. 1974. *Patterns of recruitment: A state chooses its lawmakers.* Chicago: Rand McNally.

Sloan, Lee. 1969. "Good government" and the politics of races. *Social Science Problems* 17 (fall): 161–64.

Smith, Robert C. 1978. The changing shape of urban black politics, 1960–1970. *Annals* 439 (September): 16–28.

Solanik, Gerald R., and Pfeffer, Jeffrey. 1977. Constraints on administrative discretion: The limited influence of mayors on city budgets. *Urban Affairs Quarterly* 12 (June): 475–98.

Spilerman, Seymour. 1970. The causes of racial disturbances: A comparison of alternative explanations. *American Sociological Review* 35 (August): 627–49.

———. 1971. The causes of racial disturbances: A test of an explanation. *American Sociological Review* 36 (June): 427–82.

Stafford, Walter W. 1976. Dilemmas of civil rights groups in developing urban strategies and changes in American federalism, 1933–1970. *Phylon* 37 (March): 59–72.

Stokes, Carl B. 1973. *Promises of power: A political autobiography.* New York: Simon and Schuster.

Stone, Chuck. 1970. *Black political power in America.* New York: Dell.

Taebel, Delbert. 1978. Minority representation on city councils. The impact of structure on blacks and Hispanics. *Social Science Quarterly* 59 (June): 142–52.

Taeuber, Karl E., and Taeuber, A. F. 1965. *Negroes in cities: Residential segregation and neighborhood change.* Chicago: Aldine.

Thompson, Daniel. 1963. *The Negro leadership class.* Englewood Cliffs, N.J.: Prentice-Hall.

Turk, Herman. 1970. Interorganizational networks in urban society. *American Sociological Review* 35 (February): 1–19.

Verba, Sidney, and Nie, Norman. 1972. *Participation in America*. New York: Harper and Row.

Wahlke, John, Eulau, Heinz, Buchanan, William and Ferguson, LeRoy. 1962. *The legislative system*. New York: John Wiley.

Walton, Hanes. 1972. *Black politics*. Philadelphia: Lippincott.

———. 1976. Black politics in the South: Projections for the coming decade. In *Public policy for the Black community*, ed. Marguerite Ross Barnett and James Hefner, pp. 77–100. Port Washington, N.Y.: Alfred Publications.

Washnis, George J. 1974. *Community development strategies: Case studies of major Model Cities*. New York: Praeger.

Weinberg, Kenneth. 1968. *Black victory: Carl Stokes and the winning of Cleveland*. Chicago: Quadrangle Books.

Weingarden, C. 1972. Barriers to black employment in white-collar jobs. *Review of Black Political Economy* (spring): 13–24.

Welch, Susan. 1975. The impact of urban riots on urban expenditures. *American Journal of Political Science* 19 (November): 741–60.

Welch, Susan, and Karnig, Albert. 1978. Representation of blacks on big city school boards. *Social Science Quarterly* 59 (June): 162–72.

———. 1979a Correlates of female officeholding in city politics. *Journal of Politics* 41 (May): 478–91.

———. 1979b. The impact of black elected officials on urban expenditures and intergovernmental revenue In *Urban policymaking*, ed. Dale Rogers, Marshall. Beverly Hills: Russell Sage.

———. 1979c. The impact of black elected officials on urban social expenditures. *Policy Studies Journal* 7 (summer): 707–14.

Wilson, James Q. 1960. *Negro politics*. New York: Free Press.

———. 1966. The Negro in American politics: The present. In *The American Negro Reference Book*, pp. 434–41 Englewood Cliffs, N.J.: Prentice-Hall.

Wirth, Clifford. 1975. Social bias in political recruitment: A national study of black and white school board members. Paper presented at the Southern Political Science Association meeting, Nashville, Tenn.

Wolfinger, Raymond. 1965. The development and persistence of ethnic voting. *American Political Science* 59 (December): 896–908.

Wright, Gerald C. 1977. Contextual models of electoral behavior: The southern Wallace vote. *American Political Science Review* 71 (June): 497–508.

# Author Index

# Subject Index

Albany, Georgia, 30
Albany, New York, 97
Antipoverty programs, 17, 21–24, 37–38, 49–51, 58, 59, 60, 61, 63–64, 77–79, 91, 93, 94, 96–97, 102, 105, 144, 153–56
Atlanta, Georgia, 17, 114, 139
At-large elections. *See* District elections
Attitudes of black officials, 12, 13, 109, 110–12, 114–16
Attitudes of blacks, 109, 111–12, 142, 145, 149; alienation, 9; antiwhite beliefs, 8–9; black power, 8, 9; trust, 8
Attitudes of white officials, 6, 12, 13, 110–12, 114–16
Attitudes of whites, 9–10, 20, 32, 77, 96, 100, 112, 115, 142, 145, 148–49; toward integration, 9; negative stereotypes; 10

*Beer* v. *United States*, 30
Black candidates, 33, 43, 44, 45, 46–66, 69–78, 82–86, 95, 101, 109–110, 143, 144, 145, 146
Black council equity (subtractive measure), 71–73, 93, 95, 98, 100, 101, 102, 108–9, 142
Black council equity ratio, 70–73, 75–76, 79, 81–82, 84, 87, 90, 91, 93, 95, 96, 97, 98–99, 100–103, 104–5, 116, 143, 145
Black elected officials: characteristics of, 11–13; influence of, 13–15, 34, 109–10, 139, 141, 152, 154
Black financial institutions, 31, 32, 33, 34, 39, 56–57, 87–88, 100–101, 105
Black media, 19, 31, 32, 33–34, 39–40, 56–57, 87–88, 100, 101, 148
Black officials: members of Congress, viii, 4, 24; school board members, viii, 109–10, 111; state legislators, viii, 4, 24
Black population size, 1, 2, 31, 32, 34, 39, 43, 46, 49, 50, 54–58, 59, 61, 62, 64, 66–67, 77–78, 87–88, 90–91, 93, 94–95, 100, 102, 104, 105, 106–7, 108, 142, 143, 148, 149, 150, 151
Black power, 8–9, 12, 13, 83, 104, 145

Black representation: council, 26, 27, 43–44, 70–72, 77, 82, 84, 105, 126, 128, 136, 139, 141, 142–46, 147, 150, 153; mayoral, 26–27, 28, 42–44, 84, 104, 126, 128, 136, 139, 142–46, 150, 152–53
Black socioeconomic resources, 20, 31–32, 34, 36, 39, 43, 46, 56, 58, 60, 62, 64, 66–67, 77–78, 87–88, 90–91, 93, 94–95, 99, 100, 102, 105, 106–7, 108, 144, 149, 150
*Blacks United for Lasting Friendship, Inc.* v. *City of Shreveport*, 30
*Bolden* v. *Mobile*, 30
Bradley, Tom, 10, 68, 154

Candidate equity score, 70, 80, 84–89, 90, 93–95, 102
Candidate representation rate, 70, 80, 85, 87, 88, 90, 93–94, 102, 144
Carter, Jimmy, 7
Case study approach, viii–x, 117
Charlotte, North Carolina, 154
Chicago, Illinois, vii, ix, x, 25, 97–98
Cincinnati, Ohio, 114
City manager. *See* Form of government
City size, 19, 21, 35, 36, 47, 48, 49, 74, 83, 90, 97, 104, 120, 136, 142
Civil rights acts, 4–7, 142
Civil rights organizations, 31, 32, 33, 34, 39, 56–57, 87–88, 93, 99–100, 101
Cleveland, Ohio, ix, 25, 42, 113, 114, 151, 156
Commission government. *See* Form of government
Community Action Programs (CAP). *See* Antipoverty programs
Council representation, 32, 43–44, 68–74, 80–81, 82, 83, 104, 122, 131, 136, 139, 143, 145
Council size (effect on black officials), 24, 27, 28, 31, 39, 79–80, 81–83, 97, 104

Dallas, Texas, 17
Data and methods, 35–41, 44–45, 59–60, 69–72, 90, 118–21